LONG LOST BLUES

MUSIC IN AMERICAN LIFE

*A list of books in the series appears
at the end of this book.*

LONG LOST *Blues*

Popular Blues in America, 1850–1920

PETER C. MUIR

University of Illinois Press
Urbana and Chicago

Manufactured in the United States of America

1 2 3 4 5 C P 5 4 3 2 1

♾ This book is printed on acid-free paper.

Library of Congress Cataloging-in-Publication Data
Muir, Peter C.
Long lost blues : popular blues in America,
1850–1920 / by Peter C. Muir.
p.   cm.
Includes bibliographical references and index.
ISBN 978-0-252-03487-9 (cloth : alk. paper)
ISBN 978-0-252-07676-3 (pbk. : alk. paper)
1. Blues (Music)—History and criticism. I. Title.
ML3521.M85   2009
781.64309′041—dc22   2009015046

To Judith

the Cure

for my blues

CONTENTS

ACKNOWLEDGMENTS

A book such as this is by its nature as much a collaboration as the work of a single individual. There are many people who have contributed to it, directly or otherwise, and I wish to express my appreciation to them.

First, I wish to thank a small army of collectors who have helped in my research in many ways. Among them are Audrey Van Dyke, Alex Hassan, David Jasen, Gene Jones, Nan Flint, Konrad Nowakoski, Merle Sprinzen, and Richard Zimmerman, all of whom allowed me access to their collections, generously supplied me with copies of rare material when I requested it, and helped me in various ways.

Two collectors in particular have especially supported my project. One is Thornton Hagert, a pioneer researcher and historian, who allowed me unfettered access to his unique sheet music collection. It was he who first realized the importance of Hughie Cannon and other proto-blues composers in the 1970s. He selflessly passed his research on to me, and invited me to use it. I am indebted to his generosity.

Perhaps the most important collector to influence the production of this book was Michael Montgomery of Detroit. Mike allowed me complete access to the Montgomery Archive, perhaps the finest blues sheet music and piano roll collection in private hands, over a period of many years. This provided me not only with an enormous amount of research material but also supplied several important illustrations in the book. In addition, Mike became an unofficial consultant to this project, and we discussed aspects of it for many hours. I have found his comments and suggestions always illuminating, and I greatly appreciate his warm friendship and wisdom.

Much of the initial research for this project was undertaken at the Library of Congress, and I must mention two staff members who helped me tremendously in my endeavors. The first is David Sager of the Recorded Sound Division, who has located many recordings for me. The other is Wayne Shirley, now retired, of the Music Division, who, over a period of years, was remarkably generous with his time in locating literally hundreds of blues sheets, most untouched for more than eighty years. Wayne's enthusiasm for my endeavors, along with his unparalleled knowledge of American music, has been a continuous inspiration to me.

There were a number of other people who were most generous with their time and resources. I should mention particularly Tim Brooks, who has contributed importantly to this project by giving extensive assistance in the preparation of the discography, providing insightful feedback on the drafts of the manuscript, and helping me clarify my thoughts relating to the subject through numerous discussions. I am very grateful for his friendship and involvement in my work. Another person of great help was Lawrence Gushee, Professor Emeritus of musicology at the University of Illinois. It was he who first drew my attention to the proto-blues of Hughie Cannon as well as many other related matters. I am indebted to another musicologist, John Graziano, whose tireless help and encouragement in this project has been integral to its realization. Other musicologists, scholars, and academics who have generously assisted me include Allan Atlas, Edward A. Berlin, Rebecca Bryant, Paul Charosh, John Garst, Richard Kramer, Merrilyn Pike, Richard Powers, Doug Seroff, Richard Spottswood, Jeffrey Taylor, and Leo Treitler. I am also very grateful to Elliott Hurwitt, who has offered much information and supplied one of the illustrations. I owe a special vote of thanks to my friend Michael Garber, who assisted in many ways throughout the development of this work, not least through a painstakingly thorough reading of the manuscript. I am similarly indebted to Anne Allwood for her patient and insightful feedback on the first draft of this work. John Diamond, M.D., has a special place in the genesis of this project. It was he who, more than anyone, first stimulated, and then nurtured, my interest in early blues; much of chapter 3 was suggested by his unique work in the field of music of health. Finally, I need also to thank my editors at the University of Illinois Press, Laurie Matheson and Judith McCulloh, for their patience and tact.

I owe perhaps my greatest debt to my wife Judith. For her infinite patience, unquestioning support, intelligent feedback, and much else besides, I am more grateful than I can express.

A WORD ABOUT THE MUSIC EXAMPLES

As this book is primarily a musicological study, there are of necessity many music examples. This will inevitably present a partial obstacle for many readers; however, I have attempted to minimize this difficulty in two ways. First, recordings of all the examples are available for download as audio-clips at the book's website, longlostblues.com. Second, I have deliberately structured the discussion of the examples so that the main points are made verbally without the reader needing to read the notations.

I have attempted to adopt a consistent approach in the presentation of the music examples. The following points should be noted:

- All markings and indications found in the original sheet music are usually adhered to. The fact that some of these examples are marked with many nuances, such as dynamics and pedaling, while others are comparatively sparse, simply reflects the state of the original edition. However, in instances where putting in the detailed markings would obscure a particular point being demonstrated, I have omitted them.
- Any obvious errors in the original have been corrected.
- For clarity, most of the examples have added chord symbols of the conventional "Fake Book" type. I have generally indicated just the harmonic outline: passing chords are marked only if they relate to a discussion in the text.
- For substantial examples, tempo markings are indicated wherever they are given in the original. Note, however, that "moderato," a commonly used term, does not necessarily indicate a medium speed. As I have shown elsewhere, this designation was often used as a default, indicating to the performer to select his own tempo.[1] Works designated "moderato" indicated that the work could be performed at any tempo from slow to fast, depending on the context.

LONG LOST BLUES

INTRODUCTION

This book is about what happened when blues first emerged from the black subculture and spread into the American mainstream in the second decade of the twentieth century. The result was the rise of the genre I call *popular blues.*

Popular blues is different from more familiar types of blues, such as traditional Delta blues, or postwar Chicago blues, for two reasons. First, as blues moved into the mainstream, it absorbed some of the features of popular music, thereby producing a style that contained a varying mixture of popular and folk elements. Second, folk blues at this time had not yet fully evolved and was consequently in a rather undefined state. The result of these two factors—the interaction of blues with popular music, and the malleable nature of its folk roots—resulted in an innovative body of composition that, while stylistically removed from blues as the music is thought of today, is both illuminating from a historical point of view and, in many instances, of independent worth.

Popular blues were produced in great numbers. In the period covered by this book, the first nine years of production (1912 through 1920), over 450 different popular blues works appeared, giving rise to roughly eight hundred known recordings on disc and piano rolls. Certain of these were among the best-selling records of their era. By the end of the decade, if not before, blues had become a staple of the mainstream entertainment industry and had made its way into musicals, revues, circuses, minstrel shows, and vaudeville. Its creators included some of the best-known musical talents of the day, including W. C. Handy, Spencer Williams, James P. Johnson, George W. Thomas, and Perry Bradford, along with dozens of others who are less well-known.

Yet despite this productivity, there has been very little study of, and appreciation for, popular blues. Aside from my own doctoral dissertation on the subject, there has only been one brief study surveying the genre as a whole.[1] Otherwise, what commentary there is has occurred almost entirely in the context either of blues histories,[2] where the subject is usually given short shrift, or in more general writing about black vernacular music of the period.[3] Most attention has been given to the blues of W. C. Handy, but even in his case there has been little detailed examination, especially of the music. The lack of scholarly attention is especially surprising when one considers the enormous bibliography of blues in general.

I have examined the reasons for this neglect elsewhere in some detail.[4] In essence, blues has usually been seen by critics and historians as essentially folk music, inherently at odds with the allegedly corrupting forces of the popular music industry. The idea of popular blues is therefore seen as at best a debasement of a noble art form, and at worst as an oxymoron. At a deeper level, this neglect is due not so much to the commercialization of the genre as to the medium in which it appeared, sheet music. Like the popular music industry of which it was a part, popular blues of the 1910s was sheet music-based: recordings, although numerous, came after the fact. Blues, however, is seen as an essentially oral phenomenon. In the minds of commentators, this means that blues whose basic form is a notated text, rather than a live or recorded performance, just does not compute as blues.

This is not to criticize earlier generations of blues commentators. We are all, as the astronomer Fred Hoyle once put it, prisoners of our culture, hardly able "to think outside the particular patterns that our brains are conditioned to."[5] Throughout much of its history, the definition of blues has been stringently restricted, and the idea of notated blues has been antithetical to those writing about the subject. Over the years, however, the situation has mellowed: the definition of blues has broadened considerably and has come to embrace far more than just the "pure" folk style of Robert Johnson, including boogie-woogie, rhythm and blues, the blues-derived music of 1960s rock, and much else besides. The point is, as Elijah Wald puts it, that people can use "whatever definition [of blues] they like, as long as they grant that it is not the only one."[6]

The definition of blues used in this book is very simple: it refers to titular blues, that is, works that were titled (or subtitled) blues. In other words, it comprises works that were clearly considered to be blues by the culture that produced them. It could be objected that this kind of definition is inappropriate in an era when blues music was still in the process of stabilization. The roughly 450 titular blues produced in the nine-year period covered by this book display what at first glance appears a bewildering range of forms and styles, from old-fashioned parlor ballads to hypermodern jazz, from voguish dances like fox-trots and one-steps to more conservative ones like polkas and even waltzes. Surely, then, the term *blues* was almost meaningless at this time, and in many cases it was probably little more than a convenient marketing label.

Nonetheless, there are two ways in which popular blues of the 1910s can be considered a coherent genre. First, even though the range of styles is wide, nearly all works titled "blues" have at least some relationship to folk blues styles. This relationship is sometimes remote, and sometimes not, but it is nearly always present. There is a deeper sense of coherence about the genre, too. That is what one might term the curative aspect. By the time the label "blues" was being applied to music, it had already been a buzzword in American culture for over a decade. "Blues," referring to the new illness of neurasthenia, was the fashionable malady of mainstream American society. A psycho-physical reaction to the excesses of modern life, everyone at the turn of the century had it, and everyone wanted to get rid of it. The notion of "a cure for the blues" became standard in the culture, and music was seen as having important powers in this regard. Describing a work as a blues therefore connoted more than a musical style. By tapping, usually subliminally, into the cultural code of the day, the composition's title carried with it the suggestion that the piece would cure the consumer's blues.

In addition to the term "blues," I need to define two others that are used freely in this book: *popular* and *folk*. The difference between these involves their means of transmission. *Folk music* is vernacular music transmitted "from person to person, often orally, and usually face to face over a period of time," to borrow Richard A. Reuss's classic description.[7] *Popular music,* by contrast, is vernacular music disseminated through mass media, which in the period covered by this book consists of sheet music and recordings.[8] There is obviously some overlap between these two categories as far as blues are concerned, since from the outset published and recorded (i.e., popular, in my terminology) blues were influenced by black folk (i.e., orally transmitted) music. However, despite this overlap, the two styles—folk blues and popular blues—are clearly distinct. In case this is not clear, think, for instance, of British rock blues of the 1960s. While this style was strongly influenced by African American folk blues, the two genres are obviously different: there is no way a blues performance by Cream could be mistaken for a Delta blues recording. Similarly, with popular blues of the 1910s, there are very few published examples (and no recordings whatsoever) that can be regarded as straight folk music. And I would argue that the exceptions—such as Leroy "Lasses" White's "Nigger Blues," published in Dallas in 1913 (see chapter 2, example 5)—are so rare and so far removed stylistically from typical popular blues as to confirm rather than weaken the argument on behalf of the general separation of the folk and popular idioms during this period.

In fact, the dualism between folk and popular music before the 1920s is not only valid, but rather it is the key to understanding the basic process of the emergence of blues. A new musical idiom, later to be called blues, developed in African American folk (i.e, oral) culture at the end of the nineteenth century. This idiom was at the time quite distinct from popular (i.e., published and recorded) music. However, elements of the new idiom very soon begin to spread into popular music. The most obvious example of this is the twelve-bar sequence, which was previously unknown in popular music, but which started to appear in published songs around the turn of the century. Throughout the first decade of the new century, the incorporation of these elements into popular music became more common; at the same time, the blues genre gained increased definition within folk culture. These two developments prepared the way for the rapid spread of blues within the popular idiom in the 1910s.

A word of explanation is required about this study's cut-off date at the end of 1920. On August 10 of that year, the black singer Mamie Smith recorded Perry Bradford's "Crazy Blues" for Okeh records. This was a seminal event, in part because it was the first time an African American female vocalist had recorded blues. More important, the success of the record—75,000 copies were allegedly sold in the first week of release—traditionally marks it as the beginning of the race record industry (records targeted to the black market).[9] This has had the remarkable consequence of "Crazy Blues" being identified as the effective beginning of commercial blues. Even the widely respected Giles Oakley describes this recording as "the moment the music ceased to be transmitted exclusively through local folk culture," thereby denying the existence of over four hundred blues that had been published and recorded before that date.[10] Admittedly, Oakley's revisionism is rather extreme: most commentators pay at least lip service to the pre–"Crazy Blues" blues industry. Few, if any, however, really acknowledge the true extent or importance of this earlier activity. To redress this balance, the focus of this book is the popular blues industry *before* "Crazy Blues." And while my cut-off date should, strictly speaking, be August 9, 1920, I have carried it through to the end of that year for convenience.

There is another way, aside from the period it covers, that this book redresses a deficit in blues scholarship: its musicological approach. There has been remarkably little detailed musical discussion of blues. To understand the degree of this lopsidedness, consider the case of Robert Ford's *A Blues Bibliography* (1999), at the time of this writing the most comprehensive book of its kind. Of the 758 pages of bibliographic listings, the category "Lyric Transcriptions & Musical Analysis," which lists the major musicological studies of the genre, takes up just four pages. Compared, for instance, with its listings of biographical and historical writings about blues (612 and 50 pages, respectively), musicological studies pale in significance.

This deficiency in blues scholarship is quite odd: blues is first and foremost a musical genre, after all. The obvious explanation is that the blues readership is poorly equipped to deal with detailed musical analysis, or at any rate has little desire for it. The facts, however, suggest otherwise. Three books on blues that have dared to dig deep musically—Samuel Charters's *The Bluesmen,* David Evans's *Big Road Blues,* and Jeff Todd Titon's *Early Downhome Blues*—are all regarded as major contributions to blues studies. Titon's work, for instance, originally published in the 1970s, was reissued in a new edition twenty years later, while Evans's book, which first appeared in 1982, is still in print today (2008). The focus of this book is therefore musicological, my main purpose being to explore and make familiar what is basically an uncharted genre. Having said this, I have included biographical, historical, and (especially in chapter 3) sociological discussions wherever it has seemed necessary to do so.

A brief mention is in order, therefore, about the book's content and structure. The opening chapter gives an overview of the popular blues industry of the 1910s: it defines its scope, traces its beginnings, and charts its development and dissemination. Chapter 2 examines the music and lyrics of popular blues to determine both the characteristics of its idiom and the nature of its identity in relation to the surrounding styles of mainstream popular music, on the one hand, and folk blues, on the other. This is followed in chapter 3 by a discussion of the therapeutic aspect of blues, that is, the notion of curing blues with the blues. As mentioned earlier, I consider this concept fundamental to understanding the culture of early popular blues. Chapter 4 is a musical examination of the work of W. C. Handy, the most important figure in the field at this time. Chapter 5 uncovers a host of early published blues from the South, which, being close to the folk sources of the genre, are particularly interesting and revealing. The final chapter, essentially an extended afterthought, examines protoblues, that is, works published before the start-up of the blues industry in 1912 that show significant blues characteristics. Such works have much to reveal about the development of the blues idiom in both popular and folk culture.

Finally, a word about the book's title. "Long Lost Blues" is the name of a very fine published blues from 1914 by two African Americans, H. Alf Kelley and J. Paul Wyer; the song is briefly examined in chapter 5. However, the epithet also applies more generally to the subject of this study. Popular blues of the 1910s were truly popular. Yet the near-complete neglect of that genre by historians afterwards means that, in a very real sense, these blues have been "long lost." They are, I hope, ripe for rediscovery.

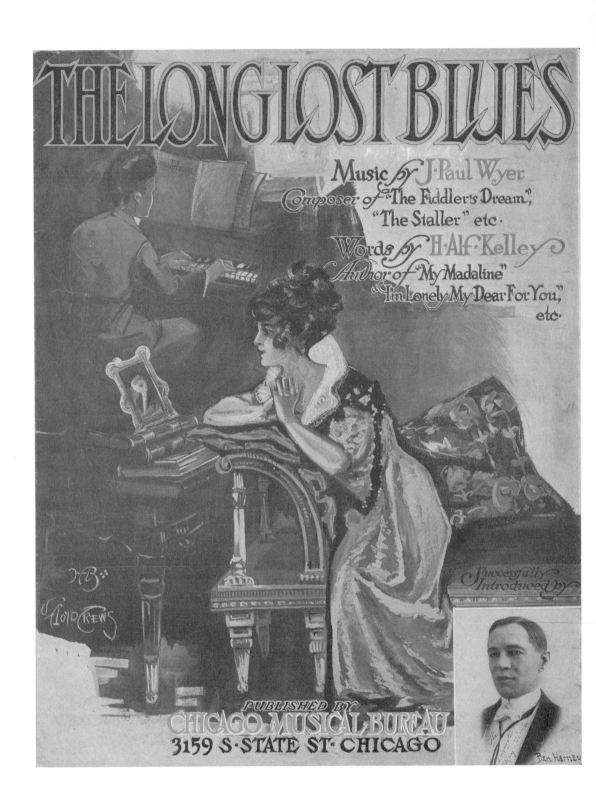

CHAPTER 1

The Popular Blues Industry, 1912–1920

THE BIRTH OF POPULAR BLUES

It is a little-known fact that the date January 12, 1912, marks a milestone in American music. It was on that particular Thursday that a certain piece of sheet music was registered for copyright at the Library of Congress in Washington, D.C. Called simply "The Blues" and published by the major New York firm of Shapiro Music, the song was the start of the popular blues industry, an industry that has, perhaps more than any other, changed the face of vernacular music in Western culture.

"The Blues" was the work of two African American writers, Chris Smith and Tim Brymn, who had both been active in the popular music industry for more than a decade. The pair had collaborated before, most successfully (with Jim Burris) on the awkwardly titled "Come After Breakfast, Bring 'Long Your Lunch, and Leave Before Supper Time" (1909), which had been the hit of a black show called *His Honor the Barber,* and which had gone on to become one of the best-selling songs of 1910.[1]

Although essentially a ragtime song, "The Blues" contains much that is blues-related. The basic scenario—a woman grieving for her lover, who has deserted her—is typical of the genre. The most telling moment is at the beginning of the chorus, when the singer declares, "I've got the blues, but I'm too blamed mean to cry" (example 1), a variant of a line much used in folk blues and first found in a field transcription published the year before this song appeared.[2] The music that accompanies this sentiment makes striking use of blue notes (circled in example 1). Such colorings are a long way removed from the idiom of mainstream popular song as it existed in 1911, and they suggest that the music for this passage was, like the text it accompa-

EXAMPLE 1. Smith and Brymn, "The Blues" (1912), chorus, mm. 1–4

FIGURE 1. The first published blues.
(Courtesy Elliott Hurwitt Collection)

nies, derived from folk sources. The inherent bluesy qualities of the song is admirably brought out by its only known recording, made for Paramount in 1926, by the black singer Iva Smith, accompanied by barrelhouse pianist Charles "Cow Cow" Davenport.[3]

The most noteworthy feature of the song is not, however, its content, but rather its title. "The Blues" boldly announces to the mainstream public the existence of a new genre. In fact, this was not the first publication to describe itself as a blues, but the second. The first was a 1909 piano rag by a white New Orleans pianist named Robert Hoffman. Its main title was "I'm Alabama Bound," but it was subtitled "The Alabama Blues" in its original edition. This subtitle is the earliest known reference to blues as a genre, and it was certainly justified, the work making extensive use of two traditional African American folk melodies. Despite this, the second edition of the composition, also published in New Orleans, makes no mention of the "Alabama Blues" subtitle, nor do subsequent editions. The fact that the subtitle was used only for the first edition implies that describing a work as a blues was at that time too obscure a notion to be used as a selling point, even for purchasers in the South. This suggests that, while the label had by 1909 gained some currency in the folk culture from which Hoffman acquired his melodies, such usage had not yet garnered enough general acceptance to make the leap into the commercial mainstream.

By 1912, however, all that had changed. Smith and Brymn's song was the first of four titular blues to appear in print that year. The other three were, in chronological order: "Baby Seals Blues" by H. Franklin "Baby" Seals; "Dallas Blues" by Hart A. Wand; and W. C. Handy's "The Memphis Blues." Another blues, "Negro Blues" by Le Roy "Lasses" White, was copyrighted in 1912 but not published until the following year under the title "Nigger Blues" (see table 1). Thereafter, published blues appeared on a continuous and increasingly frequent basis, so that by 1920 the genre had become a major branch of the popular music industry, with a new title appearing every two or three days. 1912, then, marks the beginnings of the mainstream blues industry, with January 12—the copyright date of Smith and Brymn's "The Blues"—the precise moment of its birth.

The scenario I have outlined above raises two questions. The first is one of timing. It would seem that in 1909, when Hoffman published "The Alabama Blues," the world was not ready for blues, but by 1912 it was. What had changed in those three years? The second question relates to its evolution: what exactly was the path of blues from its rural origins to the mainstream?

The answer to both questions concerns black vaudeville. At the turn of the century, the black entertainment industry was in still its infancy. But it was growing up fast, and in the first decade of the new century black theaters—that is, theaters where African American talent performed

Table 1. Blues Copyrighted in 1912

Copyright Date	Title	Lyrics	Music	Original Publisher
01/12/12	Blues (The)	Chris Smith	James T. Brymn	Shapiro Mus., New York
08/03/12	Baby Seals Blues	Baby Seals	Baby Seals	Seals & Fisher, St. Louis
08/06/12	Dallas Blues	—	Hart A. Wand	Wand Pub., Oklahoma City, Okla.
09/27/12*	The Memphis Blues	—	W. C. Handy	W. C. Handy, Memphis
11/09/12**	Nigger Blues	Le Roy Lasses White	Le Roy Lasses White	Le Roy Lasses White, Dallas

* The first edition of this composition was not copyrighted; the date given is that of publication
** Not published until 1913

for African American audiences—were springing up with increasing frequency in towns and cities all over America. African American vaudeville adopted the same basic approach as mainstream vaudeville, which was then at the height of its popularity: the entertainment offered was a variety of performances, a series of unrelated and diverse acts by a wide range of talents. These acts were by no means restricted to music, but music was undoubtedly a central attraction.

The sudden rise of black vaudeville in the early 1900s resulted in the overnight formation of a large pool of African American entertainers. Many of their acts focused specifically on materials drawn from the musical subculture. It was through the agency of these performers that the emerging genre of blues spread from its rural roots into the urban-based world of black entertainment. Furthermore, the fact that these artists were constantly touring (typically a vaudeville artist would stay no more than a week or two in one location) and doing so over a wide area (in some cases throughout much of the country) created an ideal situation for the rapid dissemination of the new genre within the black community.

It is possible to trace the spread of blues in black vaudeville through reports in the show business sections of black newspapers of the period like the *Indianapolis Freeman*. The first known reference to a blues performance in black vaudeville—it is, in fact, the earliest known account of blues singing on a stage of any kind—is in a report in the *Freeman* of a show at the Airdome Theater in Jacksonville, Florida. It describes a routine where Henry, the dummy of ventriloquist John W. F. "Johnnie" Woods, gets drunk. The report enthused: "[I]t's rich; it's great; and Prof. Woods knows how to handle his figure. He uses the 'blues' for little Henry in this drunken act."[4] The date was April 1910. After that, reports of blues in black vaudeville became increasingly common, and by 1912, less than two years later, blues had become a "rampant" phenomenon.[5]

As black vaudeville blues gained popularity, its geographic base spread. Initially confined to the South, it ventured north for the first time in May 1911 when the husband-and-wife team of Butler "String Beans" and Sweetie May were booked for a two-week run in Chicago at the Monogram Theater on State Street.[6] String Beans was a pioneer blues singer and pianist from Montgomery, Alabama, who, in the assessment of historians Lynn Abbott and Doug Seroff, was "the greatest attraction in African-American vaudeville" in the 1910s and "the first recognizable blues *star*."[7] The overwhelming success of his appearance at the Monogram "opened the floodgates for other Southern acts" to appear in the North, thereby promoting the dissemination of blues.[8] By 1912, with blues the latest craze in black vaudeville, it was inevitable that black professional songwriters would start to experiment with the commercial potential of the genre.

The catalyst seems to have been Chris Smith, co-writer of "The Blues." Smith was no stranger to blues. As early as 1901, he had experimented with a protoblues song called "I've Got de Blues: A Colored Complaint," while a composition published in 1911, "Honky-Tonky Monkey Rag," makes striking use of the twelve-bar idiom. In addition to being a successful songwriter, Smith was also a performer in black vaudeville. By coincidence, he also shared the bill at the Monogram with String Beans and Sweetie May during the first week of their May 1911 run.[9] I would suggest

FIGURE 2. Chris Smith (right), seminal early bluesman, with one of his vaudeville partners, dancer George Cooper, ca. 1915. (Courtesy Montgomery Archive)

that it was Smith's exposure to String Beans's sensational singing of the blues and its impact on northern audiences that inspired him to pen "The Blues" with Brymn a few months later.

THE NATURE AND SCOPE OF THE EARLY POPULAR BLUES INDUSTRY

The rapid growth of the early popular blues industry is shown in table 2. It lists the total number of titular blues published in sheet music and/or on recordings for each year between 1912 and 1920. We can see that the two biggest years of growth are 1916 and 1919; both of these years more than doubled the output of the preceding year. By the end of 1920, no fewer than 456 blues had been published. (Details of all these blues up to 1915 are provided in the appendix; all blues up to the end of 1920 are listed on the book's website.)[10]

Popular blues were of two basic types, vocal and instrumental. Vocal blues, also called blues songs, were, like regular pop songs, almost always published for single voice with piano accompaniment. Instrumental blues were almost always published for solo piano. Both vocal and instrumental blues were sometimes also published in arrangements for other instrumental combinations, ranging from full band to various duo combinations. This was the standard practice of the popular music industry at the time, especially if a work was particularly successful. Of the two types, vocal blues were more common, outnumbering instrumental blues three to one.[11]

Table 2. Growth of the Popular Blues Industry

Year	Number of Blues Compositions Published*	Aggregate**
1912	5	5
1913	4	9
1914	12	21
1915	21	42
1916	50	92
1917	48	140
1918	55	195
1919	114	309
1920	147	456

* Total for that year. Includes all known titles published in sheet music and/or on recorded formats. The year given is the year of copyright, except in cases where the composition was published before it was copyrighted or when the composition was not copyrighted: in each of these instances, the year of publication is used.

** Total number of all blues published up to the end of the year.

Recorded Media

In addition to appearing in sheet music form, popular blues were disseminated through recordings on the grooved media of discs and cylinders, and on player piano rolls.[12]

The discs were mostly double-sided ten-inch records made of a natural plastic called shellac. They played for approximately three minutes per side at seventy-eight revolutions per minute. There was some variation, however, given the lack of uniformity in the recording industry of the 1910s: discs could be anything from five to twelve inches in diameter, with playing times modified accordingly; some were single-sided, and some played slower or faster than seventy-eight revolutions a minute.

All known blues cylinders appeared on one particular format, the Edison Blue Amberol cylinder. Blue Amberols, which were just over two inches in diameter and about four and a quarter inches long, were the dominant type of cylinder in the marketplace of the 1910s and played for up to four minutes. However, there were few blues recordings made on cylinder, in part because cylinder sales were much lower than disc sales, but also because Edison was notoriously conservative in the music he chose to record.

Blues were prolifically recorded on grooved media, as is shown by table 3, which gives the total number for each year before 1921. There was little activity in the first half of the decade (just six recordings up to the end of 1915); thereafter there was rapid growth, with a total of 385 recordings made by the end of 1920.

The story of player piano rolls in early blues recording history is a complex one. Piano rolls are made of paper wound on spools, with holes punched into the paper corresponding to the notes to be played. Rolls are bulky, roughly twelve inches wide and about two inches in diam-

FIGURE 3. The biggest and smallest blues discs from the 1910s. On the left, white vaudevillian Marie Cahill performs "The Dallas Blues" on a twelve-inch Victor recorded in 1917, running at around four minutes. On the right, the African American jazz band of Wilbur Sweatman performs Will Nash's "Lonesome Road Blues" on a five-inch Little Wonder record, with a duration of just ninety seconds. (Author's Collection)

FIGURE 4. Blues were rarely recorded on wax cylinder. This four-minute Edison Blue Amberol is of a long-forgotten work titled "The Hula Blues," performed by Harry Raderman's Jazz Orchestra in 1920. (Author's collection)

Table 3. Blues Recordings on Grooved Media
(Disc and Cylinder) before 1921

Year	Number of Recordings*	Aggregate**
1912	0	0
1913	0	0
1914	3	3
1915	3	6
1916	27	33
1917	46	79
1918	43	122
1919	124	246
1920	139	385

* The year given is the recording date, except in instances when the recording date is not known, in which case the date of the record's issue is used.

** Total number of all blues recordings up to the end of the year.

eter and weighing several ounces, but they could play longer than grooved media of the era, the limiting factor being only the length of paper that was able to be conveniently wound on the spool. It was possible, for instance, to fit an entire symphonic movement onto a single roll. Nonetheless, most blues rolls were of about the same duration as blues discs and cylinders, that is, between two and four minutes. Player pianos were approaching the peak of their popularity just as blues were starting to gain a foothold in mainstream culture. Consequently, blues rolls from the period are numerous: a provisional listing includes roughly 450 items from before 1921, though the true total is almost certainly greater, perhaps as many as 700.[13]

A comparison between the sound of piano rolls and grooved media is interesting. Discs and cylinders of the 1910s had a muffled, indistinct sound because of primitive acoustic recording systems. Piano rolls, by contrast, played on a real piano, and the sound therefore had far greater superficial impact. In other respects, however, piano rolls were at a disadvantage.

FIGURE 5. Literally hundreds of piano rolls of blues were recorded during the 1910s. This one, an Imperial Songrecord from 1917, was composed and performed by African Americans: Maceo Pinkard's "Those Draftin' Blues," played by the prolific Chicago pianist Clarence M. Jones. (Author's collection)

Most blues rolls lacked fluctuations of tempo or dynamics; while these were supposed to be added to the performance by the operator of the player piano on playback, this was something which required considerable skill to do convincingly, and for much of the time the rolls were most likely played "flat." As a result, they tended to sound rather mechanical. The exceptions are the high-end reproducing rolls, made by companies such as Duo-Art, Welte-Mignon, and Ampico, which aimed to replicate the performer's subtleties of dynamic and rhythmic nuance. However, there are very few blues rolls of the reproducing type, as blues were not considered suitable fodder for the high-end market.

Another issue with piano rolls concerns their status as historical documents. Due to the recording process, it was possible to change piano rolls after they had been recorded (indeed, many rolls were punched directly and were not based on a live performance at all). Consequently, they were routinely edited, not just to correct any errors in performance but also at times to spice up the arrangement, adding parts and altering rhythms, with an ease unmatched until the advent of digital editing in the 1990s. It is, therefore, generally not possible to know what a performer actually played. By contrast, a disc or cylinder, however poor the recording quality, captured an actual performance: no editing options existed at the time except to rerecord the entire side.

Perhaps for these reasons, piano rolls have never attracted the attention of historians in the way disc and cylinder recordings have; as a result, the field is seriously under-researched. This is unfortunate, because the sheer number of rolls produced suggests they were important vehicles in the dissemination of blues in the 1910s, even though the sales of most were probably quite modest.[14] Furthermore, despite doubts concerning the fidelity of this mode of recording, "hand-played" blues piano rolls (that is, rolls performed by a particular artist, rather than rolls punched straight in) represent a unique body of information about early piano blues performance styles. Indeed, there are hardly any piano blues records from the 1910s, most likely because of the formidable competition posed by piano rolls.

Blues Records Versus Sheet Music

Blues, then, were disseminated in the mass-marketplace through sheet music and recordings (discs, cylinders, and piano rolls). Which of the two was the more important? This is a question central to understanding the blues industry of the 1910s, but it is not easy to answer.

When the American popular music industry started in the late 1800s, it was driven entirely by sheet music for the simple reason that sheet music was the only available medium for mass dissemination. However, with the rise of commercial recordings in the 1890s, the situation began to shift. Given that today the music industry is centered around recordings, there was obviously a point in time when records began to surpass sheet music.

In fact, it seems that the crossover point was reached in the 1910s. Important evidence for this is provided by the *U.S. Census of Manufactures*. In 1909, the total sales of sheet music slightly exceeded the combined sales of recorded media (cylinders, discs, music rolls): $5.5 million for sheet music, compared with $5.2 million for recordings. By 1914, however, that situation had reversed quite dramatically: $11.9 million of annual sales for recordings, but only $6.8 million for sheet music. By 1919 that trend had increased further, with $47.8 million earned from recordings and $12.5 from sheet music.[15] While these figures do not provide full information (it would be helpful, for instance, to know not just the total value of the media, but the number of units sold), it seems clear that recordings were more important than sheet music in the general music industry of the 1910s.

The situation within the blues industry is harder to ascertain. Popular blues emerged as a sheet music phenomenon in 1912; the first disc recordings were not made till two years later. I strongly suspect that by the end of the decade, when blues had become thoroughly integrated into the mainstream music industry, recordings dominated sheet music commercially, just as they did within the industry as a whole. When the crossover happened, however, is impossible to determine with any precision: my best guess would be around 1918.

The discussion about the shifting relationship between blues sheet music and recordings has thus far only dealt with commercial aspects. But what about creative dimensions? There the story is quite clear. Of the 456 titular blues from before 1921, 96 percent appeared in sheet-music form, but only 42 percent were recorded. As this indicates, fully 58 percent of blues appeared only as sheet music, that is, they were never recorded. By comparison, just 4 percent of blues appeared only on recordings. It is therefore no exaggeration to say that in terms of creativity, early popular blues was a medium that was essentially sheet music-based.

This is confirmed by the nature of blues recordings from the 1910s. In these, the music is mostly performed in a relatively straight manner, with close adherence to the written original. The creative input of the performer is thus secondary to that of the composer, as was the norm in recordings of this era. This is in sharp contrast to innumerable jazz and blues records of the 1920s and beyond, where the performer assumes a far greater creative prominence over—and independence from—the composition being performed.

There are some notable exceptions, however. Perhaps the most striking is the Original Dixieland Jazz Band's "Livery Stable Blues," recorded in February 1917. This is a famous recording, since it forms one side of the first jazz record ever to be made, Victor 18255 (the record's flipside, incidentally, was a non-blues titled "Original Dixieland One-Step"). What makes "Livery Stable Blues" so different from all earlier popular blues is that it is the first to be conceived around live performance. The farmyard calls that are the work's most distinctive feature (crowing clarinet, neighing cornet, and mooing trombone), as well as the frantic drive and exuberant polyphony of the jazz-based performance, are palely reflected in the published sheet music. Furthermore, that sheet music was not copyrighted till some months after the record was made, a most unusual procedure at the time, confirming that in this case the printed version was secondary to the recorded version. "Livery Stable Blues" was an indicator of things to come. So much canonic material recorded by blues artists of the 1920s, such as Blind Lemon Jefferson, Bessie Smith, and Charlie Patton, are first and foremost recordings and have only a secondary life as sheet music (indeed, many did not appear in sheet music form until decades later). I must reiterate, however, that in the popular blues culture of the 1910s, examples like "Livery Stable Blues" are rare. Indeed, the other exceptions consist largely of works recorded by jazz bands in the wake of the Original Dixieland Jazz Band, such as the prolific Louisiana Five.

DEVELOPMENT OF THE EARLY POPULAR BLUES INDUSTRY

The popular blues industry grew quite slowly at first. A crucial reason seems to be that of the nine blues copyrighted in 1912 and 1913, all except Smith and Brymn's "The Blues" were only published regionally: three in Memphis, two in different locations in Texas, and one each in Missouri, Oklahoma, and Illinois.[16] Regionally published music, not having the opportunities for promotion and distribution enjoyed by music produced in the twin entertainment centers of New York and Chicago, had little chance of national recognition. Meanwhile "The Blues," although published by a major New York house, seems to have been a relative commercial failure, if the rarity of the sheet music today is anything to go by (although the existence of the Iva Smith recording suggests the song must have had at least some mileage among black performers).

What turned the tide was W. C. Handy's "The Memphis Blues." The remarkable history of this work has been told elsewhere, most notably in Handy's autobiography *Father of the Blues,* but it worth recapping the outlines of the story.[17] It was composed in Memphis in 1909 for Handy's band—at that time regarded as one of the finest locally—to play for the mayoral campaign of Democrat Edward Crump. Originally titled simply "Mr. Crump," the work was a highly original and appealing adaptation of the emerging blues style. As a result, it acquired a local popularity that long outlasted the election. Even so, Handy waited for four years to publish the song. Perhaps he was eventually encouraged to do so by the increasing popularity of blues in the black community (his only previous foray into music publishing, a 1907 plantation song titled "In the Cotton Fields of Dixie," had not been a success). Having been turned down by several major publishing houses—the work with its twelve-bar blues sections was just too far from the norm of conventional popular music—Handy decided to publish it himself. Thinking the work a flop, he then sold it to a white midwestern publisher, Theron C. Bennett, for a mere fifty dollars shortly after the initial publication. Whether there was outright deception on Bennett's part, as Handy later claimed, or Bennett was simply taking what he shrewdly judged a good business opportunity, is debatable.[18] Either way, Handy did not reacquire the copyright until 1940.

Under Bennett's ownership and promotion, the work quickly became popular, with sales allegedly topping fifty thousand by the fall of 1913.[19] Given the ever growing interest in the composition, Bennett decided to produce a vocal version of the work and hired the wordsmith George A. Norton to create the lyric.

The choice of Norton was not random. Two years earlier, he had penned the lyric to "My Melancholy Baby," the copyright for which Bennett had also purchased from the composer, in this case a certain Ernie Burnett. Though not titled a blues, the mood of "My Melancholy Baby" is bluesy (the original title was "Melancholy," and the tempo marking on the first edition is "slow, with feeling"); this, combined with Norton's proven bankability as a lyricist, meant that he was in Bennett's eyes the obvious person to create the lyric to "The Memphis Blues." As will be discussed in chapter 4, it was a wise choice, and the song version generated even greater interest than the original for solo piano.

By 1914 "The Memphis Blues" came to the attention of the record companies, apparently due to Bennett's active proselytizing.[20] Three recordings were made that year: two, issued in July, were instrumental versions by the respective house bands of the biggest record labels, Victor and Columbia; the third was of the song version, by Morton Harvey, issued in October on Victor. These are the first blues records, and while their exact sales are not known, surviving copies are relatively common, suggesting at least a reasonable degree of commercial success. In terms of sheet music sales, Edward Foote Gardner ranks "The Memphis Blues" as the twenty-eighth best-selling song of 1914.[21] Moreover, the composition had already sold steadily in 1913, and indeed it would continue to do so for many years to come. With impressive sheet-music sales and three successful recordings by the end of the 1914, "The Memphis Blues" was undoubtedly on its way to renown, the first blues to gain national, rather than regional, prominence. Its success acted as a catalyst, encouraging the popular music industry, ever on the watch for new developments, to experiment with the genre, which it did at an ever-increasing rate.

There was a substantial increase in blues production in 1915, with a total of twenty-one publications—as many as in the preceding three years combined. Nowadays, the best-remembered blues from that year were all by African Americans: W. C. Handy's "Hesitating Blues" and "Joe Turner Blues"; Jelly Roll Morton's "Jelly Roll Blues," copyrighted on September 22, his first published work, long regarded as a jazz classic; and Artie Matthews's "Weary Blues," which also was to become a Dixieland jazz standard after a seminal recording by Louis Armstrong's Hot Seven in 1927 for Okeh. There were also many others of interest, including several by other black composers (William King Phillips, William Nash, and James "Slaps" White) and two by white folk-ragtime pianist Euday L. Bowman.

However, the blues hit of the year was a now forgotten piece of ethnic tomfoolery called "Chinese Blues" by Fred D. Moore and Oscar Gardner. A Chinese laundryman pleads with his "little Chinagirl" to let him visit her, while all the time high on opium. His outburst at the climax of the song is "I got those Ipshing Hong-Kong Ockaway Chinese Blues" (see example 2). A decade later, the song was remembered by the blues commentator Abbe Niles as being catchy but so inauthentically bluesy that it "would have made Mr. E. H. Crump [the mayoral candidate for whom Handy had written The Memphis Blues] gasp and stare."[22] Despite this—or perhaps because of it—"Chinese Blues" not only sold well in sheet music but was also prolifically recorded: nine disc recordings and ten piano rolls are known, all recorded between 1915 and 1917.[23] This made it the biggest blues hit yet and confirmed that blues, in however a trivialized form, had commercial potential as popular music.

EXAMPLE 2. Moore and Gardner, "Chinese Blues" (1915), chorus, mm. 13–16

The blues industry grew substantially in the second half of the decade: in 1916 the number of published blues more than doubled to fifty, and in 1920 no fewer than one hundred and forty blues were produced. As the industry developed, it spread northward. Blues, of course, originated as folk music in the South, and most of the first commercial blues were published there. However, as it increasingly caught on in the mainstream, its geographic center of production shifted to New York City and Chicago, the focal points of the popular music industry.[24]

The northward spread of blues leads to the issue of race. Blues were originated in black culture, and not surprisingly most of the earliest published blues, including all those copyrighted in 1912 (table 1), are demonstrably of black origin.[25] However, as the genre developed in the mainstream, it attracted the attention of an increasing number of white composers and lyricists, the popular song industry being dominated by white songwriters and musicians.

The combination of blues spreading to the North and moving into white culture resulted in a stylistic broadening of the genre. Early southern black published blues are, generally speaking, much closer to folk influences than those produced in the North by whites, which are in turn closer to mainstream popular music. This dichotomy is discussed in a 1923 article from the trade journal *Sheet Music News,* which distinguishes between what it terms "white blues" and "low down blues." The article explains that the former "are popular numbers with a ballad strain and jazz [i.e., fast] tempo," while "low down blues" are "the typical numbers of the Southern colored folks," adding that "No white man can write 'low down blues.'"[26] This taxonomy is oversimplified—many southern black composers wrote blues practically indistinguishable from popular songs, and there are at least some instances of white composers being strongly influenced by folk blues—but in the broadest terms it is valid.

The growing appetite of the mainstream public for published blues of the "low-down" type, along with the recognition that "no white man can write them," meant that black composers were much in demand. Throughout the 1910s blues and related styles provided a greater opportunity than ever before for black composers and lyricists to work within the musical mainstream. The number of published blues by black composers is therefore disproportionately high, given the white domination of the popular music industry as a whole. This in turn led to an enhanced respect for black composers, for it was understood that they had talents that white composers did not. A 1919 advertisement on a piece of sheet music produced by a major New York publisher boldly states that "GENUINE 'BLUES' SONGS are RARE INSPIRATIONS that come only to GIFTED NEGRO COMPOSERS."[27] This was the era of the Harlem Renaissance, after all, and the blues publishing industry did its part to promote respect for black creativity. At the same time, one should not overstate the black presence in early popular blues. Testimonials like the one above were rare at this time. The fact remains that a large majority of blues published in the 1910s were by whites, and even most of those that were composed by blacks were published and promoted by whites.

BLUES PERFORMANCE IN THE MAINSTREAM

Blues was disseminated into the mainstream above all through public performance. Blues performances occurred in a wide variety of settings. I will outline here three of the most important—vaudeville, musicals, and the minstrel shows—before going on to discuss black performances of blues in the mainstream.

Blues in Vaudeville

We have already seen how blues flourished in black vaudeville before appearing as sheet music, and it continued to flourish in vaudeville settings throughout the 1910s. However, black vaudeville was by definition for black, not mainstream, audiences: very few black vaudeville blues were published, and none of its performers were recorded at the time. White vaudeville, however, was a different matter. It is not known exactly when blues began to appear there, but it probably did so soon after the appearance of published blues. Certainly by 1913, the violinist Waiman, a popular vaudevillian, was featuring "The Memphis Blues" "at every performance," according to the New York instrumental edition of the work, which featured his picture on the cover. By 1915, blues had a secure footing in mainstream vaudeville: Walsh and Sherman's "Broadway Blues" was featured by the singer Sophie Tucker, who was by that time a major star in vaudeville. The cover of the piece's sheet music shows three photographs of her, proudly announcing that the work was "Originally Introduced in Vaudeville by Sophie Tucker." As the decade advanced, blues acquired an ever-increasing presence in vaudeville. Singers such as Jane Green and Nora Bayes, along with numerous jazz bands and other instrumental and vocal groups, used blues in their vaudeville acts. For many of these, blues was central. For instance, the singer Marion Harris, who was a major vaudeville performer, recorded numerous blues and blues-related songs in the 1910s and 1920s, an indication of how important the genre was to her repertoire. Another major performer, Gilda Gray, who went on have a Hollywood career, allegedly had two hundred blues in her repertoire by 1919, including all of Handy's major num-

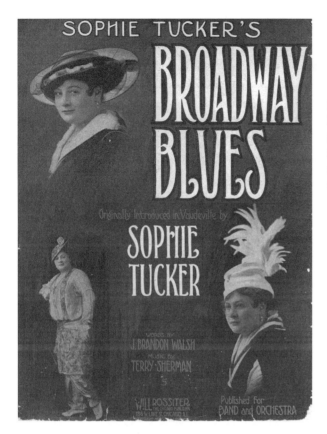

FIGURE 6. "Broadway Blues," a 1915 New York publication, featuring Sophie Tucker on its cover, is indicative of the spread of blues to mainstream vaudeville by the middle of the decade. (Author's collection)

bers and other important black-composed blues, such as Clarence Jones's "The Dirty Dozen," a toned-down version of a bawdy black song-type.[28] White vaudeville was, therefore, a central means of dissemination of early popular blues.

Blues in Musicals

Shortly after blues became popular in vaudeville, it spread to musicals. In 1915, the first show blues was published: "Old Kentucky Blues," by three African Americans, James Vaughan and brothers J. Homer Tutt and Salem Tutt Whitney. It was from a revue called *George Washington Bullion Abroad,* produced by Tutt and Whitney's Smart Set, a black company that staged numerous productions of this sort in New York between 1908 and 1929. The first white show to feature a blues was the highly successful and long-running *Chin-Chin,* starring the comedians Dave Montgomery and Fred Stone, which ran at the Globe Theater on Broadway beginning October 1914. At some point in 1916, an instrumental number, "Bull Frog Blues," was interpolated into the show, performed by a novelty saxophone sextet called the Six Brown Brothers, who were star attractions in vaudeville. The sextet made a successful recording of the composition that was released in the fall of 1916.[29]

By 1919 blues was attracting the attention of leading musical songwriters such as Rudolf Friml and Otto Harbach, whose "Laughing Blues" was featured in a show called *Tumble Inn,* which ran for 129 performances at the Selwyn Theatre in New York. By 1920 blues had become a truly widespread phenomenon on Broadway: No fewer than twelve shows from that year are known to have used published blues songs, and some of these enjoyed wide popularity. Probably the most important was Jerome Kern's "Left All Alone Again Blues," with lyrics by Anne Caldwell. This was from *The Night Boat,* one of the most successful musical comedies of the early 1920s, running for 319 performances in New York before going on the road for three years.

"Left All Alone Blues" was the hit of the show, with eleven disc recordings made in 1920 alone, along with a similar number of known piano rolls. The song is sung near the beginning of the show by the leading lady, Hazel White, and articulates her feelings of loneliness at being left alone by her husband Bob.[30] It is a typical "white blues," to use the label from the *Sheet Music News* article: basically a light-hearted popular song but hinting at blues in its musical idiom and in the theme of its lyrics (neglect by a lover; see example 3). The success of the song was deserved: it is of superior quality, with a clear, catchy melody. Kern was one of the foremost songwriters of the age, and the fact that a blues song was a central feature of an important show like this demonstrates how the genre had become assimilated into the popular mainstream less than a decade since its first appearance in published form. It also shows how popular composers were starting successfully to incorporate the blues idiom as a special flavor into their songs.

Blues in Minstrel Shows

By the second decade of the twentieth century, minstrelsy was not the force it had once been in the American entertainment industry. Nonetheless, because of its inherent, if complex, relationship with African American culture, it was still a significant disseminator of blues. For instance, the 1912 "Nigger Blues" (see example 5) was composed by Leroy "Lasses" White, a white minstrel who was later to gain fame at the Grand Ole Opry. The cover of the song features White in minstrel get-up, and there can be no doubt that he performed this song as part of his act. The work, which was, as we will see in the next chapter, influenced by folk blues to an exceptional degree, attracted the attention of other minstrel performers, notably the Washington lawyer George O'Connor, who was a favorite entertainer of presidents, and who recorded it for Columbia in 1916.[31] Perhaps the most important of the white minstrel bluesmen was Al Bernard, a New Orleans native, who performed blues extensively both live and on record. For instance, between 1919 and 1920 he made multiple recordings of Handy's "St. Louis Blues" and "Beale Street Blues" and a number of others blues, including his own "Big Chief Blues."[32]

Domestic Performance

We have so far focused exclusively on public performances. I conclude this section by emphasizing the pervasiveness of private performances of blues. As discussed earlier, the blues industry in the 1910s was driven by sheet music, and a large majority of those sales would inevitably

EXAMPLE 3. Caldwell and Kern, "Left All Alone Again Blues" (1920), chorus, mm. 1–8

have been to domestic purchasers. This was an age of great musical literacy and education, with pianos common in American households. There were hundreds of thousands, even millions, of amateur singers, pianists, and other instrumentalists eager to try the latest musical novelties flowing from the printing presses of New York and Chicago. While the result may have often been readings that were more enthusiastic than stylistically empathetic, the fact remains that domestic performance of blues was a crucial means to its dissemination in the mainstream.

African American Performance of Blues in the Mainstream

The situations outlined above have focused on whites performing blues for whites. One might be forgiven for assuming that the early dissemination of blues in the mainstream was almost entirely carried out this way: the entertainment industry at this time was, after all, almost

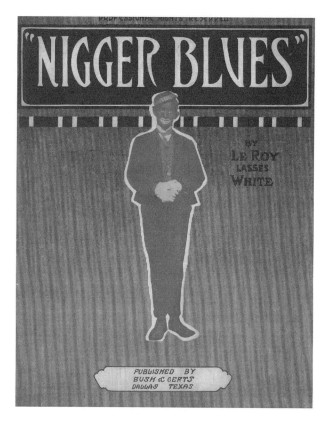

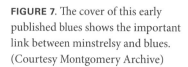

FIGURE 7. The cover of this early published blues shows the important link between minstrelsy and blues. (Courtesy Montgomery Archive)

entirely segregated. However, while it is certainly true that white blues performances dominated the mainstream, black performances of blues were regularly encountered by whites in a number of settings.

One such setting was minstrelsy. Black minstrel shows performed under tents—so-called tented minstrelsy—had developed just before the turn of the century, and the genre quickly established itself as a popular source of entertainment in the South, playing to racially mixed audiences. Beginning in about 1914, blues were featured in minstrel performances on a regular basis. In terms of vocal blues, most of the major minstrel companies carried specialist blues singers from about 1915. These included some of the preeminent blues stars of the era—and others who were soon to become leading stars, such as Bessie Smith, who performed with the Florida Blossom Minstrels in 1916. Band performances of blues were even more common, with arrangements of published blues by black composers such as W. C. Handy.[33]

Black minstrelsy also had an important presence in circus sideshows, where blacks regularly performed for mixed audiences. As in tented minstrelsy, blues were featured both by the minstrels and separately by the band that accompanied them. In fact, the presence of blues in circus sideshows predates that of tented minstrelsy by two years. A November 1912 report in a black newspaper, the *Indianapolis Freeman,* announced that John Eason's band, a black band performing in the sideshow of the Yankee Robinson Circus, was making a "daily hit" with "Baby Seals' Blues," the second blues to be published, following Smith and Brymn's "The Blues."[34] It seems that circus sideshows were important in disseminating blues over a wide area. For instance, in May 1914 the black bandleader J. C. Miles, at that time playing with Jones Bros. and Wilson's Three Ring Circus, reported to the *Freeman* that in Philadelphia blues "goes bigger . . . than it does in Bam [Alabama]."[35]

Another opportunity for whites to experience black performances of blues was provided by medicine shows. Medicine shows were a unique type of traveling entertainment, which focused on the peddling of a particular, often bogus, medicinal product through a folksy variety show. Performers tended to be folk-based and audiences often racially mixed, a combination of factors that allowed whites to encounter folk blues directly. Many of the folk musicians who recorded blues in the 1920s and 1930s cut their teeth in medicine shows, including Coley Jones, Jim Jackson, Pink Anderson, Henry "Ragtime Texas" Thomas, and Will Shade. While medicine shows were most common in the South, they were not confined there. For instance, Gus Cannon, a pioneer songster and early bluesman who began working in medicine shows in 1914, visited Chicago with Doc Benson's medicine show in 1927.[36] Whereas tented minstrelsy and circus sideshows allowed whites to experience black performance of popular blues, medicine shows allowed whites to experience blues in its rawer folk form.

In addition, there were very occasional opportunities for mainstream audiences to hear blacks playing blues in vaudeville. For instance, the Creole Band, a pioneering seven-piece outfit from New Orleans containing some of the most important jazz musicians of the era, toured extensively in mainstream vaudeville from 1914 to 1918. The band is known to have featured blues, particularly those of W. C. Handy and his associates.[37] However, this circumstance was exceptional: Black musical acts in vaudeville were unusual, and those featuring blues were even rarer. The reality is that, aside from tented minstrelsy, circus sideshows, and medicine shows, white exposure to black performances of blues was for the most part very limited.

However, this limited exposure pertained only to *live* performance. Recordings were a different matter. There were a substantial number of blues recordings made before 1921 by African American artists on disc and on piano rolls. The disc recordings are of two types, vocal and band. There was only one artist to record vocal blues before the watershed of Mamie Smith's "Crazy Blues" in August 1920. That was the African American singer-comedian Bert Williams, who waxed three titles between November 1919 and May 1920: "Unlucky Blues," "Lonesome Alimony Blues," and "I'm Sorry I Ain't Got It, You Could Have It If I Had It Blues."[38] These recordings, made by Williams for Columbia in his inimitable half-spoken, half-sung style, were top sellers: A total of 129,000 copies of "Lonesome Alimony Blues" and 183,800 of "Unlucky Blues" were shipped.[39] These enormous quantities indicate Williams's popularity with mainstream audiences, which was unique for an African American entertainer of that era. And while they are quite different in style from "Crazy Blues," I would strongly suspect that the success of these recordings paved the way for Smith's recording, whose release in the fall of 1920 opened the floodgates for African American vocal performances of blues. By the end of the year, an additional eight titular blues had been recorded, four by Smith herself (for Okeh), the others by fellow vaudevillians Lucille Hegamin and Noble Sissle (for the Arto and Emerson labels, respectively).

Band recordings of blues by African Americans in the pre-1921 era are thankfully more common than those by singers. Altogether four black bands are known to have recorded blues, those of W. C. Handy, Ford Dabney, James Reese Europe, and Wilbur Sweatman. The performances ranged from a rather square semimilitary style to something much closer to jazz. Again, a number of these records were top sellers, especially those recorded by Sweatman for Columbia. The best-selling of all seems to have been "Kansas City Blues" (Columbia A2768), which shipped 180,300 copies, but there were at least half a dozen of his other blues recordings that also sold extremely well.[40] Handy recorded five blues in the Columbia sessions of September 1917. These also seem to have been healthy sellers and are discussed in more detail in chapter 4. Europe recorded for the smaller Pathé label, and while no exact figures are known, sales were probably less than those for Sweatman's and Handy's recordings. Dabney was associated with the obscure label Aeolian Vocalion. His sales were therefore comparatively small (copies of his records are very rare today), which is ironic considering that he recorded more blues than his colleagues; indeed, he recorded more than a dozen blues between 1917 and 1919, ranging from "Rainy Day Blues," a lightly blues-inflected popular song by Frank Warschauer, to "Slow Drag Blues," a strongly folk-influenced instrumental blues by black pianist Q. Roscoe Snowden.

Finally, there were recordings on piano rolls. All told, five black pianists are known to have recorded blues before 1921: the stride pianists James P. Johnson and Charles Luckyeth Roberts, ragtimer Eubie Blake, composer Maceo Pinkard, and Clarence M. Jones, a versatile and underrated performer based in Chicago's South Side. All of these recorded one or two blues songs within the period, except for Jones, who recorded at least a dozen (Jones was, in fact, one of the most prolific roll artists of his day). As has already been noted, piano rolls on average had quite small, and often minimal, sales. The impact of these blues rolls was therefore relatively minor compared to that of blues records. This is not, however, to deny that musically they contain interesting and at times excellent performances. For instance, the five versions of his composition "Mama's Blues" that James P. Johnson recorded in 1917 for various roll labels demonstrate his dexterity and creativity to great advantage.[41]

• • •

One wonders whether Chris Smith and Tim Brymn had any sense of what was to follow when they copyrighted "The Blues" at the beginning of 1912. Less than a decade later, blues were all over America. New songs were being published at the rate of one every few days, ranging from standard popular material with a mere hint of blues to out-and-out "low down" numbers, and records and piano rolls were appearing at much the same rate. And the music was being performed everywhere: in vaudeville, musicals, revues, circuses, minstrel and medicine shows, and elsewhere, played and sung for mainstream audiences by both whites and blacks. In nine short years, the genre had permeated almost the entire entertainment industry and become, along with its close relative jazz, the musical embodiment of a new, vibrant, modernistic spirit sweeping America.

CHAPTER 2

The Identity and Idiom
of Early Popular Blues

THE MAIN INFLUENCES: FOLK BLUES AND TIN PAN ALLEY

In chapter 1, I examined the nature and development of the early popular blues industry. I now turn to the heart of the matter: the music and texts of the 456 titular blues published between 1912 and the end of 1920. This chapter provides a general overview of the identity of popular blues and examines its idiom in some detail. The starting point is a brief discussion of the two basic forces that shaped early popular blues: folk blues, on the one hand, and the popular music industry of the day, commonly known as Tin Pan Alley, on the other.

Folk blues, as noted in the introduction, are blues whose prime means of transmission has been oral, as compared with popular blues, which have been transmitted via mass media, in this case, sheet music and recordings. In terms of the pre-1921 period covered by this study, folk blues includes not only the fully integrated style well known from later recordings by artists like Blind Lemon Jefferson and Robert Johnson, but also the proto-blues styles that were its immediate antecedents, found in the recorded legacy of such performers as Ragtime Henry Thomas and Gus Cannon, who, though they did not record until the 1920s, were professionally active before 1900.

By the second decade of the twentieth century, the popular music industry in America had become a thriving, multimillion dollar enterprise. The industry was at this time creatively centered in sheet music (see discussion in chapter 1). In other words, a new song usually appeared in notated form and only recorded after the fact. The heart of the industry was in New York City, specifically the section of Twenty-eighth Street running between Broadway and Sixth Avenue, which by the late 1890s had become the location of many of the major song publishers.

The term *Tin Pan Alley* was the original nickname for the street itself: it referred to the sound of the latest hits being continuously demonstrated on music publishers' pianos, which allegedly sounded like a cacophony of tin pans being struck together. The term was then used by extension to describe first the song industry generally and then the actual music. And what a range of music it was: everything from parlor songs to the latest fox-trots, old-fashioned waltzes to snappy ragtime numbers, sentimental tear-jerkers to humorous songs, the latest operetta hits to ethnic parodies. Tin Pan Alley was a stylistic babel that truly reflected the melting-pot culture that produced it.

As mentioned in the introduction, the commercialization of blues during the 1910s—what one might term its Tin-Pan-Alley-fication—resulting in the genre I call popular blues, has traditionally been regarded with deep suspicion. This stems from a deep-rooted attitude on the part of folklorists and blues commentators, who viewed commercialism as "a cheapening and deteriorative force," to quote the jazz historian Rudi Blesh.[1] Behind this attitude lay the belief developed in the nineteenth century that folk music was the supreme artistic expression of Man, the higher embodiment of a pure, spontaneous creativity uncorrupted by the trappings of civilization. This belief was clearly expressed by the jazz writer Hughes Panassié when he argued that, "in music, primitive man generally has greater talent than civilized man."[2]

Although more recent writing about blues has not been so extreme in its idealization of folk music, nor in its demonization of popular music, the attitude persists in blues culture, albeit in a toned down form. Indeed the appeal of "roots music" for many of today's fans is that it allegedly offers a direct power of expression as compared to "sell-out" contemporary pop music.[3]

Nonetheless, it is important to realize that the dualism between folk blues and popular music is an invention after the fact. Early blues performers did not recognize any conflict between the two genres. The reason for this is that most of them were not self-conscious blues specialists, but *songsters,* musical all-rounders competent in many styles, including ragtime/jazz songs, sentimental parlor songs, gospel songs, hymns, and folk ballads.[4] Even musicians nowadays thought of as quintessential blues artists, such as Blind Lemon Jefferson and Robert Johnson, were highly versatile performers.[5] The disproportionate number of blues they recorded has often resulted in an incomplete understanding of the musical identities of many blues artists. For example, at the time of his discovery by Alan Lomax in the early 1940s, Muddy Waters, later to become one of the most famous of bluesmen, included in his repertoire such pop standards as "Chattanooga Choo-Choo," "Darktown Strutters' Ball," "Dinah," "Blues in the Night," "Red Sails in the Sunset," and "Whatcha Know Joe?" along with a slew of commercial hillbilly songs, including "You Are My Sunshine."[6]

Even more impressive was the repertoire of Howard "Louie Bluie" Armstrong, a black fiddle and mandolin player from Tennessee who recorded traditional-style blues in 1930 as a member of a string band called the Tennessee Chocolate Drops. Armstrong, who died in 2003 at the age of 96, not only played a wide range of Tin Pan Alley tunes, but also square-dance pieces, Gene Autry numbers, and an extensive selection of Italian, Polish, Hawaiian, and Mexican songs.[7] Then, as now, versatility was a key requirement for the jobbing musician, and while Armstrong may have been unusually flexible in his choice of repertoire, there were very few blues artists recording before the 1940s who were not adept at performing popular material, even if in many cases they did not record it.

In suggesting that early folk blues and popular music in general had a relatively harmonious relationship—at least as far as its performers and therefore its audiences were concerned—I do not mean to suggest that the two genres were closely related. While Tin Pan Alley songs of the 1910s covered a broad stylistic range, folk blues of the day was distinct from any of them, for it had not yet been incorporated into the melee of mainstream pop production. Indeed, one can view the entire phenomenon of 1910s popular blues as the result of the interaction of a regional ethnic culture—folk blues—with the commercial mainstream of Tin Pan Alley. How that interaction plays out in popular blues of the 1910s is the main subject of this chapter. I begin with an overview of blues songs and of instrumental blues, followed by a more detailed examination of the idiom of popular blues.

AN OVERVIEW OF POPULAR BLUES SONGS

There were nearly 350 published blues songs produced within the period (i.e., before 1921). Examples 4 and 5 offer two contrasting instances. Example 4 is a 1920 composition, "The Broadway Blues," with words by Arthur Swanstrom and music by Morgan Carey. Although now long forgotten, in its day the song was quite successful: twelve disk recordings of it were released in 1920 alone, and there are five known piano rolls. Example 5 is "Nigger Blues" by Leroy "Lasses" White. This is one of the first blues to be published, copyrighted in 1912.[8] It also enjoyed some commercial success, with four disk recordings issued between 1916 and 1919 and four known piano rolls from approximately the same period.

The overall structure of "Broadway Blues" consists of two sixteen bar verses (mm. 7–22) and a thirty-two bar chorus (mm. 23–54). From this point of view, it is identical to a regular Tin Pan Alley popular song. "Nigger Blues" is quite different. It has no chorus and consists of three twelve-bar verses (beginning mm. 10, 22, and 34, respectively). The music for these three verses is repeated with a second set of words, making six verses altogether. The fact that there is no chorus, and that the verses are twelve rather than sixteen measures in length, makes this song highly unorthodox according to the standard of Tin Pan Alley. Instead, it strongly suggests the influence of folk blues, which typically have precisely this form. It would superficially appear, then, that "Broadway Blues" is closer to a regular pop song, while "Nigger Blues" is strongly influenced by folk blues.

This impression is confirmed when the songs are examined in more detail. The harmony for each verse of "Nigger Blues" conforms to a standard twelve bar blues progression. I have

EXAMPLE 4. Swanstrom and Morgan, "Broadway Blues" (1920), complete

EXAMPLE 4. Continued

EXAMPLE 4. Continued

EXAMPLE 4. Continued

EXAMPLE 5. White, "Nigger Blues" (1912), complete

EXAMPLE 5. Continued

EXAMPLE 5. Continued

indicated this on the score for the first verse (beginning m. 10). The basic harmonic structure is given in table 4.

The harmony for "Broadway Blues" is far more sophisticated. Look, for example, at the chords for the first half of the verse, provided in table 5. Exotic colorations like the G♭ (♭III) chord in m. 8 are a long way from the earthy harmony of country blues and clearly derive from mainstream influences. No less revealing is the dramatic sustained B⁷ (♭VI) chord used at the musical turning-point of the song at m. 47. This device, much used in art music and known technically as a German sixth, seems almost operatic in its effect.

Turning to the texts for the two songs, the six verses of "Nigger Blues" use the familiar AAB form of blues. The first, for example, runs:

A: Oh! The blues ain't nothing, Oh! the blues ain't nothing but a good man feeling bad.
   [Repeated]
B: Oh! that's a feeling I've often had.

Table 4. Harmonic Structure of "Nigger Blues" Verse

Measure	10	11	12	13	14	15	16	17	18	19	20	21
Chord	B♭	B♭	B♭	B♭⁷	E♭Maj⁷	E♭⁷	B♭	B♭	F⁷	F⁷	B♭	B♭
Numeric	I	I	I	I	IV	IV	I	I	V	V	I	I
Prototype Blues	I	I	I	I	IV	IV	I	I	V	V	I	I

Table 5. Harmonic Analysis of "Broadway Blues," Chorus, mm. 7–14

Measure	7	8	9	10	11	12	13/14
Chord	E♭	G♭	A♭m/C♭	B♭7	E♭	C♭7	B♭7
Numeric	I	♭III	iv	V	I	♭VI	V

This and the other five verses of the song are traditional texts widely used in folk blues. In fact, the original unpublished copyright deposit of the song in the Library of Congress is more extensive and contains no fewer than fifteen such folk-derived verses.[9] The text for "The Broadway Blues" is quite different. It is fashioned in the manner of a popular song. The chorus, for example, is a series of pairs of short rhyming lines (beginning "When your heart is aching for the trees / When you long to hear those buzzin' bees"), climaxing with the line "You've got the Broadway Blues" in m. 51.

It is possible to analyze these two songs in more detail, but it is not really necessary. The point is clearly made that the music and text of "Broadway Blues" is heavily influenced by contemporaneous pop music and hardly at all by folk blues, while "Nigger Blues" is disproportionately influenced by folk blues. This is not to say that either song is a "pure" example of the genre from which it is principally derived. For example, "Broadway Blues" makes striking use of blue notes (such as the blues third [F♯] found in the right hand of the piano part in m. 26), a device clearly related, even if only loosely, to blues culture. Similarly, m. 9 of "Nigger Blues" uses a vamp, a continuously repeated measure (or series of measures) inserted between the introduction and the verse to give the singer extra preparation time (note that m. 9 has the indication "[play] till ready"). This device is not usually found in folk blues but is ubiquitous in Tin Pan Alley songs.

Despite these and a few other small "impurities," these two popular blues are unusually closely related to their dominant influences. Each of the 456 blues published before 1921 can be viewed as being located at a particular point on a continuum that ranges from full-fledged Tin Pan Alley songs like "Broadway Blues" to overtly folk-derived works like "Nigger Blues." To put it another way, folk blues and Tin Pan Alley can be thought of as the parents of 456 "children," each of whom displays genetic traits of its parents in varying proportions.

Looking at this question of genetics in more detail, there are four genes that determine the fundamental character of published blues songs. Two come from Tin Pan Alley and the other two from folk blues. Of the Tin Pan Alley genes, the first is responsible for the structure of the song. Nearly all popular blues follow the Tin Pan Alley structural formula, which consists of an introduction, a vamp, two or more verses, and a chorus (also known as the *refrain*), with the chorus acting as the musical and expressive focus for the entire song. It is quite different from the stanzaic structure of folk blues (i.e., one verse after another with no chorus). Thus, "Nigger Blues," which is stanzaic and yet a popular blues, is exceptional; almost all other popular blues songs have the verse-chorus structure of "Broadway Blues."

The second Tin Pan Alley gene informs the lyrics and might be termed the *gene of thematic cohesion*. Popular songs tend to thematic cohesion in their lyrics, while folk blues do not. From this point of view, "Broadway Blues" is a typical popular song. Everything in the song is an expansion of the single idea of having the "Broadway Blues," that is, being tired of city life and hankering for the country. Compare this with the lyric to "Nigger Blues." The first two verses talk about the nature of blues ("a good man feeling bad" in verse 1, "the dog-gone heart disease" in verse 2). The next two verses are concerned mainly with the train the singer takes because of his blues. The last two are concerned with the singer's death. There is no overt single theme or image here. Although one can argue that there is a thematic link between pairs of verses (for example, the train in verses 3 and 4), such links involve only part of the song. In any case, the linkages are quite weak. For example, it would make more sense to reverse the order of verses 5 and 6, so that the singer sings first of killing himself and then of the events after his death, rather than the other way round. Most popular blues are cohesively themed like "Broadway Blues," while only a very few have the seemingly disparate themes of "Nigger Blues."[10]

The two genetic components of folk blues have equally important roles in determining the character of popular blues songs as do the Tin Pan Alley genes just examined. The first component is the strongly personal flavor of folk blues. All folk blues are sung in the first person, and there is always the implication that the events, actions, and emotions of the song are ones that are happening, or have happened, to the singer. So it is with popular blues, which are usually sung in the first person and clearly have the singer as the central protagonist. For example, in the famous opening lines of W. C. Handy's "St. Louis Blues"—"I hate to see de evening sun go down / 'cause my baby, he done lef' dis town"—it is clearly meant to be the singer, not anyone else, who has been abandoned by her lover.[11] Only about 20 percent of published blues are nonpersonal, that is, sung in the third person (or, occasionally, the second person, as in "Broadway Blues"). Nonpersonal blues describe the events, actions, and emotions of others, not the singer. An example is Walter Hirsch and Spencer Williams's "Paradise Blues," which is about a pianist in an Alabama cabaret and the effect of his playing on a black female admirer.[12] The role of the singer here is one of storyteller, and though the first person is used in the chorus, it is only because it quotes the words of the admirer to her pianist. The first two lines, for example, are "Honey, don't play me no op'ra, / Play me some blue melody." Clearly songs like "Paradise Blues" are quite different from the more personal type of folk and popular blues; equally clearly, they derive from Tin Pan Alley, which often uses this approach.

The second genetic characteristic of folk blues that is dominant in popular blues is one that defines the entire genre: the assumption that the singer has the blues. Most popular blues make the same assumption, and in fact a large majority of the personal-type songs explicitly say so at some point. For example, in the opening to "St. Louis Blues," it is immediately apparent that the singer has the blues, a fact that she explicitly states in the chorus, which begins "Got de St. Louis Blues, jes blue as I can be."

A final question of genetics concerns the intensity of popular blues lyrics. An important quality of folk blues lyrics is their force and directness of expression. For example, consider the text of Blind Blake's "Early Morning Blues":

1. Early this mornin' my baby made me sore,
I'm goin' away to leave you, ain't comin' back no more.
2. "Tell me pretty mama where did you stay last night?"
"It ain't none of business, Daddy, since I treat you right."
3. When you see me sleepin', baby, don't you think I'm drunk:
I got one eye on my pistol and the other on your trunk.
4. Love you pretty mama, b'lieve me 'tain't no lie,
The day you try to quit me baby, that's the day you die. [13]

The main theme here is the faithlessness of the lover and the threat of her desertion. It is stated in uncompromising language, with the singer demanding to know where she was last night and threatening to kill her if she leaves him. The down-to-earth quality of the text is enhanced by the use of the vernacular idiom throughout, especially in phrases like "my baby made me sore" in the first line, and the racy dialogue between the couple in the second verse. Altogether, this lyric has a powerful directness of expression.

In this regard, the lyrics of folk blues are quite different from those of Tin Pan Alley, which rarely deal with emotional issues in this head-on manner. For example, take "When I Lost You," a popular song by Irving Berlin from 1912. This song is comparable with "Early Morning Blues" in that its central theme is the loss of a lover. Here, as may also be the case with "Early Morning Blues," the song was inspired by a real-life event, the death of Berlin's wife five months after their marriage from an illness contracted while they were on their honeymoon in Cuba. [14] The chorus runs:

I lost the sunshine and roses,
I lost the heavens of blue,
I lost the beautiful rainbow,
I lost the morning dew;
I lost the angel who gave me summer
The whole winter through,
I lost the gladness that turned into sadness
When I lost you. [15]

The formal language of this text, along with its sophisticated syntax (the entire chorus is one sustained series of parallel phrases) and sentimentalized imagery based on nature and religion ("angel who gave me summer") is a far cry from the visceral immediacy of "Early Morning Blues."

The lyrical content of most popular blues is located somewhere between these two extremes. On the one hand, there are lyrics like those of "Nigger Blues," which, being essentially a transcription of a folk blues performance, are of an earthy, hard-hitting style ("The blues ain't nothing but the doggone heart disease," "When a woman gets blue, she hangs her little head and cries," etc.). Clearly this is much closer to "Early Morning Blues" than "When I Lost You." By contrast, take this popular blues lyric, from the chorus of a 1916 song by Lew Berk titled "I've Got the Blues":

> I've got the blues,
> And they won't leave me,
> I've got the blues,
> And all for you.
> I want you near me,
> Come back and cheer me,
> You often told me
> Your heart was true.
> The time will come
> When you'll get lonely.
> And then you'll know
> That you were wrong.
> When you get lonesome
> Just for someone's love,
> That someone will be me,
> As sure as stars above,
> Some day you'll say,
> I've got the blues.[16]

The theme again is of desertion, as in both "Early Morning Blues" and "When I Lost You." However, instead of threatening violence as in "Early Morning Blues," here the singer's response, at least in part, is to try and win back his lover by arguing that at some point in the future she will want him again. It is an indirect and reasoned reaction, and the mood is supported by language that is never passionate and is at times quite poetic ("When you get lonesome / Just for someone's love, / That someone will be me"). Clearly, then, this lyric is closer in expression to "When I Lost You" than to "Early Morning Blues," although it avoids the former's intricate syntax and poignant imagery of roses, heavens of blue, angels, and morning dew.

THE FIVE CATEGORIES OF POPULAR BLUES SONGS

Most popular blues songs belong to one or more of five basic categories. These I have labeled *relationship blues, nostalgia blues, prohibition blues, war blues,* and *reflexive blues.* I shall discuss each in turn.

Relationship Blues

Much the most common of the five is the relationship blues. As the name implies, it deals with the tensions of sexual relationships, especially questions of separation, threatened or otherwise, from the beloved. This was the theme of Berk's "I've Got the Blues." Another example is "Washtub Blues," a 1920 blues by Arthur U. James and Frank Wright, where a woman works all day at her washtub yearning for her lover who has left her, begging him to return ("I'll buy your clothes / I'll even shine your shoes").[17] Her cry at the beginning and end of the chorus is "Daddy, come home!" This phrase is taken up on the cover of the sheet music, vividly illustrating her obsessive state: it is on a sign by her front door, on the washing hanging on the line, and in the cries of five animals gathered around her doorstep while she sits on an upturned washtub in a Rodinesque pose of grief.

There were at least 130 such relationship blues produced before 1921. The dominance of this type clearly shows the influence of folk blues, for relationship problems are overwhelmingly the most common cause of the blues in folk blues (for example, in Blind Blake's "Early Morning Blues," examined above). In the words of folk blues scholar Jeff Todd Titon, early folk blues songs "were overtly concerned with love between men and women."[18] Or, as Son House expressed it: "[T]he blues exists, and that comes between male and female bein' in love. . . . And when one has been deceived by the other."[19] Now, although "male and female bein' in love" is also a ubiquitous theme of Tin Pan Alley non-blues, the negative emotional states on which folk blues

FIGURE 8. A popular blues from 1920, whose cover graphically illustrates its theme of the desertion of a lover. (Author's collection)

are predicated—unhappiness, despair, depression, and so on—are far less common in Tin Pan Alley songs than in blues. For instance, one survey suggested that the theme of abandonment by a lover, standard in folk and popular blues, is only found occasionally in Tin Pan Alley non-blues.[20] From this point of view, Berlin's "When I Lost You" is unusual. Generally, then, the dominance of relationship blues in popular blues points to the influence of folk blues.

Nostalgia Blues

The second category of popular blues is nostalgia blues. In this type of blues, the cause for the blues is not personal relationships, but rather nostalgic yearning for the country and rural life. This theme was already encountered in "Broadway Blues," where the despondent city dweller is "aching for the trees," longs to "hear those buzzin' bees," and wants "to eat a cake / Just like your mammy used to bake." This song is atypical for a nostalgia blues in that the yearning is for the country in general. More commonly, a specific region or town is the focus. An example is "I've Got the Blue Ridge Blues," a commercially successful blues from 1918, in which the singer pines for the delights of the Blue Ridge Mountains,

> where the sunsets seem so mellow
> And all the fields are green and yellow.
> Golden Rod is rearin'
> in the cabin clearin',
> Smoke atrailin' up the valley.[21]

This kind of nostalgic longing is simply not found in folk blues, so some explanation is required as to the origin of such blues.

In fact, an explanation is easily come by. Anyone familiar with the output of Tin Pan Alley will recognize the type of lyric I just quoted. It belongs to that class of popular song arising in the early 1800s that embodied the yearning for rural roots, particularly in the South, and includes, in the pre–Tin Pan Alley era, such classics as Stephen Foster's "My Old Kentucky Home" (1853) and James Bland's "Carry Me Back to My Old Virginny" (1878). By the early twentieth century, such songs had become a staple of the burgeoning popular song industry and often depicted (or at any rate implied) the yearning of the city-dweller for his rural roots. Examples are Irving Berlin's "I Want to Go Back to Michigan" (1913) and Ballard MacDonald and James Hanley's "Back Home Again in Indiana" (1917). The song-type remained important into the Depression era with Stuart Gorrell and Hoagy Carmichael's "Georgia on My Mind" (1930) and Clarence Muse and Otis and Leon Rene's "When It's Sleepy Time Down South" (1931).

Nostalgia blues are generally titled "The X Blues" or "I've Got the X Blues," where X is the place that is remembered.[22] Spencer Williams's "Tishomingo Blues," for example, is about the town of Tishomingo, Mississippi, "among the cypress trees," where "they make you welcome all the time."[23] It is true that a number of folk blues, such as Daddy Stovepipe's "Tuxedo Blues" (Gennett 6212, 1927) or Billy Bird's "Alabama Blues" (Columbia 14381–D, 1928), also bear titles featuring place-names. However, most folk blues of this type "really deal with the relation of man and woman," as one early survey of such compositions concluded, and not with a yearning for the place itself.[24]

Nostalgia blues, therefore, took the folk blues device of titling a blues with a place-name and combined it with the long-established Tin Pan Alley theme of yearning for a place. This transference from folk blues culture was partially legitimated by the fact that this type of Tin Pan Alley song was most often about the South, and blues were perceived as a southern phenomenon. However, I would also argue that the notion of yearning for a place is simply a metaphorical extension of the yearning for a lover that is at the heart of folk blues expression. Evidence for this is provided by a number of popular blues where the longing is for both a particular place *and* a lover. For instance, in "Carolina Blues" from 1916, the singer longs to return to Carolina, stating:

> When Ah get home with Dinah,
> Carolina will look good to me.
> How Ah long to be down
> In mah little hometown
> In dear ole Carolina
> 'Neath the pine again with Dinah Brown.[25]

Here girl and state—drawn from the different traditions of folk blues and Tin Pan Alley—are effectively fused into one symbol of longing. Hence nostalgic blues are in fact related to, and partially derived from, relationship blues.

Prohibition Blues

The third type of popular blues is prohibition blues. Although prohibition was not officially enacted nationwide until 1920, twenty-six states were dry by 1916, and the topic became a preoccupation in American culture in general and popular blues in particular during the second half of the decade. The earliest reference to prohibition in popular blues is also one of the most famous: W. C. Handy's "Beale Street Blues" of 1916. Beale Street is in Memphis, the base of Handy's operations at the time; the state of Tennessee had gone dry in 1910. Thus the singer jokes:

> Goin' to the river, maybe, bye and bye
> Goin' to the river, and there's a reason why
> Because the river's wet and Beale Street's done gone dry.

After 1917, a number of blues appeared with the specific theme of prohibition. The most successful of these was "Alcoholic Blues" by Tin Pan Alley veterans Albert von Tilzer and Edward Laska,[26] a good-sized hit that received a total of twenty-two recordings up to the end of 1920.[27] In this song, as in most prohibition blues songs, the singer craves booze and laments its unavailability. The chorus begins:

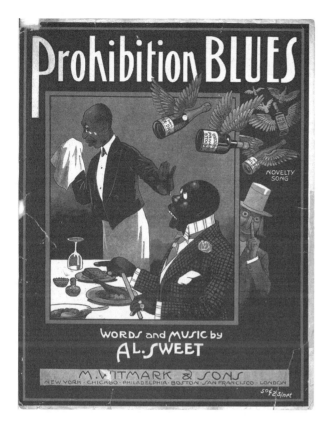

FIGURE 9. This 1917 blues deals humorously with one of the hot-button issues of the day, prohibition. The cover depicts a caricature of a well-dressed African American sitting down to eat in a restaurant and pointing to an empty wine-glass. The tearful waiter is clearly unable to help. Meanwhile, bottles of alcoholic beverages ascend to heaven on angelic wings, and a symbolic figure of The Blues (shaded grayish-blue in the original) wags a moralistic finger at the viewer. (Author's collection)

I've got the blues, I've got the blues
I've got the alcoholic blues.
No more beer my heart to cheer;
Good-bye whisky, you made me frisky.
So long high-ball, so long gin.
Oh, tell me when you comin' back agin?

The choice of drink as a subject for popular blues is presumably influenced in part by folk blues, where it is also a standard theme.[28] However, the specific focus of most commercial prohibition blues, the yearning for drink, is uncommon in folk blues. I would argue that such songs are, like nostalgia blues, a metaphoric extension of the basic blues archetype of the blues being caused by the abandonment of the lover, the bottle here taking the place of the lover.

War Blues

The fourth category of blues is war blues, that is, popular blues songs based on the theme of World War I. Tin Pan Alley responded to America's entry into the war in 1917 with a fervent outpouring of patriotic and war-related songs, and war blues are really part of this wider cultural phenomenon. They approach their topic in various ways, some dealing with it seriously, others not. "War Bride Blues," a Texas blues from 1917, deals with the despair of a wife whose husband has gone to war.[29] This lyric is particularly interesting in that it uses a number of folk blues lines. For example, the chorus ends:

> Down the road as far as I could see,
> Thought I saw my dear old used to be.

The second verse contains the first appearance in print of a familiar blues image: "two sixteen done carried poor John away"—"two sixteen" referring to the 2:16 train. The most famous instance of this device is probably that which opens Jelly Roll Morton's "Mamie's Blues": "Two nineteen done took my babe away."[30]

"Those Navy Blues," also from 1917, deals with another serious issue, the fears of a man who is shortly to be enlisted in the navy:

> Ev'ry time I try to sleep, I lie awake
> Thinkin' 'bout the lovely corpse that I would make
> If ever I sailed upon the deep blue sea,
> Think what those torpedoes could be doin' to me.[31]

Domer C. Browne and W. C. Handy's "The Kaiser's Got the Blues" is in a lighter vein, satirizing German ambitions in the war.[32] The first verse runs:

> There's a man this very minute
> Wants the world and all that's in it,
> Says his "Kultur's" gotta rule both land and sea.
> And I know it was heart-rending
> With our Uncle Sam a-sending
> All our soldier boys,
> To tell him what we'd choose.
> When we refused,
> The Kaiser's got the blues
> (He's got the weary blues).

Such war songs, humorous but with a strong patriotic undercurrent, were produced in great numbers by Tin Pan Alley. Two non-blues examples that were popular at the time are "We Don't Want the Bacon (What We Want is a Piece of the Rhine)"[33] and "The Russians Were Rushin,' The Yanks Started Yankin."[34] Clearly, "The Kaiser's Got the Blues" took this standard Tin Pan Alley genre and grafted it onto the notion of having the blues. Incidentally, in this work, the blues idiom is reflected in the music as well as the words. For example, the harmonic scheme for the verse quoted above is a standard twelve-bar sequence.

Reflexive Blues

The fifth and last category of popular blues song is reflexive blues. Such blues are a manifestation of a specialized subgenre of popular music known as *reflexive song*. A reflexive song is defined as any song that dwells upon the ingredients of the song itself—the music or lyrics—and/or some aspect of its performance, such as dance, the performers, the venue (cabaret, club, theater), or the audience. Reflexive songs are an important, if rather undervalued, subgenre of popular music, and thousands upon thousands of them were created for musicals or as independent songs during the Tin Pan Alley era.[35]

The most famous example of a reflexive blues from this era is the song version of W. C. Handy's "The Memphis Blues" (1913). George Norton's lyric focuses on a performance of the blues by Handy's band in Memphis, vividly describing the instruments and the players:

> They got a fiddler there that always slickens his hair,
> And folks he sure do pull some bow,
> And when the big bassoon seconds to the trombone's croon, croon,
> It moans just like a sinner on Revival Day.[36]

This description of the act of musical performance is absolutely typical of reflexive blues. A second characteristic is a description of the effects of the performance on the protagonist, which are usually quite extreme. For instance, "The Memphis Blues" tells how the music of Handy's band "wraps a spell" around the heart of the protagonist, and how it "sets [him] wild." In Hirsch and Williams's "Paradise Blues," the female protagonist begs the pianist in a southern cabaret to play the blues, and the song graphically describes the effects of the music on her:

> Lay right on those piano keys,
> I feel that feelin' way down to my knees,
> 'Cause when you play the Blues,
> I'm right in Paradise.

A third characteristic of reflexive blues is a preoccupation with the dance accompanying the blues and its effects on the dancer.[37] Thus, for example, the chorus of "The Hula Blues" (1920):

> Oh, Oh, Oh, those loving Hula Blues!
> Tell me, have you heard those loving Hula Blues?
> You can't imagine what you're feeling blue about,
> You simply glide and take a slide,
> And you want to shout;
> You wriggle, you giggle,
> You wriggle to the Hula Blues.[38]

Reflexive blues songs of the 1910s correspond closely with non-blues reflexive songs of the day. For example, the notion of hearing a band play African American derived music—as in Handy's "The Memphis Blues"—is strongly reminiscent of Irving Berlin's enormously influential "Alexander's Ragtime Band," a reflexive song from 1911.[39] In this song the protagonist and his unnamed partner go to hear ragtime played by the band of the eponymous Alexander, "the bestest band what am" that "can play a bugle call like you never heard before / So natural that you want to go to war." Likewise, the descriptions of the music's powerful effects on the protagonist are

FIGURE 10. "I've got the Shimmee Blues" is an example of a reflexive blues themed around dance, in this case the then fashionable and controversial shimmy, which, as discussed below, was often used to accompany blues performance. (Author's collection)

standard in reflexive non-blues. In Berlin's "Stop That Rag (Keep on Playing, Honey)," for instance, the female black protagonist fears she is "suffocating with delight" when listening to ragtime.[40] This compares closely with the protagonist being "set wild" by the playing of the band in "The Memphis Blues," and even more with "Paradise Blues," where the playing of the pianist puts the protagonist "right in Paradise." The device of describing dance steps within the song—as in "Hula Blues"—became standard in pop songs of the 1910s, particularly after the runaway success of Burris and Smith's 1913 "Ballin' the Jack," the chorus of which consists entirely of instructions to the dancer, beginning "first you put your two knees close up tight, / Then you sway them to left, then you sway them to the right."[41] All this suggests that reflexive blues are basically a form of popular song, particularly when we bear in mind that reflexivity is rare in folk blues.

AN OVERVIEW OF INSTRUMENTAL BLUES

Instrumental blues show the same wide stylistic range as the blues songs: some have a strong folk flavor, while others are indistinguishable from the standard fare of Tin Pan Alley. The folksier side is represented by example 6, "Snakey Blues," by William Nash, published in 1915.[42] There are a number of folk blues influences at work here. For instance, the first and third strains utilize the standard twelve-bar blues sequence (mm. 1–12, 29–40), with the first strain using a folk melody that first appeared in print in 1904 (see example 86). This melody uses a striking number of blue notes (for example, the blue thirds [D♯] in mm. 1, 3, 7, and 8, and the blue seventh [B♭] in m. 4). In addition, there is the slow tempo, indicated by the designation "slow" at the beginning and the mournful feel as conveyed by the Spanish term *lutoso*, meaning sad or mournful (mm. 1 and 41).[43] There is also the piano writing, which is generally rough, and almost crude at times. Take, for example, m. 32, with the unusually dissonant chord at the beginning of the second beat in the right hand; the equally dissonant chord that follows it at the start of m. 33 and the subsequent melodic plunge of nearly two octaves; and the peculiar melody line in m. 43 that clashes so eccentrically with the bass. This type of writing pervades the work. It might be tempting to dismiss it as compositional amateurishness were it not for the fact that it is found in many other early southern-published instrumental blues. This strongly suggests that it is an example of a particular regional style of folk blues piano. The most interesting and explicit connection with folk blues in "Snakey Blues" is found in its final section (beginning at m. 41). Subtitled "Fare Thee," this is a folk proto-blues whose full title is "Fare Thee, Honey, Fare Thee Well" and that is known from numerous published and recorded versions beginning in 1901. The folkiness of "Snakey Blues" explains why it had little commercial success, despite being published by W. C. Handy, the leading blues publisher of the day. It is known from just one piano roll (Ideal 6000) and one record (by Handy's band).[44]

Let us compare "Snakey Blues" with example 7, an extract from an instrumental blues from 1917 called "Bone-Head Blues" by Leo Gordon.[45] Like "Snakey Blues," this work has four sections, but in the interest of brevity I have only quoted the first two (mm. 5–20 and 21–36), which are preceded by a four bar introduction (mm. 1–4). It shows none of the folk blues influence found in "Snakey Blues." Harmonically, the two sections are of the standard sixteen-measure design—there is not a hint of the twelve-bar blues sequence in either section. There is also scarcely any use of blue notes, the only exception being the blue third (D♯) in the melody at the beginning of m. 17 (the two other sections that I have not quoted in the example are also not bluesy). In short, "Bone-Head Blues" is like "Broadway Blues" (example 4) in that there is little to distinguish it from the standard fare of Tin Pan Alley, whereas "Snakey Blues" is much like "Nigger Blues" (example 5) in that it draws directly on folk sources.

Most of the 110 or so instrumental blues that were produced before 1921 are essentially dance music. This does not mean that such blues were always used for dancing, but rather that they were composed in such a way—with a clear and consistent rhythm—that they could be used for dancing if the occasion required. In this respect, instrumental blues belong to a large family of social dances whose continuous popularity in American life since the middle of the nineteenth century had been one of the driving forces of the popular music industry. Members of this family included older style European-derived dances, like the waltz, quadrille, schottische, and

EXAMPLE 6. Nash, "Snakey Blues" (1915), complete

EXAMPLE 6. Continued

EXAMPLE 6. Continued

EXAMPLE 7. Gordon, "Bone-Head Blues" (1917), A and B strains

EXAMPLE 7. Continued

EXAMPLE 7. Continued

polka, along with innovative forms of the 1890s, such as the two-step, the cakewalk, and, in the newest wave of terpsichorean innovation, the one-step. Most compositions embodying these dance styles shared a basic structure that had became standard by the late 1800s. They were multisectional, that is, they comprised three or more sixteen-measure sections or strains, each repeated, and with at least one strain (typically the first) recurring somewhere in the structure. Most compositions contained at least one modulation, usually to a closely related key like the subdominant (e.g., F in the key of C).

Instrumental blues adopted precisely this same structure. To give just one instance, "Snakey Blues" (example 6) has four strains (beginning mm. 1, 13, 29, and 41, respectively). Each strain is repeated immediately after it is played, so we could define the work's structure as AABBCCDD. The piece begins in C Major and there are two key changes, the C strain (m. 29) being in F major (subdominant) and the D strain (m. 41) in Bb major (the subdominant of the subdominant). In fact, the structure of "Snakey Blues" is a little unorthodox. Most instrumental blues have three strains rather than four, and one key change is more common than two. It is also slightly unusual that no strain returns at a later point in the structure (for instance, if the work were typical, it would be expected that the A strain would return between the B and C strains).

Instrumental Blues and Ragtime

In general, instrumental blues are closely connected to ragtime. This is again illustrated by "Snakey Blues." For example, the A strain (mm. 1–12) uses such tell-tale ragtime traits as the "boom-chick" style left hand (mm. 3–4, 7–9a, 11a/b) and the frequent use of syncopation in the melody (for example, mm. 1, 4, 5, and 8). This connection between ragtime and blues was recognized at the time. For example, the sheet music for Ted S. Barron's "Original Blues" from 1914 has a footnote stating that "the Blues is a class of Southern Rag which derives its name from the fact that the melody contains so many socalled [*sic*] 'blue' notes."[46] Similarly, W. C. Handy in a 1916 article suggested that the main reason why his "Memphis Blues" should be considered blues rather than ragtime was because of the twelve-bar structure of two of its strains.[47] Both Barron's and Handy's compositions are subtitled "Southern Rag" to reinforce the connection, and this practice of subtitling blues as rags (and vice versa) is not uncommon in the period 1912–15 (for example, "Snakey Blues" is subtitled "An Etude in Ragtime").[48] A particularly striking instance of the interchangeability of the two genres is Handy's "Yellow Dog Blues" (1914). This song was first issued under the title "Yellow Dog Rag" and only given the more familiar title in 1919. The changed title resulted in enhanced popularity for the work. However, it was more than just a commercial ploy, for the work makes use of characteristic blues features such as the twelve-bar sequence and blue notes.[49] The fact that Handy, who was the leading figure in popular blues, was prepared to label such an obviously bluesy work a rag shows the close relationship between the two genres.

The Influence of the Fox-trot and Other Dance Styles

In addition to ragtime, there are three other genres that were major influences on early instrumental blues, and, like ragtime, they are all associated with dance. They are the fox-trot, the one-step, and jazz. I will deal first with the fox-trot.

The evidence is that instrumental blues was strongly linked with the fox-trot. For instance, a survey of thirty-eight recordings of instrumental blues (or instrumental versions of vocal blues) released before 1921 found that three-quarters were labeled fox-trots (of the remaining quarter, half were labeled one-steps, a term discussed below, while the other half did not designate a dance step). Although this sample is quite small, representing only about a tenth of the total number of blues records made before 1921, there is nothing to suggest that it is not representative: a parallel survey of blues piano rolls from the period gave similar results.[50]

Given the strong association of popular blues with the fox-trot, the question arises as to the relationship between the two genres. At first sight, this relationship might be dismissed as mere commercial opportunism, for the fox-trot, as the dance sensation of the age, was a label that could only benefit the sales of sheet music and records. However, deeper study suggests that the two genres are in fact strongly linked, through both music and dance. An understanding of these linkages sheds much light on the identity of popular blues, and I will therefore explore both sides of the musical and terpsichorean relationship in some detail, beginning with the latter.

The fox-trot emerged suddenly and triumphantly into the mainstream in the spring (or, according to some accounts, the summer) of 1914, when it garnered immediate and enduring popularity. There were a number of professional dancers who claimed to have originated the fox-trot. These include Joan Sawyer, Wallace McCutcheon, Oscar Duryea, Harry Fox (for whom the dance was supposed to have been named), and the dance team of Vernon and Irene Castle.[51] In fact, the strong likelihood is that the fox-trot was not created by an individual, but that it was adapted from folk culture, like almost every other important vernacular dance of the era. This

FIGURE 11. This fox-trot from 1914, one of the first to be published, shows a version of the dance on its cover by two early practitioners. Fox-trots and blues are intimately linked in terms of both music and dance, and the two genres became popular at around the same time. (Author's collection)

would account, in large measure, for the phenomenon of multiple claimants for the dance. As historian Reid Badger puts it, "roughly the same dance was evolving . . . from several sources at the same time."[52] Sawyer, McCutcheon, and all the other claimants are therefore to be thought of as adaptors of the dance from folk culture, not as its inventors. Of particular significance for the present inquiry is the role of the Castles.

The Castles apparently developed their version of the fox-trot while on tour in April and May 1914. It was directly inspired by W. C. Handy's "The Memphis Blues." The Castles's African American bandleader James Reese Europe, who was apparently an early champion of the work, suggested that they might experiment with a dance step that would fit the song's slower tempo and unusual rhythmical feel. Although skeptical about the public demand for a new dance at this speed, the Castles devised it anyway and tried it out at some private engagements, where, to their surprise, it enjoyed overwhelming success. They first performed the new dance publicly in vaudeville in August 1914.[53]

The foregoing account is probably an accurate description of what happened. It is essentially confirmed by all parties concerned: Handy in his autobiography *Father of the Blues*; Europe in a 1914 article in the *New York Tribune*; and Irene Castle in a 1920 letter to entertainer Noble

Sissle.[54] Furthermore, Vernon Castle was never proprietary about his contribution to the new dance. He readily acknowledged its folk origins, admitting in a 1914 interview that it "had been danced by negroes . . . for fifteen years," and attributing its discovery to Europe.[55] In fact, the three parties involved in the account—the Castles, Europe, and Handy—were unusually deferential, all attributing the main role in creating the dance to the others. Thus, Vernon Castle credited Europe; Europe, in response, recognized Handy for his pivotal role as the composer of "The Memphis Blues";[56] while Handy acknowledged the role of both the Castles for devising the dance and Europe for encouraging the Castles to fit steps to "The Memphis Blues."[57] As Rebecca Bryant points out: "The triangle of transferred credit between Handy, Castle, and Europe is curious, particularly for a popular phenomenon that so many entertainers disingenuously claimed as their own. . . . [T]he existence of their integrated stories lends credibility to the connections."[58] Given this, and the central importance of the Castles as the leading society dance team of the era, their blues-focused account is valuable evidence for the argument of a strong connection between the blues and fox-trot.

The initial attraction of the blues for the Castles seems to have been one of tempo. In order to understand this, we need to go back a few years. The major vernacular dance to emerge over the previous decade had been the one-step.[59] Although it had apparently been in existence since at least the 1890s, the one-step first emerged into mainstream culture through a succession of animal dances, such as the grizzly bear, bunny hug, and turkey trot, all of which enjoyed a brief vogue, beginning with the grizzly bear in about 1909. The craze for animal dances was on the wane by 1912; they were superseded by the "straight" one-step and its offshoot, the Castle Walk, introduced by the Castles in 1912. The origins of the animal dances are obscure. Some, like the turkey trot and grizzly bear, may have derived from black culture, as the music historian Thornton Hagert has argued.[60] Other authorities, such Richard M. Stephenson and Joseph Iaccarino, have strongly disagreed with this assumption.[61] Either way, the dances were scandalous in their encouragement of close physical contact, and their impact was consequently enormous: their appearance marks the first wave of the revolution in social dancing that was to transform mainstream American culture in the era just before the First World War.

The main characteristic of the one-step and all its animal variants was that it was fast, about sixty-six measures per minute. Its dominance from about 1910 rapidly created a need for a slower dance that would complement it. One candidate was the Argentinean tango, whose enormous popularity in North America began about 1910.[62] The tango was indeed slower, but was too exotic and specialized to fully complement the easily learned and flexible one-step.[63] What was required, then, was a dance that was not only slower, but relatively simple to master. The fox-trot, with comparatively easy steps and an average speed of around forty measures a minute, answered the need perfectly.[64] And, as will be seen, it was ideal for dancing to the musical pre-jazz style that was then emerging into the mainstream.

Blues was associated with slower tempos, and by 1914 it was beginning to gain serious exposure in the mainstream. It was, therefore, the natural musical partner of the fox-trot. As I have argued in chapter 1, "The Memphis Blues" was the first blues to attain widespread popularity, and it did so in the period immediately before the appearance of the fox-trot, following the publication of the song version in 1913. Given this fact, it was almost inevitable that "The Memphis Blues" would be the specific inspiration for the Castles.

Yet the compatibility of blues with the fox-trot involved more than just its slower tempo. A more fundamental connection was its blackness. As already mentioned, the fox-trot, was, according to Vernon Castle, of black folk origin, as of course was the blues. This view was also consistently supported by James Reese Europe.[65] The fact that both Castle and Europe, who were so central to the development of the new dance, were adamant on this point encourages us to look further to see what the connection between the fox-trot and black folk culture might be—and if that connection might relate to blues. For example, could it be that the component steps on which the fox-trot is based are somehow connected to dance styles that were associated with the earliest folk blues or proto-blues? Although there is no conclusive evidence, the following argument is suggestive.

One of the characteristics of the fox-trot, then and now, is its combination of fast and slow steps. In an interview with the *Ladies Home Journal,* Vernon Castle described the component slow step as a "drag" in a 1914 interview, commenting that it was "a very old negro [*sic*] step, often called the 'Get Over, Sal.'"[66] The term *drag* suggests the *slow drag,* a black dance from the turn of the century. If so, this is the missing link, for in African American culture the slow drag is intrinsically associated with blues. Indeed, there is evidence that the dance and musical styles were coevals. The ethnomusicologist Alan Lomax described how in 1902, when his father, the pioneering folklorist John Lomax, was on a field trip in Texas, he was taken by a white planter to "a tightly shuttered sharecropper cabin, where they were allowed to peep in and see the tenants doing 'the blues' or the slow drag."[67] (The dance was so shocking that Lomax's father only told his mother about it years later.)[68]

This seems quite straightforward. The earliest blues were danced to the slow drag, elements of which influenced the choreography of the fox-trot, and so the two genres—blues and fox-trot—are linked at a deep level. I would stress, however, that the above evidence scarcely amounts to proof for such a connection: more research is needed to back up the theory. Nonetheless, it is suggestive.

Leaving the issue of dance-steps aside for the moment, what is the relationship between the music of blues and that of fox-trots? The outstanding musical feature of the earliest fox-trots was their heavy reliance on melodies with dotted rhythms. This was in contrast to the one-step, for example, which tended to use even notes, not dots. This distinction was maintained with instrumental blues from the period. Those that are labeled fox-trots on the sheet music tend to be dotted. For instance, "Bone-Head Blues" (example 7) is subtitled a fox-trot, and you can see that there are frequent dotted rhythms in the melody in both the A and B sections. In contrast, example 8 is the first strain of a 1919 blues called "Bevo Blues," by Louis Katzman, which is subtitled a one-step.[69] It uses no dotted notes at all.

EXAMPLE 8. Katzmann, "Bevo Blues" (1919), A strain

Crucial to understanding the musical connections between instrumental blues, fox-trots, and one-steps is understanding the relationship of all three genres to ragtime. As previously discussed, early instrumental blues are closely allied with ragtime. So are fox-trots. In fact, a typical fox-trot, as in example 7, is actually very close to regular ragtime. It makes frequent use of the rhythmical "boom chick" left hand pattern of ragtime, and there is much use of syncopation. There are in fact only two significant differences. The first is in the use of dotted rhythms. Traditional ragtime, such as that found in "Snakey Blues" (example 6), does not normally use dots. The second difference is one of meter: ragtime is usually in 2/4, not 2/2. To demonstrate this, example 9 gives the first eight measures of the first section of "Bone-Head Blues" (the equivalent of mm. 5–12 of example 7) with those characteristics altered (i.e., the dotted notes evened out and the meter altered to 2/4 by halving the note values). The resulting music looks and sounds remarkably like ragtime. In fact, if I told you the work as it is presented in example 9 was called "Bone-Head Rag" rather than "Bone-Head Blues," I do not think it would occur to you to doubt my word.

Unlike fox-trots, one-steps generally have little in common stylistically with ragtime. This can be seen by examining the passage from "Bevo Blues" (example 8). The extract uses no syncopation other than the tied chord in the right hand between mm. 9 and 10, nor does it make any use of a leaping ragtime-like "boom-chick" bass part. From this I conclude that fox-trots are in general musically much closer to ragtime than are one-steps. As instrumental blues are also closely related to ragtime, it follows that instrumental blues are in general more closely related to fox-trots than to one-steps, as is confirmed by the fact mentioned above that far more blues are labeled fox-trots than one-steps on sheet music and recordings.

All this seems relatively clear-cut, but there is a complication. It was stated above that traditional ragtime rarely uses dotted rhythms. By *traditional ragtime,* I refer to the type of ragtime that evolved before 1910. This earlier ragtime is what most people would instinctively associate with the term and includes the so-called "classic" piano rags of Scott Joplin and his ilk. According to Edward Berlin, who has studied the musical idiom of ragtime in depth, only 6 percent of pre-1910 rags use dotted rhythms to any extent. However, after 1910 ragtime becomes increasingly dotted. In 1911, the number of dotted rags suddenly doubles to 12 percent. The proportion increases steadily for the next few years, so that by 1916, a clear majority (58 percent) of new rags is dotted.[70] In such cases, the relationship between rags and fox-trots is even closer than I suggested earlier.

EXAMPLE 9. Gordon, "Bone-Head Blues" (1917), A strain, mm. 1–8, ragtime arrangement

Why did ragtime become dotted in the 1910s? And why were dotted rhythms such a strong feature of early fox-trots (and instrumental blues in fox-trot style)? These two questions need to be addressed if the triangular relationship between ragtime, instrumental blues, and the fox-trot is to be understood. Fortunately, both questions can both be answered by a single word: jazz.

The Jazz Influence

The conventional wisdom of American music historiography is that ragtime, which first emerged into the mainstream in the late 1890s, evolved into jazz over the first two decades of the new century. By about 1920, give or take a few years (depending on which records and/or bands meet your particular definition of authenticity), jazz had come of age. In doing so, it rendered ragtime obsolete. The most important difference between jazz and ragtime is the rhythmical feel. Jazz has that irresistible rhythmical forward momentum called "swing," which is lacking in ragtime—or, if it is there in ragtime, is in a less developed state than in jazz (historians argue endlessly on this point).

A crucial characteristic of swing is the phenomenon of "swung" notes. If a jazz musician performs a passage notated rhythmically, as in example 10a, his tendency will be to make each pair of notes uneven, the first note being approximately twice as long as the second, so that the first note of the pair takes approximately two-thirds of the beat, and the second note takes a third, instead of the usual fifty-fifty split.[71] The result will be played as in example 10b. Swung notes give the music that distinctive forward-moving fluid quality that is the basis of melodic playing in jazz and related styles.

This swung note subdivision of the beat into two thirds and a third, as seen in example 10b, can be compared with example 10c, which uses the same pitches as before, but in which the rhythm is dotted so that each subdivision is divided three-quarters to a quarter. If this rhythm is played literally, the effect is jerky and unswingy, compared with the fluidity of the triplet rhythm of example 10b. However, the use of such dotted notation in fox-trots, instrumental blues, and ragtime of the 1910s is deceptive. In reality, it is simply a convenient way of notating the same type of triplet feel as in example 10b.

This explains the fact that the notation of the melody of many fox-trots and rags combine runs of triplets with dotted notes. For example, example 11a is an extract from the end of the

EXAMPLE 10. Ascending C major scale:
  a. eighths;
  b. triplets;
  c. dotted eighths and sixteenths

EXAMPLE 11. Fry and Yarborough, "Sterling Fox Trot" (1915), A strain, melody, mm. 13–16:
a. as written; **b.** as performed

first section of a 1915 fox-trot called "Sterling Fox Trot."[72] If interpreted literally, the change from triplet eighth runs (on the fourth beat of each of the first three bars) to the dotted eighths/ sixteenth note pairs would sound peculiar, a schizophrenic flipping back and forth between two fundamentally different approaches. This makes little sense, especially for dance music, where a consistent rhythmical feel is required. The only sensible solution in performance is to relax the dotted eighths/sixteenth note pairs so that they conform approximately to the triplet feel. The result would be as notated in example 11b.[73]

The same convention seems to be operant in rags that are dotted. Example 12 shows an extract from the commercially successful "Ragging the Scale" by Edward B. Claypoole from 1915, the same year as "Sterling Fox-trot."[74] Example 12a quotes the published notation; example 12b provides its implied realization.

There is nothing unusual in notating pairs of notes that are meant to be performed in the proportion two-thirds-to-a-third as three-quarters-to-a-quarter. It is a convention known to musicologists as *underdotting,* and reaches back at least to the time of Bach.[75] For the entire second half of the nineteenth century, it was standard in the notation of the *schottische,* one

EXAMPLE 12. Claypoole "Ragging the Scale" (1915), B strain, melody, mm. 1–4:
a. as written; **b.** as performed

of the most popular social dances of the era.[76] For instance, a popular schottische from 1907, "Four Little Blackberries," uses precisely the kind of notation found in fox-trots (a representative fragment of the melody line is quoted in example 13a; the realization is provided in example 13b).[77] Given this, and the fact that schottisches were still being regularly produced almost up to the time of fox-trots, it may in fact be possible to trace a musical lineage from schottisches to fox-trots (and other dotted styles of the 1910s), although to do so is beyond our purpose here. Suffice it to say that underdotting was standard in sheet music of the era.

What I am suggesting, then, is that the dotted notation of fox-trots, rags, and instrumental blues in the 1910s reflects the tendency to perform music in a "swung" rather than "straight" manner. Such a swinging style became increasingly widespread in the vernacular as ragtime evolved into jazz in the 1910s. I will give two examples to lend weight to my argument. The first is Euday L. Bowman's "Twelfth Street Rag." This rag, one of the most popular of all rags, was first published in 1914.[78] In its original edition, it has no dotted notes in the melody. However, in 1919 it was reissued in a dotted version subtitled "Slow Fox Trot Arrangement."[79] Example 14a gives the first part of the A strain melody as originally published. It uses even eighth notes. Example 14b gives the same passage in fox-trot version, where it is dotted. The swingy feel, as realized in example 14c, is found in several hot jazz and dance band recordings of the work from the 1920s,[80] including versions by Louis Armstrong (1927),[81] Abe Lyman (1926),[82] and Ted Lewis (1923),[83] along with a vocal performance by the black vaudeville singer Eva Taylor (1923).[84] This rhythmical approach is even found in a rather stilted British dance band recording of the composition from 1921 by an obscure group called the White Coons.[85]

Even more revealing is the case of Jelly Roll Morton's "Jelly Roll Blues."[86] The original sheet music edition from 1915 labels the work a fox-trot on the front cover, and, as would be expected, it uses dotted rhythms and triplet notation extensively, as is evident in example 15a, the first four measures of the opening strain. All major recordings of this work (the earliest disc recording is from 1924), including several by the composer, swing the rhythm of this opening section in a manner that corresponds closely with example 15b.[87] Given Morton's status as a pioneer of jazz, there seems little doubt that the notation of the rhythm in the original edition is an attempt to

EXAMPLE 13. O'Connor, "Four Little Blackberries" (1907), B strain, melody, mm. 1–2: **a.** as written; **b.** as performed

EXAMPLE 14. Bowman, "Twelfth Street Rag" (1914), A strain, mm. 1–4:
  a. original version; **b.** fox trot arrangement (1919, arr. Wheeler); **c.** swung realization

EXAMPLE 15. Morton, "Jelly Roll Blues" (1915), A strain, mm. 1–4:
  a. as written; **b.** as performed

convey the swing feeling that must have been an integral part of Morton's compositional and performing style by the time the piece was published.[88]

All this can be summarized as follows. As African American-derived vernacular music transitioned from a "straight" ragtime feel to a "swung" jazz feel in the second decade of the twentieth century, dotted rhythms, a convenient way of approximating swing feel in music notation, became increasingly prevalent in printed music. This initially affected ragtime, which became increasingly dotted after 1911. The fox-trot, which entered mainstream culture in 1914, was invariably dotted, and it can thus be thought of as proto-jazz: although the swung rhythms of the fox-trot hint at jazz, the style had not yet fully emerged, and contemporaneous performances of fox-trots rarely swing as strongly as the best jazz recordings of the late 1910s and early 1920s. In other words, with historical hindsight, it can be said that the fox-trot is a midway point between ragtime and jazz; viewed teleologically, it emerged when it did to ease the transition between the two styles.

The suggestion that the fox-trot is in essence an embryonic form of jazz is confirmed by the fact that early jazz was danced to the fox-trot, which was ideally suited to it since the creative freedom the dance style encouraged paralleled the semi-improvisatory, spontaneous character of the new music.[89] As one observer noted: "What is termed 'jazz' dancing is really glorified 'foxtroting' [*sic*]—that is to say, the foxtrot with a few extra steps thrown in."[90]

So where does early instrumental blues fit into this complex web of interrelated genres? It must first be remembered that jazz had been closely connected with blues since the first jazz record, the Original Dixieland Jazz Band's "Livery Stable Blues" (1917). In fact, it is possible to date the connection between the two back before that time. A recently discovered article from the *Chicago Tribune* from July 1915 bears the title "Blues is Jazz and Jazz is Blues."[91] The writer, Gordon Seagrove, is trying to discover more about blues. He asks at a music publishing house what blues are, and he receives the answer "Jazz!" A pianist elaborates on this with the following insightful comment: "The blues are never written into music, but are interpolated by the piano player or other players. They aren't new. They are just reborn into popularity. They started in the south [*sic*] half a century ago and are the interpolations of darkies originally. The trade name for them is 'jazz.'" The article marks the earliest proven instance of the word "jazz" in a musical context, and it is entirely to the point that the word is treated synonymously with blues.

Blues, of course, is at the heart of jazz, as is acknowledged by all writers on the subject. Superficially the influence is manifested at the level of musical idiom, especially the blue note, an integral element in the expression of jazz melody and harmony, and the twelve bar blues progression, the basis of so many jazz numbers. However, blues also operates in jazz at a paramusical level: it gives it soul. The depth of expression that tinges great jazz recordings and performances ultimately derives from the blues.

Early fox-trots, however, lack this depth, at least to judge from contemporaneous recordings. But what they do have is the proto-swing feel that was to flower so spectacularly in jazz in the 1920s. Looked at this way, the interrelationship of ragtime, the fox-trot, and instrumental blues makes sense. Jazz is ragtime, combined with the rhythmical feel (and dance step) of the fox-trot and the soulful feeling of the blues (as manifested in commercial instrumental blues of the 1910s).

SOME DISTINCTIVE COMPONENTS OF THE POPULAR BLUES IDIOM

The discussion of popular blues songs and instrumental compositions has so far dealt with broad issues: the type of themes used in the song lyrics, for example, or the relationship of instrumental blues to other styles of dance music. This final part of the chapter takes a more detailed look at the idiom of popular blues, focusing on certain distinctive musical and textual components whose presence helps to separate the genre from the mass of popular music. By "distinctive," I mean both that the components can be clearly defined and that they are found much more frequently in popular blues than in other styles of popular music. There are a number of such devices, and a detailed examination of all of them is beyond the scope of this study. In the interest of brevity, therefore, I will focus on a handful of the most striking. They are: the twelve-bar sequence; blue notes; the barbershop ending; the four-note chromatic motif; and the phrase "I got the blues."

The Twelve-Bar Sequence

The single most distinctive musical feature of popular blues is the twelve-bar sequence. In a survey of the genre, it was found in slightly less than half of popular blues from the 1910s.[92] Its presence clearly separates popular blues from regular Tin Pan Alley material, which hardly ever makes use of the device.[93]

The sequence is derived from folk blues. It is given in table 6 in its most basic form, along with commonly found variants. In table 6a the chords are presented numerically, and in table 6b they are presented as regular chords symbols in the key of C.

In a typical folk blues, the sequence forms the harmonic basis of each stanza and is repeated throughout the song. Each blues is based on a single melody that is adapted to fit the words of each stanza. There are only a few instances in published blues of the twelve-bar sequence being used in this way. An example is "Nigger Blues" (example 5), which uses a twelve-bar sequence throughout and employs a single melody for all six of its stanzas. In the vast majority of cases, however, usage of the sequence in popular blues differs significantly from that in folk blues.

First, in cases where the sequence is used for the entirety of the composition, the melody usually changes at least once. For example, the instrumental composition "Original Blues" by Ted S. Barron has three strains and uses a twelve-bar sequence throughout.[94] However, it uses independent melodies for each strain. Similarly, W. C. Handy's 1915 song "Joe Turner Blues" uses a twelve-bar sequence for both verse and chorus, but a different melody for each.[95]

In fact, relatively few popular blues using the twelve-bar sequence do so for their entirety. In about two-thirds of cases, the sequence is used for only a part of the composition, either for the verse or for the chorus in songs, or for one or two strains in the case of instrumental compositions. For the remainder of the composition, conventional sixteen-bar or thirty-two-bar sequences are employed. In instrumental blues, this has already been demonstrated in "Snakey Blues" (example 6), which used the twelve-bar sequence for two of its strains (mm. 1–12 and 29–40) and a sixteen-bar structure for the other two strains (mm. 13–28 and 41–57). Example 16, "The Tennessee Blues" by William Warner and Arthur S. Holt, is a typical instance of the twelve-bar sequence in a blues song.[96] The verse for this song consists of two twelve-bar sequences (mm. 1–12 and 13–24; harmonic analysis is marked in the score for the first sequence).

Table 6. Prototype Twelve-Bar Blues Sequence with Common Variants

a. Chords presented numerically												
Measure	1	2	3	4	5	6	7	8	9	10	11	12
Chord	I	I	I	I	IV	IV	I	I	V	V	I	I
Variants		IV				iv			II	IV		
b. In the key of C												
Measure	1	2	3	4	5	6	7	8	9	10	11	12
Chord	C	C	C	C	F	F	C	C	G	G	C	C
Variants		F				Fm			D	F		

EXAMPLE 16. Holt and Warner, "Tennessee Blues" (1916), verse and chorus

EXAMPLE 16. Continued

EXAMPLE 16. Continued

The two sequences use identical melodies, just as they would do in a folk blues. The chorus (mm. 25–40), on the other hand, uses a regular sixteen-bar structure and an unrelated melody.

Why was the blues sequence used differently when it was transplanted from the folk to the commercial medium? One reason seems to be that using the same melody and chord sequence as the basis for an entire composition was firmly at odds with the conventions of Tin Pan Alley, which assumed that the piece needed musical variety in order to hold the attention of listeners. W. C. Handy states as much in his memoirs when he says that he added the famous sixteen-measure tango section of "St. Louis Blues," which would otherwise have been entirely twelve-bar in structure, "to avoid monotony."[97] Furthermore, popular songs and instrumental compositions of the period were structured around the easy-on-the-ear symmetry of sixteen and thirty-two bar structures. Building a piece entirely on an asymmetrical twelve-bar structure (three lines of four measures each) was considered too commercially risky.

Therefore, it is not surprising that in many popular blues the twelve-bar sequence is expanded to sixteen bars. Example 17 shows a way in which this was often done. It is the melody of the first half of the thirty-two measure chorus of Spencer Williams's "Tishomingo Blues," a commercially successful song that is still performed by traditional jazz bands.[98] The first twelve measures comprise a regular blues sequence (the only unconventional element is the colorful ♭VI chord in m. 6). However, the sequence is then extended for four measures: instead of resolving in m. 12, the melody rises at the end of the measure and the words carry through to the next measure ("Oh how I wish that I was back again / with a race . . . ."). The sequence does not cadence till the beginning of m. 16.

Another way of adapting the twelve-bar structure to the demands of commercialism was to take just the opening part of the sequence and graft it onto a Tin Pan Alley harmonic formula. This is demonstrated in example 18, the opening eight-bar period of a popular blues titled "Profiteering Blues."[99] The period begins as a regular blues sequence before departing from it in m. 6 and cadencing in a typical Tin Pan Alley fashion in m. 8.

Blue Notes

The second distinctive element of the popular blues idiom is the blue note. Blue notes are defined as microtonally lowered diatonic pitches; they are, of course, an integral expressive element in folk blues, deriving from African American vocal style. Because of their microtonal nature, they can neither be notated accurately by conventional means, nor accurately performed on fixed-pitch instruments like the piano. Instead, in early popular blues sheet music, their effect is approximated by flattening the relevant note by a half step. Thus, the blue third, the most common blue note, is notated as a minor third, that is, a major third lowered by a half-step (E♭ in the key of C major: see example 19a). Similarly, the blue seventh, the next most common blue note, is a minor seventh, that is, a major seventh lowered by a half-step (B♭ in C major: see example 19b). The less common blue fifth is a diminished fifth, that is, a perfect fifth lowered by a half-step (G♭ in C major: see example 19c).

EXAMPLE 17. Williams, "Tishomingo Blues" (1917), chorus, mm. 1–16

EXAMPLE 18. Wilson and Bibo. "Profiteering Blues" (1920), chorus, mm. 1–6

According to ethnomusicologist David Evans, blue notes are used in four ways in folk blues. First, they are expressed "as a slur, usually upward from the flat towards the natural"; second, "as a wavering between flat and natural or two other points within the interval"; third, "as the simultaneous sounding of the flat and natural pitches"; and fourth, "[as] the sounding of a flat where a natural should be expected."[100]

Three of these four approaches are to be found in popular blues of the 1910s. They are demonstrated in example 20, using the blues third (E♭ in C major). Evans's first type, the upward resolving slur, is usually notated as in example 20a. This is the type called the slurred blue note. His third type, which consists of the simultaneous sounding of the flattened note and the diatonic, is approximated in example 20b. Notice that the use of the crushed note (the technical term is *acciaccatura*) means that the two notes are played almost, rather than completely, at the

EXAMPLE 19. Blue intervals

EXAMPLE 20. Four types of blues notes

same time. This type I call the crushed blue note. Example 20c represents Evans's fourth type and is simplest of all, consisting of just the blue note. This type is the most striking, because, unlike the other two types, it never resolves to the natural and hence creates the most tension. This is the unresolved blue note. Evans's second type, the wavering between the blue note and the natural, would probably be notated like example 20d. This type is not found in popular blues of the 1910s, perhaps because it is hard to execute, especially when sung.

All three types of blue note used in 1910s popular blues—slurred, crushed, and unresolved— are to be found in example 21, the famous opening of W. C. Handy's "St. Louis Blues."[101] The example starts with a crushed blue third in the melody (A♯–B over a G chord), while the first two and last two melody notes of m. 2 are of the slurred type (the D♯–E at the beginning of the measure is a blue third,[102] while the B♭–A at the end is a blue seventh;[103] both occur over a C chord). The accompaniment is even richer in blue notes. An unresolved seventh (F) is held throughout the first measure in the right hand. While the voice holds its long G over mm. 3 and 4, the tension is maintained in the accompaniment with slurred blue thirds in the right hand (A♯–B in mm. 3 and 4) and an unresolved blue seventh in the left hand (F in m. 4).

Nearly all popular blues use blue notes to some extent. In their mildest form, they are virtually indistinguishable from regular chromaticism. At their most intense, however, as in

EXAMPLE 21. Handy, "St. Louis Blues" (1914), verse, mm. 1–4

the examples just discussed, they effectively communicate the raw emotion of blues with an intensity at odds with the popular music aesthetic of the day.[104] While blue notes are also found in other styles of popular music, they occur with neither the frequency nor the intensity with which they appear in popular blues.[105]

The Barbershop Ending

The "barbershop ending"[106] is a harmonic figure found in about a third of popular blues, about twice as often as in non-blues.[107] It is basically an expansion of the final tonic chord of a piece (or section of a piece) characterized by chromatically descending chords over a tonic pedal. Example 22 provides a notable instance. It comprises the last three measures of W. C. Handy's "The Memphis Blues" (instrumental version). The barbershop ending occurs in the penultimate measure. A triple octave tonic B♭ sounds at the beginning of the measure and is held till the beginning of the next measure. Meanwhile, over the tonic pedal, there are a series of four chromatically descending chords in the inner three voices. The chords are: B♭7 (I7), B♭°7 (I°7), E♭m6/B♭ (iv6), and the final tonic B♭ (I) at the beginning the final measure.

The device is also found in "The Tennessee Blues" (example 16), where it appears at the end of both halves of the verse and of the chorus (mm. 11–12, 23–24, and 39–40). The presentation of the device in this song is rhythmically more sophisticated than in "The Memphis Blues." Here there are only two inner parts ("The Memphis Blues" had three), but they are rhythmically independent of one another, and the upper part is quite syncopated.

The barbershop ending is frequently found in folk blues. For instance, the Delta bluesman Skip James frequently made use of it in various guises.[108] Its popularity in both folk and popular blues is explained by the fact that its mood is one of wistful contemplation. This makes it particularly well suited to the expression of melancholic introspection that is so characteristic of blues.

The Four-Note Chromatic Motif

Example 23 is the opening of one of the oldest popular blues, Hart Wand's instrumental composition "Dallas Blues" (1912). The melody begins with a particular motif of four descending chromatic notes (F–E–E♭–D). Whether rising or falling, this motif is common in popular

EXAMPLE 22. Handy, "The Memphis Blues" (1912), C strain, mm. 22–24

EXAMPLE 23. Wand, "Dallas Blues" (1912), A strain, melody, mm. 1–3

blues, occurring with varying degrees of prominence in well over half the total from the period between 1912 and 1920. In popular non-blues, it is far less common.[109] It can, therefore, be thought of as a distinctive component of popular blues. Along with "Dallas Blues," the device is prominently used in two other instances of the earliest popular blues: Smith and Brymn's "The Blues," the very first popular blues to be published, where it is used to open the verse (example 24); and the beginning of the A strain of the instrumental version of Handy's "The Memphis Blues" (1912, example 25).[110] Both these examples differ from example 23 in that the motif ascends rather than descends. In other respects, however, the parallels are striking. All three examples have three notes occurring before the barline, with the downbeat on the final note, an effect reinforced by fermata over the first three notes in example 23; all three travel either from the fifth to the third of the tonic chord (example 23) or from the third to the fifth (examples 24 and 25); and all three use the motif at a structurally vital moment (at the beginning of the work as a whole, in example 23; at the beginning of the verse, in example 24; and at the beginning of the first strain, in example 25).

In fact, when used in popular blues, it is surprising how often this motif occurs at a significant moment in the work. Aside from the examples already quoted, in "Profiteering Blues" (example 18), it is used in ascending form at the start of the chorus and then immediately inverted (it recurs at m. 6). In "The Tennessee Blues" (example 16), it is used in ascending form to mark the second half of the chorus (mm. 32–33).

It is unclear why this motif should be so prevalent in popular blues, for unlike the other devices discussed thus far (the twelve-bar sequence, blue notes, and the barbershop ending), it is not a significant element in the melodic make-up of folk blues. One possibility is that the device

My   hon - ey   left   me   this   morn - ing

EXAMPLE 24. Smith and Brymn, "The Blues" (1912), verse, melody and text, m. 1

EXAMPLE 25. Handy, "The Memphis Blues" (1912), A strain, melody, mm. 1–3

exploits a loose semiotic relationship between chromatic melodic writing and the heightened emotional state associated with the concept of feeling blue. In fact, there is evidence that the motif is meant to suggest a "super-blue-note," a "wail," as it were, over four chromatic notes rather than one. Evidence for this is provided by the chorus of a song called "Those Draftin' Blues" from 1917, the first few measures of which are quoted in example 26. The three B quarter notes on the last beat of mm. 0, 1, and 2 are in each instance preceded by two chromatic grace notes, A and A♯. This is basically a crushed blue third (as in example 20b) on a G chord, that is, A♯ to B. The extra note, A, is added to enhance the effect, and a note to the performer on the sheet music asks him or her to "observe [the] grace notes with moaning effect."

"I've Got the Blues"

The final component of the popular blues idiom is textual, not musical: the phrase "I've got the blues." The phrase is widely used: my earlier survey suggested that approximately four-fifths of popular blues songs make use of it.[111] The phrase makes explicit the basic assumption of blues songs, namely, that the singer has the blues. This is sometimes stated plainly. For example, in Smith and Brymn's "The Blues," the chorus begins "I've got the blues / but I'm too blamed mean to cry" (example 1). More often, however, the phrase takes the form "I've got the X blues," where X specifies the type of blues as related in the song's title. For instance, the chorus to Handy's "St. Louis Blues" begins: "Got de Saint Louis Blues / jes blue as I can be." Similarly, at the start of the chorus of Wilson and Bibo's "Profiteering Blues" (example 18), the singer declares: "I've got the profiteering blues. / High prices make me sick."

The importance of the device is such that it usually occurs at a focal point in the song. For instance, all three of the examples I just quoted—"The Blues," "St. Louis Blues," and "Profiteering Blues"—use the device at the start of the chorus. Another approach is to place it at the very end of the song. For instance, Tom Delaney's "Jazz Me Blues" concludes with the climactic phrase "I've got those dog-gone, low down jazz me, jazz me blues."[112] In "Broadway Blues" (example 4), the line is also placed climactically at the end of the chorus (mm. 51–54), although it is changed to the second person ("You've got those Broadway Blues"; the whole song uses the second person, which is unusual in popular blues).

An important feature of the "I've Got the Blues" phrase is that, in popular music culture of the 1910s, it is rarely, if ever, used in non-blues. Hence, more than any other aspect of the

EXAMPLE 26. Pinkard, "Those Draftin' Blues" (1917), chorus, melody and text, mm. 1–4

lyric, its presence marks a song as a blues. In this, the device is the verbal equivalent of the twelve-bar harmonic sequence, which is common in popular blues but seldom found in any other popular genre.

It is because of this ability to mark a song as a blues that the phrase is often used as the title. Examples are: "I've Got the Army Blues,"[113] "I've Got the Cryin' Blues,"[114] "I've Got the Single Man Blues,"[115] and" I Got the Blues, the Soda Pop Blues."[116]

The device, of course, derives from folk blues, where it is found in many guises. However, unlike the other folk-derived elements (the twelve-bar sequence, blue notes, and the barber shop ending), the device is found much less frequently in folk blues than in popular blues. For instance, of the forty-five recordings of folk blues transcribed by Jeff Todd Titon for his book *Early Downhome Blues,* only two use the device.[117] This finding is confirmed by Michael Taft's exhaustive analysis of verbal formulae in folk blues. Drawing on the information Taft provides in his fifth chapter, the formula "I have the blues" is used far less frequently than formulas associated with travel (which Taft essentializes as "I come to some place," "I go away from some place," "Everywhere I go," "I will be gone," "I'm going home," and "I'm leaving town") or relationships (essentialized by the phrases "I have a woman," "I quit my woman," "I love you," "I tell you," and "I treat you good/bad").[118] This suggests an important difference between folk and popular blues: while the assumption is always that the singer has the blues, in folk blues this is not usually explicitly stated, whereas in popular blues it usually is.

• • •

I must stress that the five distinctive elements I have discussed—the twelve bar idiom, blue notes, the four-note chromatic motif, the barbershop ending, and the phrase "I Got the Blues"—are not the only characteristic components of the popular blues idiom. However, they are undoubtedly among the most important in that they appear frequently in popular blues and much less often (or not at all) in popular non-blues. In addition, four of the five elements derive from, or are at least closely connected to, folk blues. Their presence, therefore, in a popular blues strengthens the identity of the work as a blues. The exception is the four-note chromatic motif, which has no obvious counterpart in the folk idiom.[119]

Any given blues will utilize these elements in different combinations and to different degrees. The result helps determine the work's individual genetic make-up, which I discussed earlier in the chapter, and it helps determine just how "bluesy" the work is. For instance, the extract from the chorus of "Profiteering Blues" provided in example 18 uses three of the five elements: the phrase "I've got the blues," which appears here as "I've got the profiteering blues"; the four-note chromatic motif, which is used in the melody in mm. 0, 1, and 5; and the twelve-bar sequence, here adapted to eight measures. Compare this song, then, with "Broadway Blues" (example 4). The latter uses the "I've got the blues" device in an unusual, modified form in the second person ("you've got the Broadway Blues") at the end of the verse and the chorus. The only other element used in "Broadway Blues" is blue notes, which are found occasionally in the accompaniment (the F♯s—blue thirds—in the right hand in mm. 25 and 26, for instance). In other words, "I've Got the Profiteering Blues" uses more blues elements than does "Broadway Blues," and it does so in a much more concentrated way. It could therefore be said that "I've Got the Profiteering Blues" (at least judging by the extract in example 18) has a stronger identity as a blues; there is by comparison little to distinguish "Broadway Blues" from a regular pop song.

• • •

In this chapter, popular blues have been examined both at a general level, with the global survey of songs and instrumental works, and at a more detailed level, with a close analysis of the idiom. The next chapter focuses on a fundamental issue that underpins the culture of both folk and popular blues: the notion of using the blues to cure the blues.

CHAPTER 3

Curing the Blues
with the Blues

"'Blues' music was created to chase away gloom"
—W. C. Handy, 1919

A truth widely acknowledged, if little discussed, is that the basic purpose of blues is to cure its performers, and by extension its audience, of the condition of the blues. As Paul Oliver, the doyen of blues historians, puts it: "It is generally understood that a blues performer sings or plays to rid himself of 'the blues.'"[1] Ethnomusicologist Harold Courlander elaborates on this premise: "At its base, the [blues] song is a sort of exalted or transmuted expression of criticism or complaint, the very creation or singing of which serves as a balm or antidote."[2]

I suspect that it is the curative power of the genre, or at least the aspiration to achieve a cure, that gives blues its deep potency, and that best accounts for its central place in the development of Western vernacular music for more than a century. This is not to imply that blues are unique in being in some sense therapeutic: almost every musical style has at some point in its development been claimed to have therapeutic value. But, of the major styles of vernacular music, blues is the only one whose basic raison d'etre is explicitly to alleviate emotional negativity. This has resulted in an extraordinary linguistic phenomenon: that the genre is named after the very condition it attempts to alleviate. This approach to nomenclature has little parallel in Western music or, to my knowledge, in any of the arts.

The obvious exception is the tarantella, a lively seventeenth century dance from southern Italy.[3] The tarantella was used to cure tarantism, a type of hysterical condition characterized by an irresistible desire to dance and supposedly produced by the bite of the tarantula spider. The main cure seems to have been frenzied dancing, particularly to the accompaniment of the tarantella, often for several days. We could thus argue that there is a linguistic parallel between the tarantella and blues in that both are named for the condition they attempt to cure. Even so, the former is a very minor cultural phenomenon compared to the latter.[4]

In short, its self-consciously therapeutic aspect is absolutely integral to blues and one of its most unusual features. It is the focus of this chapter not only because I consider the subject rewarding in its own right, but also because I believe we cannot appreciate the culture of early popular blues without taking it into account. I begin with a historical examination of the term "blues" and of the notion that music can be used to cure it. I then suggest two ways in which it can effect such cures. I conclude by applying this information to the culture of early popular blues.

ORIGINS AND DEFINITIONS OF THE TERM "BLUES"

We begin, then, with the term "blues" itself. Where does the term come from? How, historically, has it been used? And what range of meanings did it have in American culture of the 1910s, the culture of early popular blues?

However, before discussing "blues," we must turn first to its parent word, "blue." Although the word has acquired a plethora of meanings and connotations over the centuries, when it emerged into Middle English in the thirteenth century it possessed only two closely related meanings, both relating to color. The first was livid or blackish blue (earliest known usage ca. 1250). The other meaning is its basic one today, that is, the color of the sky (earliest known reference ca. 1300).[5] Although authorities disagree, it has been argued, for example by the linguist Theodore Thass-Thienemann, that the first of these two definitions was the fundamental one.[6] The primary association of this definition was the discoloration of skin as a consequence of cold or especially injury. In this respect, Thass-Thienemann argues that the phonemic relationship between *blue* and *blow* is central: blue is the color skin turns after receiving a blow.[7]

This is particularly relevant for our subject as it implies that the notion of physical and, by extension, spiritual suffering is inherent in the word "blue." By 1550, the word was being used in this metaphorical way to mean affected with fear, low-spirited, depressed, or miserable.[8] By the beginning of the seventeenth century, the concept arose of a "blue devil" (earliest known reference 1616), originally a malignant demon, which, in the plural form, later acquired a metaphorical meaning of despondency—inspired, I suspect, by the age-old belief in the relationship between mental depression and demonic possession. An early example of this usage is from the novelist Frances D'Arblay, who in 1781 wrote in her diary that "generous wine will destroy even the blue devils."[9] By the middle of the eighteenth century, "blue devils" was being shortened to "blues" or "the blues." The earliest known reference to this usage is from 1741, in a letter written by the British actor-manager David Garrick: "I am far from being quite well, tho not troubled wth ye Blews as I have been."[10] References to "the blues" as an emotional state thereafter become increasingly common, and by the last decades of the nineteenth century the usage was standard in American English.

At around this time, the phrase "the blues" became closely intertwined with the medical disorder neurasthenia, a condition that was sweeping America. It was first named in 1869 by

George M. Beard, whose treatises on the subject, *A Practical Treatise on Nervous Exhaustion* (1880)[11] and *American Nervousness* (1881),[12] were enormously influential in reifying, and raising the public perception of, the new illness. Neurasthenia, coming from two roots, *neuro* (nerve) and *asthenia* (weakness), was an illness allegedly caused by depletion of the nervous system. It had a diversity of symptoms, of which some of the most basic were depression, chronic fatigue, weakness, and muscle pain. The disease was considered stress-related and sociological in its ultimate causation. "The primary cause of neurasthenia in this country," wrote the physician A. D. Rockwell in 1893, "is civilization itself, with all that the term implies, with its railway, telegraph, telephone, and periodical press intensifying in ten thousand ways cerebral activity and worry."[13] In the belief of the times, the pressure of the new fast-paced, industrialized, urbanized American lifestyle drained the nerve-force of sensitive individuals, and the result was neurasthenia. As one commentator has suggested, it was "the price Americans paid for progress."[14]

By the turn of the century, neurasthenia had become *the* fashionable malady of America, with its sufferers numbering in the hundreds of thousands. "Not without reason has nervous prostration been called the 'National Disease,'" declared the *New York Times* in 1907. "Wherever Americans work and worry, and especially in New York, where the pressure is at its worst, thousands of men, women, and children throw down their tools and leave their desks prostrated, to go to hospitals and sanitariums."[15] It was, in fact, probably the most widely diagnosed medical condition of the era in America, and it remained common as a diagnosis for the first two decades of the new century, whereupon it rapidly fell victim to the recategorization of neurotic disorders that followed in the wake of psychoanalysis.[16]

The relevance of neurasthenia for our investigation is that it was commonly known by the name "the blues," probably because its major symptoms included fits of depression and despondency. One of the most popular books on the syndrome, which ran to several editions, by a Dr. Albert Abrams, was titled *The Blues: Its Causes and Cures.*[17] By the turn of the century, the phrase "the blues" had two meanings in American culture. The first was the older, more general definition of a depressed state; the other referred to the condition of neurasthenia.

In reality, there was an enormous overlap between these two meanings, for neurasthenia was what Tom Lutz has referred to as a "bit of a catch-all category," with a truly bewildering array of symptoms.[18] Beard's *A Practical Treatise on Nervous Exhaustion* lists no fewer than seventy-five symptoms for neurasthenia, including mental irritability, morbid fears, sleeplessness, desire for stimulants and narcotics, dryness of the skin, heaviness of the limbs, rapid decay and irregularities of the teeth, impotence, and tremors, among many others. The basic point is that by the turn of the century, "the blues" was a remarkably fashionable term that covered everything from serious mental illness to passing feelings of sadness or depression; moreover, to varying degrees, enormous numbers of people at all levels of society were suffering from it. In short, it was a word on everyone's lips.

It is a fact, therefore, that blues in the musical sense emerged in American culture just as Americans were suffering acutely from blues in the medical sense. These facts are not coincidental. There is a sense in which one was created to cure, or at least relieve, the other at a societal level.

MUSICAL ALLEVIATION OF THE BLUES

There is nothing new about using music to alleviate the blues. Almost two thousand years ago the Greek historian Plutarch described how "the threnody and the mourning aulos [a double-piped reed instrument] at first stir up the emotions and make the tears flow, but then they gradually calm sorrow."[19] A particularly interesting parallel to the situation in early twentieth century America was that of sixteenth and seventeenth century England, which was stricken with a condition known as melancholy (or *melancholia*). Melancholy was, in the words of one commentator, "the fashionable malady of the Elizabethan age," just as neurasthenia was for turn-of-the-century America.[20] The symptoms of melancholy—loosely defined but firmly rooted in depression and despondency—were essentially the same as the core symptoms of neurasthenia. Like neurasthenia, the ultimate causes for the epidemic were seen as recent radical changes in society, specifically the religious, political, and cultural turbulence of the era as Europe transitioned out of the Renaissance.

Another parallel between the two syndromes involved the status of its victims. Two of the immediate causes of melancholy were allegedly an excess of concentrated thinking and solitude, and therefore writers, philosophers, and intellectuals were believed to be especially susceptible to it.[21] Indeed, melancholia was essentially an aristocratic complaint. Similarly, classic neurasthenia was supposed to affect the most sensitive individuals, that is, the intellectual and cultural elite. Consequently the roster of neurasthenic sufferers includes some of the most distinguished figures of the early twentieth century, such as Mark Twain, Henry James, Charles Ives, William James, Theodore Dreiser, Edith Wharton, and Theodore Roosevelt.

A particular relevance of melancholy for our present inquiry is that it was thought to be curable by music. In fact, music was believed to be a prime cure. Richard Burton, whose exhaustive *Anatomy of Melancholy* (1621) is regarded as not only the single most important commentary on the condition but also one of the most important literary works of the era, memorably described music as "a roaring-meg against melancholy, to rear and revive the languishing soul" (*roaring-meg* was an Elizabethan term for an enormous cannon).[22]

The condition of "the blues" was similarly assumed to be helped by music. The earliest reference to this that I have been able to find is on the cover to a pop song called "Billy's Request," with lyrics by Billy Birch and music by W. F. Wellman, Jr.[23] The date is 1879, exactly the time that neurasthenia was starting to permeate mainstream consciousness. An announcement in elaborate letters at the top of the song's title page boldly declares it to be "A Cure for the Blues."

FIGURE 12. An 1879 song, whose cover declares it "A Cure for the Blues." This is one of the earliest examples explicitly to link music with the notion of curing the blues. (Author's collection)

The song is a lighthearted one about a dying boy who makes various bizarre and at times non-sensical last requests of his mother. The fifth verse, for example (the song has eleven verses and no chorus), runs as follows:

> Roll me up in a nice light pie-crust,
> Slather me over with jam;
> Hit me with a hundred cream cakes,
> Bounce me with a ham;
> Take me to an old-time clam-bake,
> Sheep's head, lobster and gin—
> Drown me in a watermelon,
> And then "wipe off your chin!"

Both the lyricist and composer of "Billy's Request" were members of the San Francisco Minstrels, one of the most successful (white) minstrel troupes of the day (according to the cover of the sheet music, at the time of publication the song had been sung by them "with Unbounded Success for two Consecutive Years"). The song would therefore have originally been performed in blackface, and this connection, however indirect, with black culture is interesting, given the stated purpose of the song to cure the blues. However, this connection is not manifested in the song itself. It is a conventional waltz in the salon style of the day, and it contains nothing that in any way suggests the later idiom of blues. There is not even any use of pseudo-black dialect, as there is in many minstrel songs from the period.

By the early twentieth century, with neurasthenia now firmly established in American culture, references to music curing the blues start to become more common. A typical example is given in figure 13, an advertisement from a 1904 stage-bill for Cecilian Player Pianos.[24] A central message of the sales pitch, important enough to be highlighted in bold letters in the advertisement, is that "Blues [are] dispelled" by player piano music.

The notion that music dispels blues is one that became increasingly prevalent in American culture as the new century progressed. One manifestation of this that has direct relevance to popular blues is in popular song. The theatre historian Michael G. Garber traced the development of the music-cures-blues motif in the lyrics to songs from musicals written between 1898 and 1942. Garber found that the motif is found only intermittently in the first decade of the 1900s, but that during the 1910s it becomes far more common, especially after 1917.[25] This timeline is essentially that of blues, which starts in the 1900s and grows rapidly in the second decade, especially after 1917. The evidence clearly suggests that as far as musical theater is concerned, the rise of the notion that music cures the blues closely parallels the rise of the musical genre of blues. This is particularly interesting given the close relationship between popular blues and songs from musicals. Both were products of Tin Pan Alley, and indeed some of the most

FIGURE 13. By the early 1900s, the notion of using music as a cure for the blues was sufficiently established in mainstream culture to be used in advertising, as in this 1904 advertisement for player pianos. (Montgomery Archive)

commercially successful blues from our period, such as Jerome Kern's "Left All Alone Again Blues" (1920), were show tunes.[26]

We turn from the notion of music in general curing blues to the more specific one of blues music curing blues. The earliest known reference to this is from 1908. It is in a piano work titled "I Got the Blues," written and published in New Orleans by Antonio Maggio, a local piano teacher and music store owner. The work is a milestone in blues history in that it is the first both to be titled a blues *and* to use a twelve-bar blues sequence, which it does in the first of its three strains. We will examine this work in more detail later. Our interest here is that its title page, reproduced in figure 14, announces that the work is "Respectfully Dedicated to all those Who have the Blues." The implication of this dedication is that the music—which is essentially upbeat ragtime—will dispel the blues of the performer/listener.

In fact, there was general understanding in mainstream culture of the 1910s that blues music was therapeutic in intent. This is evident in two ways. First it is found in contemporaneous statements like the one made by W. C. Handy with which this chapter began ("'Blues' music was created to chase away gloom"). The earliest example of the sentiment I have been able to find is from a 1915 article from the *Chicago Daily Tribune* that simply states: "That is what 'blue'

FIGURE 14. This up-tempo ragtime composition from 1908 was the first to combine a titular blues with the use of the twelve-bar blues sequence. The composer's intention was to cure the blues, as is implied by the work's dedication in the upper right. (Author's collection)

music is doing for everybody—taking away what its name implies, the blues."[27] The second indication of the therapeutic intent of blues comes from the songs themselves, specifically from the lyrics of reflexive blues songs.

Reflexive blues, it will be recalled from our brief discussion of the topic in chapter 2, is a special category of popular blues song whose lyrics celebrate the ingredients of the song itself, that is, the music and lyrics, or some aspect of its performance, particularly dancing or the band performing. Such songs are quite common in the commercial sector within our period, and the therapeutic potential of blues is a motif in of a number of them. For example, the first verse of "Kansas City Blues," a reflexive blues from 1915, tells how "it soothes when you hear / Those old Blues called the 'Kansas City Blues.'"[28]

The therapeutic theme is central to the first and probably the most influential reflexive blues, the song version of Handy's "The Memphis Blues" (1913). George Norton's lyric is among other things a paean to the power of blues. The chorus describes both the emotional playing of Handy's band (the bassoonist moans "just like a sinner on Revival Day") and its strong effects on the listener ("Here comes the very part / that wraps a spell around my heart. / It sets me wild / to hear that lovin' tune again"); similarly, the second verse refers to the lasting effect of the experience on the listener ("[I] simply can't forget that blue refrain"). While the lyric stops short of actually stating that blues music cures the blues, it strongly implies it. A popular song from 1916, "Oh! Those Blues! (Lazy Blues, Crazy Blues)," states the matter more explicitly: "When you're feeling blue / and want a tune / to fill you full of joy . . . / take a good old tune of blues," adding that "if that tune don't set you right / there's no excuse."[29]

Once the jazz craze hit in 1917, such references to blues being fixed by blues became more common. One reason was that there was an upsurge of popular blues production at around this time. Another more complex reason was that the radical power of jazz had raised public consciousness about its alleged effects, therapeutic or otherwise. These effects were extensively debated in the media and, in fact, became one of the hot-button topics of the age. One consequence of this debate was an increase in references to the effects of music in the lyrics to jazz songs and songs in related styles, including blues songs and jazz-inflected show tunes.[30] To take one example, "Jazzin' the Cotton Town Blues," a reflexive blues song from 1917, concerns a black dance in Mississippi given by "Andy's Jazz Band," pictured on the song's cover (figure 15).[31] The chorus refers to "blue notes that cry / make you wear out your dancing shoes," and it tells how "there is some joy / on the Levee, boy, / When Andy's band in Dixieland / is Jazzin' the Cotton Town Blues." It is typical of such jazz-era songs that the references to jazz and blues are inextricably interwoven.

In sum, the evidence overwhelmingly suggests that it was widely understood that, from the time of its emergence into mainstream culture, the blues's central purpose was to cure the blues. Having established this, we need to consider the vital question of how the blues achieved, or was supposed to achieve, its curative effect; for, as will be seen, an understanding of this enables us to view popular blues culture of the 1910s in an entirely new light.

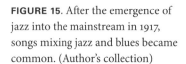
FIGURE 15. After the emergence of jazz into the mainstream in 1917, songs mixing jazz and blues became common. (Author's collection)

HOMEOPATHIC AND ALLOPATHIC BLUES

Imagine an archetypal scene. A blues singer has the blues because his lover has run off with another man. He is feeling sad, depressed, and lonely. He feels like he wants to die. So he picks up his guitar and sings a mournful blues. Having played and sung for a few minutes, he somehow feels better. He no longer feels as depressed as he did. Life seems bearable again, if perhaps only for a time. Thanks to his music-making, he wants to live. Such is the power of the blues.

But how has this happened? How has the blues achieved its cure? The basic mechanism is termed *homeopathic,* from *homeopathy* (or *homoeopathy*), a kind of alternative medicine founded by a Leipzig physician named Samuel Hahnemann in about 1800, in which diseases are treated with agents that, taken on their own, produce similar symptoms. It is based on the Latin adage *Similia similibus curantur*—"likes are cured with likes"—and comes from two Greek roots: *homo,* meaning "like"; and *patheia,* meaning "suffering". This is precisely what happens with our blues-stricken singer: he treats his depressed state of mind with depressed music. This I call *homeopathic blues*.

By contrast, imagine that the same singer in the same forlorn state uses an up-tempo, lively number to repair his mood, rather than a mournful blues. Many of the important early blues performers occasionally recorded such numbers: think, for example, of Blind Lemon Jefferson's "Hot Dogs,"[32] a virtuoso piece of guitar ragtime quite different from the soul-searching slow blues for which he is best known, or Robert Johnson's "They're Red Hot,"[33] a medicine show hokum song, its lighthearted mood again at odds with the rest of his recorded legacy. This approach we might term *allopathic,* from *allopathy,* "a method of treating disease with remedies that produce effects different from those caused by the disease itself" (from the Greek, *allo,* meaning "different").[34] In other words, allopathic songs treat a depressed mood with lively music.

Of these two approaches, homeopathic and allopathic, homeopathic seems to be the term generally applicable to much folk blues. That is not to say that all folk blues are slow and sad, but very many are. I would therefore characterize folk blues as a predominantly homeopathic genre. This is interesting, because the homeopathic principle is a far more subtle one than the allopathic. Put simply, if I have a headache, it seems counterintuitive to treat it with an agency that in another context will give me the very symptom I am trying to get rid of; but this is what homeopathy recommends. Similarly, if I am feeling depressed and decide to go to the theater to cheer myself up, I am more likely to want to see a comedy than a tragedy. In short, the homeopathic approach in music (and indeed in medicine generally) is unusual, and its presence in folk blues is one of the most distinctive—and one of the least discussed—characteristics of the genre.

Despite the fact that it is counterintuitive, musical homeopathy has a long and venerable tradition in the West. It was acknowledged by Plato.[35] It was also championed by Aristotle, who recommended the homeopathic treatment of victims of religious frenzy by the playing of melodies that produce such frenzy.[36] As a result, Aristotle claimed, such patients would be "restored as though they had found healing and purgation."[37] This is essentially the same as the treatment of tarantism by the frenzied dancing of the tarantella. We also find it in many kinds of religious expression, from Shamanic rituals to the emotionalism of Revivalist meetings. In all these instances, the basic process is *catharsis,* an Aristotelian term from the Greek *kathairein,* to purify or purge, referring to an emotional purgation brought about by an intense release of feelings.

In addition to the treatment of a frenzied condition with frenzied music, catharsis is also the basic process behind the curing of a depressed condition with depressed music, our main interest here. From this viewpoint, blues is a musical manifestation of the old adage that "a good cry" makes you feel better. There are a number of historical precedents for this. Plutarch's reference, quoted earlier, to the use of threnody to "at first stir up the emotions and make the tears flow, but then . . . gradually calm sorrow" presupposes essentially the same cathartic process as folk blues. However, the most illuminating parallel to the homeopathy of folk blues that I have been able to find is not from classical antiquity, but from seventeenth-century England, specifically in the work of the composer John Dowland (1563–1626).

At this time England was in the grip of an epidemic of melancholia, which, as I have already suggested, poses a strong parallel both in terms of its symptoms and its societal causes to the blues (i.e., neurasthenia) in early-twentieth-century America. The cult of melancholy strongly influenced the arts, most famously in the works of literary figures like Shakespeare and John Donne. Its greatest expression in music is in the work of Dowland, who is generally regarded as one of the outstanding composers of his era.

FIGURE 16. Hendrick ter Brugghen, *A Man Playing the Lute* (1624). The painting of this solitary and clearly singing performer presents a striking visual parallel with the familiar twentieth-century image of the solitary guitar-playing blues vocalist. (The National Gallery, London)

FIGURE 17. *Stavin' Chain Playing Guitar and Singing the Ballad "Batson,"* Lafayette, La., June 1934. (Library of Congress, Prints & Photographs Division, Lomax Collection)

The analogy with blues begins with the fact that Dowland's output centers on songs for solo voice and lute. The lute was an ancestor of the guitar; indeed, in European culture of the time, it functioned in approximately the same way that the guitar does in ours, as a relatively inexpensive, accessible domestic instrument used mainly for song accompaniment. Dowland was an excellent lutenist, and, in an interesting parallel with a folk blues guitarist, he "performed his own music in a semi-improvised manner from a memorized 'gist.'"[38] His compositions are often strongly melancholic, as one can see just from their titles: "In Darkness Let Me Dwell," "Burst Forth, My Tears," "Woeful Heart with Grief Repressed," "Sorrow, Stay Awhile," and, most famously, "Flow My Tears, Fall from My Springs," which, originally for solo lute, was reworked as a song and became one of the most celebrated compositions of the age. Dowland's melancholia was not restricted to his compositions, but rather spilled over into his life. He titled one of his songs "Semper Dowland, Semper Dolens" ("Always Dowland, Always Mourning") and signed himself "Jo: dolandi de Lachrimae" ("John Dowland of Tears").

Furthermore, there is a clear sense that Dowland approached his compositions therapeutically. Much like a blues artist, he regarded the curing of melancholy as a prime reason for composing. In fact, in the dedication to *Lachrimae* ("tears"), a set of pieces for instrumental ensemble, Dowland was explicit about the therapeutic intent of his music and the homeopathic means by which a cure was to be achieved: "Though the title does promise teares, . . . yet no doubt pleasant are the teares which Musicke weeps, neither are teares shed in sorrowe, but sometime in joy and gladnesse."[39] As a commentator has stated: "One of the functions of [the *Lachrimae*], presumably, was to cure the melancholy they so powerfully evoke."[40] Indeed, there is a striking parallel with blues in that the title of this particular work, *Lachrimae,* is a very rare example of the linguistic phenomenon I discussed at the beginning of this chapter, that is, of a name that describes the condition it seeks to cure.

The cause of Dowland's melancholy in his songs, when stated, is nearly always love: the coldness or infidelity of a lover, or the pain of parting—identical, in fact, to the themes of many blues songs.[41] Central here is the intimate relationship between melancholy and lovesickness. "Melancholy has long been linked to love," writes Linda Austern, "both the desire for sublime spiritual union with the Divine, and the earthly hunger for sexual satisfaction." Conversely, the essential nature of lovesickness "as the dark and solitary agony of a lone soul yearning for fulfillment has . . . rendered it an adjunct to melancholy."[42] This, of course, has profound resonances with blues. In the last chapter, for example, I showed that the essential theme of both commercial and folk blues was the yearning for the beloved.

No less interesting than Dowland's overtly lovesick songs are those that are simply an outpouring of melancholy and are not concerned with its cause. An instance from Dowland's work is the song "In Darkness Let Me Dwell":

In darkness let me dwell, the ground shall sorrow be,
The roof despair to bar all cheerful light from me.
The walls of marble black that moisten'd still shall weep,

My music hellish jarring sounds to banish friendly sleep.
Thus wedded to my woes, and bedded to my tomb,
O, let me, living, living die, till death do come.
In darkness let me dwell.[43]

The unremittingly morbid tone of Dowland's song recalls folk blues like Blind Lemon Jefferson's "See That My Grave Is Kept Clean."

Dowland's approach to word setting means that at times he uses some unusual musical effects that are remarkably evocative of blues. Example 27 provides an instance of this from "In Darkness Let me Dwell." In both mm. 30 and 32 in the accompaniment, there is a minor third that starkly clashes with the simultaneously sounding major third. This device is not uncommon in music of Dowland's era; it is technically known as a *false relation*. In a different context, however, it would be termed a blues third, and a very striking example it is too (G over an implied E^7 chord in m. 30; and F over a D chord in m. 32). Clearly the false relations quoted in example 27 are meant to reflect the anguished sentiment of the lyric; this is precisely how they would also function in a blues.

In fact, given three centuries of cultural divide and linguistic evolution, it is surprising how effective this lyric is when we convert it into a blues. This can be done quite easily by repeating the first line of each couplet of the quoted example, so as to devise a standard AAB structure. In example 28 I have done just that, turning the first couplet into a twelve-bar verse by setting it to a generic folk blues melody. The result, while unconventional because of the archaic language, is in its way remarkably effective.

I do not want to push the analogy between Dowland's music and folk blues further. There are obviously vast differences between the two styles, and in fact there is not the least likelihood that a bar of one could be mistaken for the other. Nevertheless, the fact that Dowland

EXAMPLE 27. Dowland, "In Darkness Let me Dwell" (1610), mm. 28–33

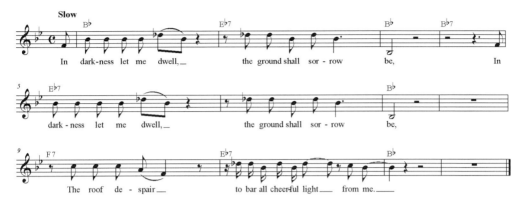

EXAMPLE 28. "In Darkness Let Me Dwell": blues reworking

composed mainly songs for voice and the guitar-like lute, the accompaniments for which were at least partly improvised in performance; that his songs were intended as homeopathic cures for melancholy; that he at times produced musical devices that are remarkably similar to blue notes; that he was the product of a society that was suffering from the Elizabethan equivalent of the blues—all of these factors offer illuminating parallels with the blues phenomenon of twentieth-century America. It encourages us to place the emergence of folk blues in a broader historical context, as but one example of a musical response to a human psycho-emotional imbalance that has surfaced at various times and in various cultures throughout history.

• • •

However, if folk blues is predominantly homeopathic, is that also true of early popular blues? Example 29 is the first section of Dorothy Harris's "Just Blues" (1915), a composer-published piano blues from Hondo, Texas. This is a highly original and expressive work, replete with blue notes. In the first three bars, for example, there are three blue notes in each hand (in the right hand, the blue thirds A♯ over implied G chord in m. 0, D♯ over an anticipated C chord at the end of m. 2, and E♭ over a C chord in m. 3; in the left hand, the blues third B♭ and the blue fifth C♯ in m. 1 and the blue third E♭ in m. 3). The frequency and starkness of these notes combine with the very slow tempo and other expressive elements to make a work of cathartic intensity. It should therefore be regarded as homeopathic. The same is true of "Snakey Blues," the piano blues examined in the chapter 2 (example 6). It, too, is slow and has the additional designation *lutoso*—"mournful"—placed at the beginning of the work and at the start of its fourth section (m. 46).

Two examples of piano blues that examined in chapter 2 stand in sharp contrast to "Just Blues" and "Snakey Blues." "Bonehead Blues" (example 7), with its lively fox-trot feel and absence of expressive devices like blue notes, is obviously allopathic. The one-step "Bevo Blues" (example 8) is, if anything, even jauntier in feel, an impression confirmed by a recording of

EXAMPLE 29. Harris, "Just Blues" (1915), A strain, mm. 1–16

the piece by the Yerkes Jazzarimba Orchestra, the only group known to have recorded this work; with its snappy tempo, complete avoidance of blues sentiment and idiom, and whirling xylophone counterpoint, this performance is as unhomeopathic as one could imagine.[44]

The song "Broadway Blues" (example 4) offers a more subtle case. The words for this song are serious, the basic theme being the yearning of the worn-out city dweller for the tranquility of the countryside. The speed indication at the beginning of the song is "Tempo di Blues," which we would assume implies a slow tempo. However, the internal evidence of the music suggests otherwise. The opening chords of the verse (mm. 7–9) last a whole measure each, and unless the tempo has some momentum the work will quickly become stagnant. The dotted fox-trot rhythms that occur in the melody of the verse also suggest a relatively cheerful mood. At the start of the chorus, the melody in the left hand of the piano part (which doubles the vocal melody) is marked *dolce,* meaning "sweetly," and indeed this appears to be the mood of the chorus as a whole: sweet, dreamy, and smooth, a comforting evocation of the pastoral bliss hankered after by the singer, not a homeopathic depiction of his depressed state to bring about catharsis. "Broadway Blues" would therefore seem to be basically allopathic in nature. This conclusion is confirmed by one of the most important recordings of the song, a performance by the African American vaudeville duo consisting of singer Noble Sissle and pianist Eubie Blake (Emerson 10296, 1920). The performance is unambiguously allopathic, cheerful in tone and taken at a very brisk, almost virtuoso, tempo.

What should we say about allopathic blues like "Broadway Blues," "Bevo Blues" and "Bone-Head Blues"? The temptation is to dismiss them as somehow inauthentic, for their cheerful mood is entirely at odds with what we associate with "real" (i.e., traditional folk) blues. However, in order to understand these blues, we need to relate them not to the aesthetic of our times, but to the aesthetic of the culture that produced them.

According to the aesthetic of the day they certainly were authentic blues, since calling a composition a blues suggested only that a prime intention of the work was to cure the blues of the performer and his or her audience. It made no difference whether this process happened allopathically or homeopathically: in either case it was still a blues. In fact, no less an authority than W. C. Handy even went so far in a 1916 article as to define blues in allopathic terms, calling them "the happy-go-lucky, joyous songs of the southern Negro."[45] Much in keeping with Handy's comment, the evidence suggests that the allopathic approach was not only considered legitimate in popular blues of the 1910s but in fact was predominant.

The most powerful evidence for this is the recorded legacy. Nearly all recordings of blues made during the pre-1921 era are allopathic. This is generally the case even when the original sheet music from which they derive suggests a homeopathic approach. An example is "St. Louis Blues," Handy's landmark song from 1914. In its original printed form, this work is unmistakably sad in tone. The lyrics center around the desertion of the (female) singer's lover for another woman. She is clearly depressed. The song famously begins:

I hate to see de evening sun go down,
Hate to see de evenin' sun go down,
Cause my baby he done lef dis town.
Feelin' tomorrow lak ah feel today,
Feel tomorrow lak ah feel today,
I'll pack my bag and make my getaway.

The intensity of the lyrics is enhanced by the powerful use of blue notes (see example 21) and a slow tempo that is indicated at the beginning of the score.

Nonetheless, nearly all of the eighteen disc recordings of the work released before 1921 are allopathic. For instance, Al Bernard's vocal version on Emerson (7477, 1919) is medium fast and "raggy" in feel. An instrumental version by the All Star Trio (Lyric 4208, 1919) is even faster and raggier. Even the two recordings of the work by African American bands—Ciro's Club Coon Orchestra (Columbia 699, 1917) and Jim Europe's Band (Pathé 22087, 1919)—which we might expect to be homeopathic given the ethnicity of the performers, are allopathic. In fact, of the eighteen recordings, the only one that is not allopathic is one made by the singer Marion Harris (Columbia A-2944, 1920). It is basically a serious performance that is quite faithful to the emotional intensity of Handy's original; and although her performance does not have the intensity of certain later recordings, such as Bessie Smith's extraordinarily cathartic 1925 recording (Columbia 14064–D), it is still fair to call it homeopathic. Harris was a leading white vaudeville performer whose blues recordings are in fact consistently homeopathic, and although largely forgotten now she was widely admired by both blacks and whites in her own day. W. C. Handy, for instance, commented that "she sang blues so well that people hearing her records sometimes thought that the singer was colored."[46]

FIGURE 18. Marion Harris, unknown date. A major attraction in vaudeville, Harris recorded blues extensively, and with such feeling that, according to W. C. Handy, people hearing them sometimes "thought the singer was colored." (Library of Congress, Prints & Photographs Division, Bain Collection)

In fact, Harris's recordings are almost the only ones within our period that are homeopathic. One has to search hard to find others. A possible exception is an obscure recording from 1917 on the cut-price label Little Wonder. It is of a work called "Southern Blues" played by the Hawaiian guitar duo of Frank Ferara and Helen Louise, played at a medium slow tempo and in quite serious a mood.[47] This is almost the only pre-1921 recording of blues that uses any sort of guitar, and the fact that it is a Hawaiian slide guitar, which produces faint associations in the mind of the listener with African American bottleneck style, reinforces the blues connection. This recording and Marion Harris's work aside, there is very little else on record from the period that might be regarded as homeopathic.

This then leads to the question of why the homeopathic approach is so rarely found in early popular blues, given its centrality in folk blues. There are basically two answers to this question. The first is that, as I have already mentioned, the homeopathic approach is a much less obvious one than the allopathic. Consequently, when we find references to curing the blues in the culture of the time, the suggested means of cure was usually allopathic. As this is a basic point, it is worth exploring in a little more detail.

The fundamental image behind the notion of curing the blues allopathically was that of creating a good mood in the sufferer by driving away or chasing out his blues or blue devils. This could be achieved by a variety of stimuli. One was humor. We have already seen this notion at work in "Billy's Request," where a humorous song is suggested as "A Cure for the Blues" (figure 12). Another such cure—and a very basic one—was amorous fulfillment. This is graphically illustrated by figure 19, the cover for a popular song from 1916 titled "I Found Someone to Chase the Blues Away."[48] A girl with a blissful countenance is protectively held by her lover in an idyllic rural setting as three "blue devils"—in the original illustration they are a sickly livid color—trudge off sulkily, the middle one turning back to look at the happy couple with an embittered look on his face.

One of the most commonly touted allopathic cures for the blues was lively dancing and the music that accompanied it. The popularity of this notion coincides with the dance craze that first hit America around 1908 and that continued well into the Depression, along with the parallel emergence of ragtime followed by jazz. Together these were seen as "a rhythmic tonic for the chronic blues," to quote a line from a 1918 song dealing with the topic by George and Ira Gershwin.[49] A partial list of song titles from the era reflecting this approach has been compiled by Michael Garber; it shows the extent to which the allopathic use of dance and music to cure the blues pervaded popular culture:

Dancing the Blues Away (1914)
Jazz All Your Troubles Away (1918)
Jazzin' the Blues Away (1918)
Chasin' the Blues (1920)
Shimmy All the Blues Away (1920)

FIGURE 19. In this 1916 song, the man's blues are cured allopathically by love. Note the iconographic similarity between the ghostly "blue devils" here and the solitary figure also representing the blues on the right of figure 6. (Author's collection)

Dance Off the Blues (1921)
Dance Your Troubles Away (1921)
Dancing My Worries Away (1922)
Strutting the Blues Away (1923)
Jazz Your Troubles Away (1923)
Shuffle Your Troubles Away (1924)
Kicking the Clouds Away (1925)
Blowin' the Blues Away (1926)
Steppin' on the Blues (1926)
Shaking the Blues Away (1926)
Dancing the Devil Away (1927)
Kicking the Blues Away (1930)
Dancing the Devil Away (1930)
Dance Your Troubles Away (1930)[50]

In comparison, the homeopathic approach is rarely mentioned in popular songs and titles as a means of curing the blues. An exception is "Tears of Love" a 1918 tear-jerker that contains the following maudlin quatrain:

Tears may mean a heart is broken,
Tears may drive the blues away,
Tears may fall when you remember
One you loved is a bygone day.[51]

Such sentiments are also rare in the culture as a whole. The following quotation from the *Ladies' Home Journal* is exceptional. It specifically relates to the treatment of neurasthenia by musical homeopathy: "Music as a medicine in the home [is] better than any system of mental therapeutics. . . . In all nervous illness music is very potent as a sedative, and, strange to say, in cases of despondency and melancholia the minor chords are most effective and act as a tonic."[52]

Occasional references to the homeopathic treatment of blues through music are also found in fiction. In an 1889 novella, the author Mary Dickens, daughter of the famous novelist Charles, describes how her heroine, Margery, has "got the blues," and how she decides to practice the piano to see if it will help. However, "although she picked her brightest little songs, she could not get on; and by-and-by she took out a book of plaintive Irish melodies. They were quite out of her line as a rule; but to-day the foreboding, prophetic wail in them seemed to suit her better, and half an hour later, she was singing away with all her heart."[53]

Clearly, then, while the homeopathic treatment of blues was known and accepted in mainstream society of the period, the dearth of references to it shows that it was considered an uncommon approach.

The second reason that the homeopathic principle was shunned in popular blues involves the inherent power of the approach. For the cure to work, the music must be strongly cathartic, and for it to be cathartic it must be earthy and passionate. While we associate those qualities with folk blues, such direct emotionalism was removed from the standard aesthetic of Tin Pan Alley. In a penetrating essay on American popular song, the critic Gene Lees discusses the ideal of love in popular song and movies of the Tin Pan Alley era. He describes a "strange vision of love that never seems to have a physical fulfillment," that is more courtly than sexual in nature, and that is ultimately the product of mainstream (i.e., white) American protestant culture.[54] As a result of this repressed culture, overt references to sex are rare in popular music (or movies) before the rock and roll era. Tin Pan Alley songs are full of lighthearted, joyous romance ("Yes, Sir, That's My Baby!") and some flirtation ("Gimme a Little Kiss, Will Ya, Huh?") with a measure of melancholy rejection ("My Sweetie Went Away, She Didn't Say Where, She Didn't Say When"), but they hardly ever contain anything stronger.

Because Tin Pan Alley tended to avoid powerful emotion, popular blues usually distanced itself from the homeopathic power of folk blues even while drawing creatively from the genre. If the sheet music was homeopathic, as with "St. Louis Blues," the distancing occurred during performance by speeding the music up and generally lightening it. More often, however, the distancing took place at the compositional level. In chapter 2 we examined how the musical and textual idiom of popular blues was adapted from the folk medium. These adaptations usually had the effect of decreasing the cathartic intensity of the original. In terms of the text, for example, we saw how the earthiness of folk blues is only rarely mirrored in popular blues; most of the time, the lyrics are considerably less intense. Similarly, when incorporating elements of the blues musical idiom, such as blue notes, popular blues did so in considerably more lightweight and less jarringly dissonant ways than in folk blues.

"Nigger Blues" (example 5) gives a specific example of how the homeopathic intensity of folk blues is moderated when transferred to the commercial medium. As discussed, this song draws closely from the folk blues idiom both musically and textually, using standard twelve-bar stanzas with the traditional AAB structure and unhappy lyrics consisting entirely of floating folk formulas. We would therefore expect "Nigger Blues" to be a regular homeopathic blues. However, the homeopathic effect is at least partially undermined by the tempo indication "allegro moderato" (moderately fast), the "boom-chick" ragtime-style left hand of the piano accompaniment, and the jerky dotted notes in the melody at the beginning of each phrase. So this blues ends up being allopathic in nature, and indeed all four known disc recordings of this work from the period—by two military bands and the singers George O'Connor and Al Bernard—are also allopathic.[55]

An important ingredient in the process of allopathizing folk blues is humor. Take for instance the 1920 "Washtub Blues," the front cover of which was reproduced in figure 8. The song is about the feelings of a woman abandoned by her lover. This is obviously a serious subject matter, and there are literally hundreds of folk blues on record dealing with this issue homeopathically. However, the effect here, as exemplified by the cover, is humorous, and hence the treatment of the subject is allopathic. Similarly, "Suicide Blues," a 1919 blues with words by George Norton (of "Memphis Blues" fame) and music by Peter de Rose, takes a potentially tragic theme and makes it humorous by exaggerating it to the point of absurdity.[56] The chorus runs:

> I'm gonna bathe ma'self in carbolic acid,
> And eat a pound of Paris Green,[57]
> Chew all the heads off a box of sulphur matches,
> And wash 'em down with gasolene;
> Den I'll hang ma'self to a weeping willow tree,
> And stab ma'self a time or two,
> And I'll weep and sigh till I droop and die,
> Cause I've cert'nly got the Suicide Blues.

In extreme form, this process of allopathization in popular blues takes the form of parody. For example, the lyrics of "Tennessee Blues" (example 16) are a caricature of black dialect. The second verse, for instance, has "Ah got anudder nigger, / han'somer an' bigger, / Some classy kid am Benny, / Swellest coon in Tennessee." This kind of lyric has the effect of undermining the seriousness of the music, which in its use of blue notes and the twelve-bar sequence has considerable homeopathic potential. Lyrics like these recall the denigrating parody of black dialect found in an earlier generation of minstrel songs, and it is interesting to remember that many of the performers of early popular blues, such as Leroy "Lasses" White and Al Bernard, were themselves minstrels.

However, the targets of racial parody in popular blues were by no means limited to African Americans. The most important and bestselling ethnic-stereotype blues from this period is Moore and Gardner's 1915 song "Chinese Blues," which, as mentioned in chapter 1, is about an opium-imbibing Chinese laundryman begging his girl to let him see her. Following the success of this song—in fact, it was one of the first published blues to achieve major success—a number of other such blues appeared targeting different ethnicities, including "Big Chief Blues,"[58] "Yiddisha Army Blues,"[59] and "Irish Blues—The Meanest Kind, the Greenest Kind."[60] One common feature of many of these blues is that each takes the "I've got the blues" trope that we found to be central to popular blues and gives it the appropriate ethnic coloring. Thus "Chinese Blues" climaxes on "I got those Ipshing Hong-Kong Ockaway Chinese Blues" (see example 2); "Big Chief Blues" starts its chorus with "Got um Big Chief Indian Blues"; while "Yiddisha Army Blues" predictably sings "Oi vey! I got the Yiddisha Blues." Blues like these are part of the much wider Tin Pan Alley phenomenon of ethnic parody songs, which poked fun at the Irish, Jews, Italians, Germans, Chinese, Native Americans, and many other ethnic groups, and which were churned out by the thousands within our period.

A final factor when considering allopathy in blues of the 1910s is the influence of jazz. Jazz of the period is strongly allopathic, being generally fast, light, fun, and very danceable. At times it is even explicitly humorous, most famously in the Original Dixieland Jazz Band's "Livery Stable Blues," the first jazz record ever to be released.[61] A major reason for the record's success was the humor found in the imitation cries of rooster, horse, and cow by the clarinet, cornet, and trombone, respectively. All jazz bands of the era recorded blues, and some of these recordings were extremely popular, especially "Livery Stable Blues," "Bluin' the Blues,"[62] and "Mournin' Blues"[63] by the ODJB; "Beale Street Blues" by Earl Fuller's Famous Jazz Band;[64] and "Kansas City Blues" by Wilbur Sweatman's Jazz Band (as mentioned in chapter 1, this last recording alone is known to have sold 180,000 copies).[65] The Louisiana Five jazz band, run by clarinetist and former ODJB member Alcide Nunez, recorded more blues than any other band within our period, an astonishing twenty-nine recordings of nineteen blues compositions made in just a single year between December 1918 and December 1919. Of these, the nine that were composed by the band were published in a special series of "Jazzensations" by the leading New York firm of Leo Feist. Most of the blues recorded by early jazz bands were fox-trots and labeled as such on records and sheet music. This meant that while they were performed quite fast, they were not as fast as compositions designated as one-steps. So in a general way, while such blues are allopathic, they are less so than the one-steps; and even at their most lighthearted they are often played with an intensity that at least hints at the cathartic folk material from which they ultimately derive.

In sum, homeopathy was generally avoided in early popular blues, at least with the intensity found in folk blues. Popular blues were either allopathic at the level of performance, as we have found with the recordings of "St. Louis Blues," or during the process of composition, as with "Nigger Blues" and "Suicide Blues." In general, this "de-homeopathizing" process consisted of making the music faster and lighter, and of introducing humorous elements in the lyrics and music or, in extreme cases, resorting to parody and often ethnic stereotyping. I should add that there is a geographical factor in all this. Blues published in the South, or at any rate composed by southern musicians like W. C. Handy, tended to be more strongly influenced by folk blues than were blues published in the North; it follows, therefore, that southern popular blues are on average more homeopathic than northern ones. It is therefore not a coincidence that the three popular blues we have examined that are clearly homeopathic—"Just Blues," "Snakey Blues," and "St. Louis Blues"—are all southern in origin.

It is tempting to view the allopathic/homeopathic issue in racial terms. According to this line of argument, the homeopathic quality—and hence the core emotional power—of folk blues is compromised when transferred to the commercial sector. Moreover, as folk blues are essentially African American, and as the popular blues industry was dominated by whites, it is equally tempting to view the commercialization of blues as the trivialization, even castration, of black culture by white.

While there may be some truth to these arguments, they are simplistic, for allopathic blues was an integral part of black, as well as white, culture. Pre-1921 recordings of blues by black artists such as Wilbur Sweatman, W. C. Handy, Noble Sissle, and James Reese Europe are nearly all allopathic (as we have already seen with Sissle's recording of "Broadway Blues" and Europe's recording of "St. Louis Blues"). Moreover, there was a strong tradition in black vaudeville of the 1910s—and thereafter—of allopathic blues. One has only to remember the 1910 report I quoted in chapter 1 of Henry, the ventriloquist's dummy, singing the blues and getting drunk at a black vaudeville show in Florida. Finally, not all kinds of folk blues of this era were homeopathic. Subgenres that were basically allopathic included "hokum" blues, championed on record in the 1920s and 1930s by performers like Thomas A. Dorsey, Bo Carter, and the Hokum Boys, and which were typically humorous in mood, often with a bawdy undertone; and raucous piano blues styles like barrelhouse and boogie-woogie that were popularized by artists like Clarence "Pine Top" Smith and Charles "Cow Cow" Davenport in the 1920s. In the 1910s, both hokum and piano blues were in the process of development in the black subculture. With these factors in mind, we cannot seriously argue that allopathic blues were confined to white culture.

Popular blues culture gradually became more homeopathic in the 1920s. What mainly precipitated the change was the rise of the race record market, which for the first time allowed the mass dissemination of recordings of African American homeopathic blues performers like Bessie Smith, Blind Lemon Jefferson, Ida Cox, and many others. In fact, the very first race record, Mamie Smith's "Crazy Blues" from October 1920, while not as cathartic as many later recordings, was, with its slow tempo and Smith's powerful vocal delivery, still strongly homeopathic when compared to nearly all of the hundreds of blues recordings that preceded it. Even so, race records were by definition mainly bought by black consumers, and despite a very few blues artists like Bessie Smith who had some crossover appeal, their impact was limited within the wider marketplace at this time.

The question that remains to be discussed involves the origins of the homeopathic strain in folk blues, given that musical homeopathy was comparatively alien to mainstream culture. The answer is simple: the homeopathic approach is endemic to African American culture and dates back at least to the time of slavery. For the slaves, music-making was imbued with the special significance that it has with many oppressed peoples. Both religious music (e.g., spirituals) and secular music (e.g., work songs and field hollers) were regarded not just as entertainment; instead, they had essential social and therapeutic functions. As the ex-slave and abolitionist Frederick Douglass wrote in 1855, "Slaves sing more to *make* themselves happy, than to express their happiness."[66] And Douglass was clear that the basic process by which this happiness was achieved was homeopathic: "The songs of the slave," he wrote, "represent the sorrows, rather than the joys, of his heart; and he is relieved by them, only as an aching heart is relieved by its tears."[67] It is precisely these musical "sorrows" that form the expressive and therapeutic basis of blues.

I suspect that the origins of the homeopathic approach can be traced even further back than African American slave culture—in fact to the African societies from which the slaves were taken. In African culture, the therapeutic function of music assumes an importance it lacks in mainstream Western society. Consider the following example, reported by ethnomusicologist Michael T. Coolen, about a *fetisher* called Noche Fanne. In the Wolof society of Senegambia, a *fetisher* is a musician (*gewel*) who also has a role as, among other things, a healer. According to Coolen: "When someone is possessed by a spirit, Fanne is called to the house to treat the illness. Beginning late in the evening, he will start to play his *xalam*, seeking out those strings and those notes that will please the spirit and entice it to leave the body of the sick person. He knows that every spirit has a tune or melody that is uniquely its own, and when played, the tune will compel the spirit to leave the body of the sick person."[68] It does not seem far-fetched to propose this approach to healing as a cultural model for curing the blues with the blues, particularly when one considers that Wolof society was an important source of slaves in America, and that the xalam is a guitar-like instrument considered a likely prototype for the banjo.[69]

I have a final point to make about the issue of blues and race. Early in this chapter I discussed the etymology of the term *blue*. I pointed out that the word carries within it the notion of physical and spiritual anguish, mainly through its relationship with *blow*. The original meaning of blue was blue-grey or livid, the color skin turns as a result of being struck. Therefore *blues* is a wonderfully appropriate term for the musical style of African Americans, for in a metaphorical sense the race turned *blue* from the oppression, the *blows* literally inflicted on it by whites. And this is especially so when we consider that *blue* and *black* derive ultimately from the same etymological source, namely, the Indo-European root *bhel*.[70] Thus blues could only be called blues, for this word alone combines the defining characteristic of the race that created it—the color of its skin—with the anguish, sorrow, pain, and oppression suffered by that race.

CHAPTER 4

The Blues of W. C. Handy

William Christopher Handy (1873–1958) was, more than any other individual, the man who made popular blues popular. By successfully combining careers as composer, publisher, and performer, Handy influenced American culture in a unique way, raising popular awareness of the new genre while at the same time helping to define it. Due to these achievements, he had acquired by the 1930s (if not before) iconic status as "The Father of the Blues," an epithet by which he became universally known, and which furnished the title of his widely read autobiography. In the mind of mainstream America, he was for some decades *the* symbol for the blues, the one name that everybody associated with the genre.

Handy's posthumous reputation rests on a relatively small number of blues compositions that, taken together, form a remarkable body of work, including some of the best-loved songs in American culture. Of these, the most celebrated are the trinity of "The Memphis Blues" (composed 1909, published 1912), "St. Louis Blues" (1914) and "Beale Street Blues" (1916), closely followed by others like "Yellow Dog Blues" (1914) and "Aunt Hagar's Blues" (1920). However, the extraordinary popularity of these songs has rather overshadowed the rest of Handy's creative achievement. He wrote approximately twenty other blues-related works, the last published when he was eighty, whose average artistic standard is remarkably high, and which at their best must be ranked as major, if in most cases lesser known, contributions to the genre (see table 7). And then there are his other compositions, which encompass an unusually wide range of genres: patriotic material, numerous arrangements of spirituals, stirring songs of racial uplift, jazz songs, instrumental compositions, and various art-songs. I cannot honestly claim that all of these are neglected masterpieces—some, in fact, are quite undistinguished—but they are nearly always engaging, and some are outstanding. In short, Handy's compositional achievement goes far

FIGURE 20. W. C. Handy, 1941. (Library of Congress, Prints & Photographs Division, Carl van Vechten Collection)

beyond that of the average Tin Pan Alley composer—or blues musician, for that matter—in both its depth and scope.

It is, therefore, surprising that Handy's music has been given little scholarly attention over the years, with even his major compositions only rarely receiving anything other than a superficial examination.[1] My aim in this chapter is to redress the balance by focusing almost entirely on his music: consideration of space precludes any comprehensive summary of his biography, which is readily available elsewhere. Of Handy's compositions, I will naturally concentrate on his blues. And of his blues, I will deal first with those written while he was in Memphis (1909–1917). The blues written after the move to New York (1917–1953) are considered later in this chapter.

BLUES FROM THE MEMPHIS PERIOD (1909–1917)

"The Memphis Blues"

Named after the city which had been Handy's home since around 1905, "The Memphis Blues" was not, as the composer was to claim for years, the first blues to be published: Smith and Brymn's "The Blues," Franklin Seals's "Baby Seals' Blues," and Hart Wand's "Dallas Blues" had

Table 7. W. C. Handy's Published Blues and Blues-Related Works

Publication	Title[1]	Words	Music
1912	Memphis Blues (or Mr Crump)[2]	—	Handy
1913	Memphis Blues (song)	George Norton	Handy
1913	Jogo Blues	—	Handy
1914	Saint Louis Blues	Handy	Handy
1914	Yellow Dog Blues[3]	Handy	Handy
1915	Hesitating Blues	Handy	Handy
1915	Joe Turner Blues	Handy	Handy
1915	Shoeboot's Serenade	Handy	Handy
1916	Beale Street Blues[4]	Handy	Handy
1918	The Kaiser's Got the Blues	Domer C. Browne / Handy	Domer C. Browne / Handy
1920	Aunt Hagar's Blues[5]	Handy	Handy
1921	Loveless Love	Handy	Handy
1922	John Henry Blues	Handy	Handy
1923	Atlanta Blues	Handy / Dave Elman	Handy
1923	Darktown Reveille[6]	Walter Hirsch	Chris Smith / Handy
1923	Feelin' Blues	William Farrell / Handy	William Farrell / Handy
1923	Harlem Blues	Handy	Handy
1923	Sundown Blues	Handy	Handy
1924	Basement Blues	Handy	Handy
1926	Golden Brown Blues	Langston Hughes	Handy
1926	Blue Gummed Blues	Handy/Dave Elman	Handy
1926	Friendless Blues	Mercedes Gilbert	Handy
1929	Wall Street Blues	Handy	Handy
1942	Go and Get the Enemy Blues	Clarence M. Jones / Handy	Clarence M. Jones / Handy
1942	Woo-Loo-Moo-Loo Blues	Clarence M. Jones / Handy	Clarence M. Jones / Handy
1953	Newspaperman's Blues	Charles L. Cooke / Handy	Charles L. Cooke / Handy

1. Not included are blues-related works that are straightforward arrangements of folk material, such as "East St. Louis," included in *Blues: An Anthology,* 53.

2. Originally titled "Mr Crump" and composed in 1909.

3. Originally titled "Yellow Dog Rag."

4. Originally titled "Beale Street."

5. Originally titled "Aunt Hagar's Children."

6. Adaptation of Handy's unpublished "Bugle Blues."

all been copyrighted earlier in 1912. Handy's work was, however, almost certainly the first of these to have been composed, having been created as early as 1909. Perhaps more important, it was far and away the most successful of this first wave of popular blues. In fact, as I have argued in chapter 1, it was this work more than any other that introduced the genre of blues to mainstream popular music.

So what is it about this work that made it such a success? We need first to be clear that "The Memphis Blues" exists as two separate works: the original published version of 1912 for piano, itself based on an earlier version for Handy's band; and the song version, with words by George Norton, that appeared in 1913 after Handy sold the work to publisher Theron Bennett. The two works, while sharing much music in common, have major differences, and I will examine each in turn.

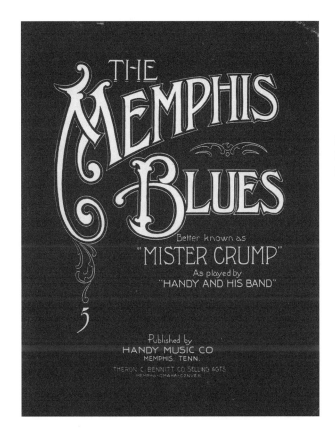

FIGURE 21. The cover of the original Handy edition of "The Memphis Blues." (Author's collection)

The original, instrumental version of "The Memphis Blues" is essentially a piano ragtime composition. It has three strains, and, as is conventional in ragtime, each strain is repeated immediately after it is first played. Also conventional is the work's tonal structure: the first two strains are in the tonic, F major, while the third strain is in the subdominant, B♭ major. In many other respects, however, the work is most unconventional. First, there is its unusual structure. In a ragtime instrumental composition, it is customary for at least one of the strains—usually the first—to be reprised later in the work. Thus a typical format for a three-strain rag is ABAC. This is a surefire way to give the rag at least a superficial structural coherence. In "The Memphis Blues," however, there are no such reprises—the structure is just ABC.[2] Instead, Handy finds a much more subtle solution to the problem of structural cohesion by making repeated use of the four-measure phrase that introduces the work (example 30). It is reintroduced as the last four measures of the A strain and turns up again quite unexpectedly at the end of the second strain, where it acts as a transition into the third strain. The reprise of four-bar units is not unknown in ragtime: a particularly famous example occurs in Scott Joplin's "The Entertainer," where the final four measures of the B strain are reprised as an interlude between the C and D

EXAMPLE 30. Handy, "The Memphis Blues" (1912), intro., mm. 1–4

strains (example 31). However, using an introduction to underpin the structure, as Handy does in "The Memphis Blues," is a highly original touch, elegantly weaving a thread of coherence throughout much of the work without resorting to the large-scale reprise of entire sections.

However, the most distinctive aspect of "The Memphis Blues" is none of the above, but rather its use of the blues idiom. Both the first and third strains employ the twelve-bar blues form: the first as a straight twelve-bar sequence, the third using the sequence twice through, thereby producing a twenty-four-bar strain. This in itself was revolutionary. Ragtime instrumental strains were usually sixteen measures in length. Although thirty-two and eight measure strains were also used, twelve-bar strains were very unusual in published ragtime, being considered jarringly asymmetrical. For a published piano rag to use a twelve-bar format for two of its three strains was almost unheard of.[3]

No less striking is the use of blue notes, which are featured prominently in the first and third strains, especially in the melody. At times their use leads to some thoroughly raw dissonance, such as that found at m. 2 of example 30, where, on the first beat, Handy oscillates between the blues third and regular third in the melody while the accompanying F major chord in the left hand clashes starkly; the inner voice played simultaneously in the right hand (E-D-C) only adds to the confusion. Unusual though this is, the most memorable use of blue notes in the work is not in this passage but in the third strain, in a pair of two-bar breaks at mm. 7–8 and 19–20 (examples 32 and 33). These breaks were apparently the invention of Handy's violinist Paul Wyer.[4] They are based on a repeated pattern of three sixteenth notes, consisting of the blues third C♯, its resolution D, and B♭, the root of the implied harmony. Such shifting three-note

EXAMPLE 31. Joplin, "The Entertainer" (1902), B strain, mm. 12–16, and transition between C and D strains

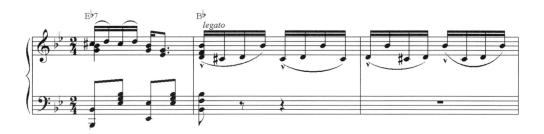

EXAMPLE 32. Handy, "The Memphis Blues" (1912), C strain, mm. 6–8

EXAMPLE 33. Handy, "The Memphis Blues" (1912), C strain, mm. 18–20

patterns are a common feature of instrumental ragtime, where they create a strong rhythmic tension, and where they are technically known as *Secondary Ragtime*.[5] Example 34, for instance, shows the first four measures of the first strain of George Botsford's "Black and White Rag," a very popular rag that appeared in 1908, the year before "The Memphis Blues" was composed. The quoted passage utilizes two secondary ragtime three-note cells, each played four times, the first (mm. 1–2) consisting of the pitches C-D-F♯ and the second (mm. 3–4) of A♯-B-E. The second cell in particular is reminiscent of the "The Memphis Blues" breaks in that it uses the blues third (A♯) and regular third (B) of the underlying harmony (G).[6]

The second strain of "The Memphis Blues" is much less bluesy than the first and third strains, having a conventional sixteen-bar structure and making much less use of blue notes. Despite this, it is just as influenced by black music as the surrounding strains, being based on a folk melody commonly known as "Mama Don't Allow." When "The Memphis Blues" was first performed by Handy's band in the mayoral campaign of Edward Crump, listeners spontaneously adapted the traditional lyrics to this new political context:

> Mr. Crump won't 'low no easy riders here,
> Mr. Crump won't 'low no easy riders here.
> We don't care what Mr. Crump don't 'low,
> We gon' to bar'l-house anyhow—
> Mr. Crump can go and catch hisself some air![7]

EXAMPLE 34. Botsford, "Black and White Rag" (1908), A strain, mm. 1–4

In this form, it acquired enduring popularity in the folk sector independent of "The Memphis Blues," as is shown by a 1927 recording by the black Memphis-based songster Frank Stokes.[8]

The question arises of the extent of Handy's creative involvement here: was his source material essentially the same as the version in "The Memphis Blues," that is, did he just arrange it, or did it require some adaptation? Musically, there are three basic forms of this song. The best known is "Mama Don't Allow It," copyrighted by blues pianist Charles "Cow Cow" Davenport in 1929, which has long been a jazz standard. It is known from a plethora of recordings from the 1930s on. The second version flourished in folk-based recordings from the mid-1920s to the mid-1930s by both black and white artists. Although it has been given various names, the generic title given to it by discographer Guthrie Meade is "No Low Down Hanging Around."[9] The third version of the song is the most obscure. Titled "Mama Don't Allow No Easy Riders Here," there are only three known recordings, all dating from 1929, two in groups led by guitarist Tampa Red (Vocalion 1429 and 1430), the other by the black piano-vocalist John Oscar (Brunswick 7104). Musically speaking, Handy's version of the song has no relationship with the first version, "Mama Don't Allow It," some relationship with the second, "No Low Down Hanging Around," and is very closely related to the third, "Mama Don't Allow No Easy Riders Here."[10] The implications of this are unclear. It could be that the second strain of "The Memphis Blues" and "Mama Don't Allow No Easy Riders Here" are simply different manifestations of the same pre-existent folk song. If so, Handy's role was presumably to insert it into "The Memphis Blues" essentially unchanged. However, if such a folk song did preexist "The Memphis Blues" and was also the inspiration for the recorded versions of "Mama Don't Allow No Easy Riders Here" in 1929, it suggests that this particular version of the song was current in folk culture from early in the century till the Depression. If so, how come there are no other recordings of it?

It is more likely that the third version of the song was either adapted, directly or otherwise, from "The Memphis Blues." This suggests that Handy's original inspiration was the second version of the song—by far the most prevalent in early twentieth century folk culture, if the recorded legacy is anything to go by—which he adapted substantially to produce the second strain of "The Memphis Blues." If this is the case, as seems likely, he must be credited with a more active role than just that of arranger.

"The Memphis Blues" was apparently Handy's favorite blues.[11] There are two probable reasons for this. First, despite, or more likely because of, Handy's reliance on folk sources, the work displays remarkably fresh creativity: the various innovative musical and structural elements I have discussed, along with many more that I have not mentioned, combine synergistically to produce a work of powerful impact. The second likely reason for "The Memphis Blues" being Handy's favorite is the context of the work's creation. Handy was thirty-eight when "The Memphis Blues" appeared, a remarkably late age for a composer to achieve his first hit. Even more impressive is the fact that the work was apparently only his third serious attempt at composition. The previous two pieces were an unpublished and long-lost "Roosevelt Triumphal March"; and "In the Cotton Fields of Dixie," an undistinguished plantation-type song co-written with Handy's future business partner, Harry Pace, which had been published by the Cincinnati firm of George Jaberg in 1907, and which had quickly disappeared into commercial oblivion. Usually when a popular music composer achieves a hit, it is after years of hard compositional toil and numerous flops. Handy's achievement in having a hit with what was only his second publication and—even more remarkably—his third composition is, as far as I know, unique for a major composer of popular music in the Tin Pan Alley era. Before "The Memphis Blues," Handy had been a minor figure on the American musical landscape. As a result of its publication and subsequent success, he suddenly began to acquire a national reputation. It is not surprising, then, that he viewed the work so fondly.

The song version of "Memphis Blues," which appeared under Bennett's aegis, is a highly effective, even ingenious, adaptation of Handy's original, simplifying it while at the same time preserving at least a modicum of its individuality. In order to conform to the Tin Pan Alley song structure of verse and chorus, Handy's A strain is omitted so that the B strain becomes the verse and the C strain the chorus of the song. Such omissions were common when turning a ragtime instrumental composition into a song. What is most unusual, however, is that the song preserves the link between the original B- and C strains (the one taken from the introduction and quoted in example 30), seamlessly extending the verse by an extra four measures. This adds tremendously to the quirkiness of the whole and means that both verse and chorus have unusual lengths, the verse being twenty measures (sixteen-measure original plus four-measure link) and the chorus twenty-four (two twelve-bar blues sequences). George Norton (if it was Norton who was responsible for the adaptation of the music from Handy's original, and not just for the addition of the words) and/or Theron Bennett deserve much credit for this idea.

In addition to the altered structure, there are various musical changes made in the song version of "The Memphis Blues," but they are mostly quite minor. The raw edge of Handy's original scoring (such as the dissonances in the passage examined in example 30) is toned down, and the melody is sometimes tweaked to make it more singable. A particularly effective instance of melodic reworking occurs at the start of the chorus. This moment in the song is compared with its equivalent in the original version (the beginning of the C-section) in example 35. In the original (example 35a), Handy wrote four repeated Fs; in the song version (example 35b) this is changed to four rising half-steps. This change clearly adds character to the melody, and the pause over the first three notes in the song version builds tension, making a stronger

EXAMPLE 35. Handy, "The
Memphis Blues," C strain, m. 1:
  a. Instrumental original
       (1912), melody;
  b. Song version (1913),
       melody and text

emotional release on the F when the music moves back into tempo. This is an example of the four-note chromatic motif (as discussed in chapter 2), which is an important expressive element in early popular blues; indeed it is also used in the A strain of the instrumental version of "The Memphis Blues" (example 25).

The single most striking element of the song version of "The Memphis Blues," however, is not in the musical adaptation, but in Norton's lyric. The lyric is a celebration of the new genre of blues in general and of Handy's band in particular. As discussed in chapter 2, this focus on a single bandleader almost certainly reflects the influence of Irving Berlin's 1911 smash hit "Alexander's Ragtime Band." But whereas Berlin's Alexander was fictitious, "The Memphis Blues" was innovative in that it celebrated a real band and bandleader. There was little precedent for this in the realm of popular music. It is true that there had been a trickle of songs around the turn of the century celebrating the band of John Philip Sousa.[12] That band, however, was at the time the most celebrated in America; Handy's band, by contrast, was little known outside Memphis when the song version of "The Memphis Blues" appeared. The popularity of the song was therefore excellent, if indirect, publicity for Handy and his band; and, even more important, the song's celebration of Handy as the quintessential purveyor of the blues marks the beginnings of his iconic status as "Father of the Blues."

"Jogo Blues"

Three and a half months before the song version of "The Memphis Blues" appeared, Handy copyrighted his second blues, an instrumental composition titled "Jogo Blues." According to Handy, *jogo* was a slang name used by blacks for an African American, being closely related to other such terms as *jig, jigwawk* (or *jigwalk*), and *jigaboo*.[13] Thus the title has some parallel to that of Leroy "Lasses" White's "Nigger Blues" (example 5), which appeared the same year. However, unlike "Nigger Blues," "Jogo Blues" was a commercial failure. Only one recorded version was made at the time, by a military band as part of a medley with the later (and far more successful) "Beale Street Blues."[14] "Jogo Blues" is in fact today remembered almost exclusively for the fact that its first strain was subsequently transformed with spectacular results into the chorus of "St. Louis Blues." Yet despite its obscurity, it is one of Handy's most interesting and original compositions.

Like "The Memphis Blues" before it, "Jogo Blues" is essentially a folk rag for piano, and indeed the tempo marking at the beginning of the original edition is "Tempo di Rag (a la Memphis

Blues).” There are four strains, each being repeated, with the third and fourth strains having written-out, varied repeats. In addition, the first strain is also reprised after the second, as is common in instrumental ragtime. There are two other sections: a four-bar introduction to the work as a whole, and an eight-measure transition linking the second and third strains. The overall structure, therefore, is: introduction-A-A-B-B-A-transition-C-C-D-D. The third strain is eight measures in length, while the other three strains use twelve-bar structures (although of these only the first uses a straight blues sequence). This means that the work is unconventional, perhaps unique, for a published four-strain rag, in that none of the strains use a regular sixteen-bar structure.

As with “The Memphis Blues,” the influence of black folk music is pervasive. According to the folklorist Abbe Niles, the last strain is based on a folk melody whose text runs:

Lawdy, Lawdy
Lawdy, Lawdy
Lawdy, Lawdy, Lawd!
I’ll see you when yo’ troubles all ’ll be like mine![15]

This melody is clearly blues-related, using a regular twelve bar structure except in mm. 5–6, where, instead of the expected subdominant chord (IV), Handy uses an unorthodox sequence of seven rapidly changing chords (example 36). The best-known blues influence in “Jogo Blues” is the first strain, both in its use of the standard twelve-bar sequence and in the famous melody, later to furnish the chorus of “St. Louis Blues.” The strain is built on a three-note rhythmic cell consisting of a blues third, its resolution, and a fall to the root (A♯-B-G; see example 37). While Handy apparently first encountered this specific motif in an A. M. E. church in the early 1890s, the melody of the strain as a whole seems to be related to a specific published source, as I shall demonstrate in the discussion below on “St. Louis Blues.”[16] That same source was also an influence on the B strain, which is one of the most eccentric of Handy’s conceits (example 38). The form is again twelve-bar, but this time the chord sequence has merely a tangential harmonic relationship to blues, as is shown by table 8: only mm. 3–5 and the second ending correspond even loosely to a prototypical blues sequence.

In his autobiography, Handy suggests that “Jogo Blues” failed commercially because it was too hard to play and because white audiences did not understand its title.[17] This is perhaps true, but there are some serious compositional issues too. The most basic of these is that only one

EXAMPLE 36. Handy, “Jogo Blues” (1913), D strain, mm. 5–7

EXAMPLE 37. Handy, "Jogo Blues" (1913), main motif of A strain

EXAMPLE 38. Handy, "Jogo Blues" (1913), B strain

Table 8. Harmonic Analysis of "Jogo Blues," B Strain

Measure	1	2	3	4	5	6	7	8	9	10a 10b	11a 11b	12a 12b
Chord	D⁷	D⁷	G⁷	G⁷	C	D⁷	E♭	E♭	D⁷	Em D⁷	A⁷ G	D G
Numeric	V	V	I	I	IV	V	♭VI	♭VI	V	vi V	II I	V I
Prototype Blues	I	I	I	I	IV	IV	I	I	V	V	I	I

of the four strains has strong melodic content. This is, of course, the first strain, and it has the unfortunate consequence of the work having nowhere to go melodically after the first strain. I assume Handy thought the climactic rendition of the "I'll see you when yo' troubles all 'll be like mine" melody, with which the work ends, would be the answer; but it simply does not have the sense of release that, for example, is found in the final strain of "The Memphis Blues." Consequently, "Jogo Blues" is unsatisfying overall, and I cannot help thinking that the work would have been better structured with the first and last strain swapped, so that the melodically potent section occurs at the structural climax. This is, of course, precisely what Handy did in "St. Louis Blues." The situation in "Jogo Blues" is not helped by the eccentricity of a structure consisting only of twelve- and eight-bar strains, which, lacking the glue of melodic coherence, seems meandering. Probably the worst moment in the work—it is, I think, one of the weakest moments in any of Handy's blues—is the transition between the second and third strains (example 39). Melodically this consists of a single note—G—endlessly repeated underneath an unchanging G harmonic pedal. Melodic and harmonic stasis is the last thing the music needs at this point, and it reminds us starkly of Handy's compositional inexperience (it would seem that "Jogo Blues" was only his fourth or perhaps his fifth completed work).[18]

Yet despite its immaturity, "Jogo Blues" is fascinating and revealing. In attempting to build on the individuality of "The Memphis Blues," Handy produced his most experimental and idiosyncratic composition. And while it must be ultimately classed as a heroic failure, this can easily be forgiven, for the work possesses the same restless striving of the creative spirit that was the following year to manifest itself in one of the most remarkable achievements, not just in blues, but in all American music: "St. Louis Blues."

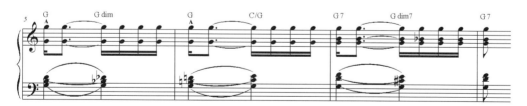

EXAMPLE 39. Handy, "Jogo Blues" (1913), transition between B and C strains

"St. Louis Blues"

"St. Louis Blues" is a unique cultural phenomenon. One authority describes it as "one of the most notable of popular music landmarks."[19] Another goes still further, calling it "the most influential American song ever written."[20] Statements like these are easier to make than to prove, but in the case of "St. Louis Blues," the recorded legacy provides graphic documentation of the song's preeminence. Tom Lord's jazz discography lists nearly fifteen hundred recordings of the work, making it the most recorded composition in the history of the genre. And those are only recordings in the jazz field. There have over the years been innumerable recordings by dance bands, popular singers, close harmony groups, and hillbilly artists; there have even been classical and ethnic reworkings. There can, in fact, be no doubt that "St. Louis Blues" is one of the most celebrated of all songs, with its popularity stemming in an unbroken line from 1914 to the present.

Yet on the surface the work is a most unlikely candidate for megastardom. Created in a single night of feverish activity, in a humble room on Beale Street that Handy rented specifically for the purpose, "St. Louis Blues" shatters the conventions of popular songs in so many ways that it would, I believe, have been impossible to predict its spectacular success.[21] It uses a most unusual three-section form that is neither the verse-chorus structure of a popular song nor the repeated verse structure of folk blues. Instead, it is some sort of hybrid of the two. Its tonal scheme is thoroughly unorthodox; it is also rhythmically highly eccentric, dramatically shifting its feel from fox-trot to tango and back again to fox-trot; and then, of course, there is the wealth of musical and textual innovation, ranging from the jarring use of blue notes to twelve-bar structures. Last but not least, there is the issue of inventiveness. As Elliott Hurwitt remarks, "St. Louis Blues" "is packed with enough memorable phrases to have carried two or three . . . songs to success."[22] It is precisely the wealth of creativity and abundance of ideas that were found in "Jogo Blues." But whereas in "Jogo Blues" the material never integrates into a dynamic whole, in "St. Louis Blues" it does so quite brilliantly. The result is a song that is both original and utterly compelling, and which has proved to have a chameleon-like adaptability to the ever-evolving styles of vernacular music in the near century since its creation.

As has already been mentioned, "St. Louis Blues" has a most unusual form. It is basically in three sections: a twelve-bar structure in G major, which I will term "A," sung twice with different words; a sixteen-measure tango section in G minor, "B"; and a twelve-bar "chorus" that moves back to G major, labeled "C." Handy provides the words for two choruses in the original edition, both of which are often performed, making the final section twenty-four bars in length. The piece as a whole is preceded by an eight-bar introduction derived from the tango (B) section, so that the overall structure is Introduction-A-A-B-C-C. Note that—rare for a popular song of the period—there is no vamp between the introduction and the A section. Handy steadfastly refused to include one, despite pressure on him to do so, apparently sensing that it would interrupt the dramatic flow of the work.[23]

It is possible to think of the song as loosely corresponding to the verse-chorus structure of a regular popular song, with the verse consisting of the two A sections and B, and the chorus of section C. However, this distinction is misleading for a number of reasons. For one thing, the B (tango) section is so musically, textually, and tonally distinct from the A (blues) section that it is hardly meaningful to group them as a unit. For another, in a standard Tin Pan Alley format the verse and chorus take on particular roles, the verse being more lightweight while the chorus is usually the emotional and musical focus. For this reason, the verse is often optional, and in many cases—classics like Gershwin's "I Got Rhythm" or Fats Waller's "Ain't Misbehavin'"—it is usually dispensed with altogether in performance. "St. Louis Blues" is quite different. The "verse" is an integral part of the song, so much so that despite its length (forty measures), it is nearly always included in performance. From this point of view, "St. Louis Blues" is structurally closer to a ragtime instrumental number, with several contrasting sections of equal importance. Indeed it shares the same overall structure as "The Memphis Blues," which in its original form is essentially a ragtime instrumental number: a central sixteen-bar strain flanked on either side by a twelve-bar blues strain.

The A section of "St. Louis Blues" is, as mentioned, a twelve bar blues. Its first line—"I hate to see de the evening sun go down"—has become one of the most famous in all blues and is set to a melody of great richness taken straight from folk blues (example 21). It is particularly impressive that Handy made no attempt to water down the emotionalism of the folk blues style in this section: the stark use of blue notes is uncompromising and brilliantly encapsulates the anguish of the singer, whose lover has left her for another woman. The folk blues influence is also felt in the structure of the text, which uses the AAB format of folk blues. This is in fact only the second example in print of this device, the first being Leroy "Lasses" White's "Nigger Blues," published in 1913, the year before "St. Louis Blues" (example 5).

The other blues section of "St. Louis Blues" is the chorus (C section), which Handy first used for the A strain of "Jogo Blues." It reappears here little changed apart from the addition of words. These lyrics seem to be largely of folk origin. For instance, the second line of the first chorus, "Dat man got a heart lak a rock cast in the sea," Handy originally heard while down on his luck in St. Louis some years earlier, uttered by an inebriated woman "whose pain seemed even greater" than his own.[24] This raises the question of the origin of the melody for this section: was it Handy's own, or was it adapted from pre-existent sources? There is no known folk melody quite like it. However, there is an interesting similarity between it and the first strain of a 1908 New Orleans ragtime composition called "I Got the Blues," composed and published by Antonio Maggio. The latter work is a milestone in blues history in that its first strain is built on a twelve-bar blues sequence: this is the first known instance in print of the sequence being associated with the notion of having the blues (example 40; the title page for the work is reproduced in figure 14). Example 41 compares "I Got the Blues" and "St. Louis Blues" side by side, and there are suggestive parallels between them. First, of course, there is the fact that the two extracts are based on the same three-note motif A♯-B-G (example 37). More specifically, the first phrase of Handy's melody (mm. 1–3) is a busier version of Maggio's, while the second phrases of the two melodies (mm. 5–8) are also closely linked, the pitches G, A, and B♭ being the focus of mm. 5–6, and the phrase coming to rest in both instances on G in m. 8. The melodies diverge for the first half of the third phrase (mm. 9–10, first beat) but then reunite in the second half (from m. 10, second beat).

What is to be made of this connection? There is enough in common between the two melodies to suggest that Handy's melody may have been in some way influenced by Maggio's. With the evidence I have so far presented, however, this remains just a possibility: the similarity between the two could be coincidental, or they might have been independently derived from the same folk source. There is, however, an additional piece of musical evidence that effectively proves a direct link between the two works. That evidence concerns not "St. Louis Blues" itself, but "Jogo Blues," published the year before, where Handy first used the "St. Louis Blues" theme. The first four measures of the B strain of "Jogo Blues" (example 38) bear a remarkable resemblance to the first four measures of the C strain of Maggio's work (example 42): not only are the melodies for these passages strikingly similar, based as they are on the same motif, but they are treated in an almost parallel fashion over essentially the same chord sequence (example 43).

EXAMPLE 40. Maggio, "I Got the Blues" (1908), A strain

EXAMPLE 41. **a.** Maggio, "I Got the Blues" (1908), A strain, melody;
  b. Handy, "St. Louis Blues" (1914), chorus, melody

EXAMPLE 42. Maggio, "I Got the Blues" (1908), C strain, mm. 1–4

EXAMPLE 43. **a.** Handy, "Jogo Blues" (1913), B strain, melody, mm. 1–4;
  b. Maggio, "I Got the Blues" (1908), C strain, melody, mm. 1–4 (original C major)

The motif upon which the two passages are based, unlike the three-note cell used in the cho-rus of "St. Louis Blues" and the A strain of Maggio's work (example 37), is not one that was in common currency at the time. Indeed, I know of no other blues or proto-blues that uses it. In addition to all this, both passages use a device that is exceptionally rare in piano ragtime and blues: the placing of the melody in the left hand underneath the accompaniment. This occurs in all four measures of the "Jogo Blues" extract, and in mm. 3–4 of the "I Got the Blues" quote. These can be seen by comparing examples 38 and 42.

Maggio, in fact, claimed much later that Handy heard his work on a visit to New Orleans, and that this in turn influenced the writing of "St. Louis Blues."[25] While it seems almost certain that Handy did not visit New Orleans at the time in question, it is entirely plausible that he encountered the work in Memphis either in sheet music form or as played by an itinerant band or musician from the Crescent City. It is interesting that Handy, in his only known discussion of Maggio's claim—a letter written to composer William Grant Still—does not explicitly deny having encountered the work.[26]

This is not to suggest that Handy was guilty of plagiarism. The inexact nature of the cor-respondences between the passages in Maggio's and Handy's works suggests that the borrow-ings were unconscious on Handy's part. "I Got the Blues" was just one of hundreds of pieces, folk and commercial, he must have experienced during this period. It was encountered by him and probably made a particular impression due to its use of the twelve-bar sequence, and perhaps also due to its blues title. It then reemerged in a creatively reworked form from his unconscious at a later date. Such a phenomenon is in fact part of the normal creative processes of a composer; but it is particularly so for a composer like Handy who was used to drawing on pre-existent material like folk music in his compositions.

"I Got the Blues" may also have influenced one other distinctive aspect of "St. Louis Blues": its key structure. As is conventional in ragtime, Maggio's A strain is reprised between the B and C strains. However, when it returns, it does so in the tonic minor (G minor, example 44). To repeat in the minor a whole section that was originally in the major is, to my knowledge, unique within the literature of ragtime and related styles. I suspect that it reflects Maggio's classical background, for this kind of alteration of mode is quite common in nineteenth-century art music (Maggio was apparently a mainstream music instructor and performer/bandleader).[27] Whatever its derivation, the moment when the music moves into the minor in "I Got the Blues" is probably the most memorable in the entire work. Similarly, the abrupt change from G major to G minor in "St. Louis Blues" at the beginning of the tango (B) section is also one of the most striking features of the piece. This is partly due to the dramatic change in rhythmic feel, a point I will discuss further in a moment. But it is also because of the key change, which is unexpected for two reasons: because it launches into the new key without any preparation whatever; and because the new key is the tonic minor (G minor), which is far more jarring than the much more common relative minor (E minor).

Yet the most remarkable aspect of the B section of "St. Louis Blues" is not the key scheme but its brilliantly effective use of tango rhythm. Handy had long been aware of the power of

EXAMPLE 44. Maggio, "I Got the Blues" (1908), A¹ strain

Latin music. He had visited Cuba with Mahara's Minstrels in 1900, and while there he had become fascinated with the indigenous styles.[28] In Memphis he had noted the potent effect on dancers of Latin-based music like "La Paloma" or Will Tyer's "Maori."[29] By 1914 the tango had become a national craze, and Handy correctly calculated that inserting it into the middle of "St. Louis Blues" was likely to be popular with dancers. This is, however, not in any way to suggest that his inclusion of the device was merely a gimmick. On the contrary, its use seems absolutely integral to the work as a whole. Furthermore, it ties in beautifully with the lyric. The A-sections have dwelt upon the depressed feelings of the singer. Suddenly, from the beginning of the B-section, her mood changes to anger as she expresses her frustration at the "St. Louis woman with her diamond rings" who has stolen her lover. The tango rhythm encapsulates the exotic allure of the rival, just as the key change to the minor at that point captures her mood of angry defiance.

The inclusion of the Latin element was one that Handy experimented with constantly in his blues. He had already used it in a somewhat disguised form for a few measures at the end of "The Memphis Blues" (example 45).[30] It was also to become a recurring feature of his blues compositions, being found, for example, in the chorus of "Beale Street Blues" (1916, example 53) and a succession of works in the 1920s starting with "Aunt Hagar's Children," the original piano version of the work later retitled "Aunt Hagar's Blues," which evinces a tango feel in its A strain.[31]

EXAMPLE 45. Handy, "The Memphis Blues" (1912), D strain, mm. 13–17

This persistent use of Latin rhythms recalls the statement made by jazz pioneer Jelly Roll Morton that their inclusion gave "the right season for jazz music" (and, by implication, blues).[32] Many of Morton's compositions included at least one section utilizing what he referred to as the "Spanish tinge," including two of his best-known blues, "Jelly Roll Blues" (copyrighted in 1915, a year after "St. Louis Blues") and "New Orleans Blues" (which was not published or recorded till the 1920s, but was probably written much earlier). Morton's claims about the importance of the "Spanish tinge" are backed up by the testimony of other early jazz musicians, such as the drummer Warren "Baby" Dodds and pianist Willie "The Lion" Smith, who both confirmed that it was in the earliest blues.[33] It would seem, then, that, whether consciously or not, Handy grasped the importance of the "Spanish tinge" in African American vernacular music and, like Morton, used it in his blues as an important expressive element.

In his autobiography, Handy mentions the "flood of memories" that filled his mind as he was composing "St. Louis Blues." Prominent among them was his own time down-and-out in St. Louis in the 1890s, one of the low points of his life. He was "broke, unshaven, wanting even a decent meal."[34] It is perhaps for this reason that "St. Louis Blues" is imbued with a sense of personal sincerity that is rarely found in popular music. It is this sincerity, combined with Handy's remarkably successful adaptation of the folk blues idiom, that has helped to ensure the unrivaled success of the song, and that has allowed it to speak across the generations in untold thousands of performances.

"Yellow Dog Blues"

"St. Louis Blues" would not have been an easy act to follow for any composer, and it is entirely to Handy's credit that his next blues, "Yellow Dog Blues," copyrighted less than three months later, is quite different in conception from its predecessor, yet in its way just as fresh and creative.

There were two main inspirations for the song. The first was a musical fragment that Handy had heard while waiting for a train at the railroad station in Tutwiler, Mississippi, in about 1903, and that had made a deep impression on him. Sung by an African American whose face, according to Handy, "had on it some of the sadness of the ages," the song consisted of one repeated line— "Goin' where the Southern cross the Dog"—and was accompanied by the singer on bottleneck guitar, a style Handy thought "the weirdest music" he had ever heard.[35] The song's lyric was an oblique reference to the town of Moorhead, Mississippi, where the Southern railroad line intersected with the Yazoo Delta railroad, the latter being known as the "Yellow Dog," or just "Dog" in black slang, because of its initials, Y. D.

The more immediate inspiration for "Yellow Dog Blues" was a hit song from 1913 titled "I Wonder Where My Easy Rider's Gone" by Shelton Brooks, one of the major African American popular song composers of the era. The heroine of "Easy Rider" is one Miss Susan Johnson, whose lover, a jockey called Lee, deserts her. "Yellow Dog Blues" was intended as a sequel to Brooks's hit. In Handy's song, Miss Johnson makes frantic inquiries as to the whereabouts of Lee and eventually receives a letter from an informant in Tennessee telling her that her lover has been seen "where the Southern cross' the Yellow Dog."

It is not hard to see the appeal of Brooks's song for Handy. "Easy Rider" is effectively a blues in all but name. The lyric centers around the prototypical blues theme of desertion by a lover. At one point (during the second chorus), the protagonist even sings the trope "I've got the blues, but I am to damned mean to cry," a standard plaint found in dozens of folk blues lyrics.[36] The song's main melody, which occurs at the beginning of the chorus (example 46a), is clearly

EXAMPLE 46. a. Brooks, "I Wonder Where My Easy Rider's Gone" (1913), chorus, melody and text, mm. 1–8 (original Bb);
   b. Handy, "Yellow Dog Blues" (1914), verse, melody and text, mm. 1–8;
   c. Handy, "Yellow Dog Blues" (1914), chorus, melody and text, mm. 5–8

blues-related, revolving around a blues seventh (the C in mm. 1–2 and the F in mm. 4–5) and using a regular twelve-bar blues sequence that is extended to sixteen measures. Meanwhile, the imagery of the "Easy Rider," a slang term meaning a sexually satisfying lover, is one found frequently in folk blues.[37] While on the surface Brooks uses "rider" in a literal sense, that is, jockey, nevertheless the double entendre would have chimed with African Americans and gives the song a powerful, blues-related sexual charge.[38]

In addition to continuing the story-line of "Easy Rider," "Yellow Dog Blues" ties into it in two ways. First, the key phrase "I wonder where my easy rider's gone" is quoted in Handy's verse. Second, at a musical level, Handy permeates his melody with the blues-derived motif of Brooks's chorus, using it in a slightly varied form for the main melody of his verse (a comparison between the two is given in examples 46a and b) and again for two measures in his chorus (example 46c). These borrowings aside, Handy's song is very much his own. It uses a twelve-bar structure for all its themes, the first of his compositions to do so. The verse is based on two melodies (A and B), with the first one repeated, and there is an independent melody for the chorus (C), which is also repeated. The whole song is preceded by a standard eight-bar introduction and two-bar vamp. The overall structure is therefore: introduction—vamp—verse (AAB)—chorus (CC).

Probably the most impressive moment of "Yellow Dog Blues" is the beginning of the chorus (example 47). Its first three notes ("Dear Sue, your . . . ") are held back (each is marked with a pause), the music being wound to a point of maximum tension before being released on the fourth note as it returns to regular tempo (on "ea" of "easy"). It is a remarkably effective musical depiction of Susan Johnson's feeling of suspense as she opens the letter, and of the consequent relief and excitement that floods over her as she realizes her quest for her lover has finally yielded fruit.

In fact, this moment is obviously derived from George Norton's song adaptation of Handy's "The Memphis Blues," which uses the same device at the identical moment, that is, at the beginning of the chorus (example 35b). Norton's use of it is purely musical, however: it is not used for the additional purpose of conveying the emotional tension of the lyrics, as it is in "Yellow Dog Blues." Furthermore, even at a musical level, Handy trumps Norton. The pitches used in both songs are chromatic, and they are therefore both examples of the four-note chromatic motif, a device commonly found in popular blues.[39] Handy manipulates the device in a most original way, for having used it once, he immediately repeats it with the pitches reversed (indicated in example 47). The whole eight-note sequence is richly and imaginatively harmonized,

EXAMPLE 47. Handy, "Yellow Dog Blues" (1914), chorus, melody and text, mm. 1–4

making the opening of the chorus of "Yellow Dog Blues" one of the outstanding moments in all of Handy's music.

The only mystery regarding "Yellow Dog Blues" is its title. It was, of course, originally named "Yellow Dog *Rag*" and only retitled a blues five years after its initial publication.[40] Why did Handy not originally call it a blues when the work is so strongly based in the blues idiom? One answer might be that, while it is bluesy in terms of musical idiom, the tone of its lyrics is lighthearted, in stark contrast to the lamenting quality of "St. Louis Blues." However, given that Handy had previously also titled purely instrumental works blues ("Jogo Blues" and "The Memphis Blues"), this explanation can be at best only part of the reason. The other factor is that blues as a genre had not yet caught on, whereas "rag" was in 1914 a more promising title to the sheet-music-buying public, and, given the close relationship between the two genres at that point in their evolution, either would have been suitable as a title to the work. According to this line of argument, Handy wanted to experiment to see if titling it a rag would help sales. If so, it was apparently a misjudgment, for the work only became widely popular after its renaming.

"Shoeboot's Serenade"

Handy's next blues-related work after "Yellow Dog Blues" was "Shoeboot's Serenade," copyrighted in March 1915. This song had little success at the time of its publication—only a single recording is known from the era—and has failed to gain much attention since.[41] It has a standard popular song format with a verse and chorus, each of thirty-two bars, and concerns Shoeboot Reader, a black bandleader and trombonist. In the first verse, we learn he has been rejected by his girl, Melinda. To woo her back he sings to her a "serenade" that comprises the chorus of the song. His efforts are successful, and in the second verse we are told that he has married her.

The work has a much looser relationship to blues than "Yellow Dog Blues" or, indeed, any of Handy's earlier blues. The verse has no discernible blues influence in either the music or lyrics (unless one counts the basic theme of the protagonist being rejected by his lover). The chorus, however, is another matter. It uses such familiar folk-derived tropes as "I woke up this morning with the blues all 'round my bed" and "I'll have to leave this town just to wear you off my mind." And while the music does not use a twelve-bar structure, it has a wistful quality that is thoroughly bluesy. This is best seen at the chorus's start (example 48), which, with its slow tempo, gently syncopating piano accompaniment and expressive melody, is an original and highly effective evocation of the singer's melancholy. Particularly striking is the F in the melody in the fourth measure, which is in stark contrast to the F♯ of the accompaniment in the previous measure. It is not strictly accurate to describe either note as a blue note, for neither clashes with the prevailing harmony. Nevertheless, its effect is thoroughly ear-grabbing.

Despite all this, the dominant influence in "Shoeboot's Serenade" is not folk blues, but rather from the opposite end of the musical spectrum. Franz Schubert's "Serenade" ("Ständchen" in the original German) was one of his most celebrated songs. It seems that Handy got into an argument with a white musician who questioned his musical competence. Handy's response

EXAMPLE 48. Handy, "Shoeboot's Serenade" (1915), chorus, mm. 1–4

was to challenge the man to name any classical melody, to which he would then give "a Negro setting." The man named Schubert's song, and Handy produced his parody of it in reply.[42] Handy draws on Schubert in two ways. First he mangles the composer's name in the title, *Schubert* becoming *Shoeboot*. Second, he takes the famous opening of Schubert's melody and makes it the backbone of his verse, expanding and syncopating it (examples 49 and 50). Incidentally, the borrowing is not only musical. Handy takes the last word of the first phrase of the original, *Lieder* ("*songs*"), and at the equivalent point (mm. 3–4 of example 50) transforms it into the homophone *leader*. This is quite an ingenious pun, especially as both words have musical associations ("leader" refers here to a *band*leader). I wonder if Handy's challenger got the joke.

Schubert's melody is brought back halfway through the verse, and again at the end of the chorus. Handy uses it, then, as a structural binder for the work, just as he did in "The Memphis Blues" with the passage quoted in example 29, and in "Yellow Dog Blues" with the quotation from "I Wonder Where My Easy Rider's Gone" (example 46). Unlike these earlier examples, however, the use of the device in "Shoeboot's Serenade" is a liability that I suspect helps account for the song's commercial failure. For a regular popular song—as opposed to a blues—to be a hit, it had to have a chorus that was able to survive independent of its verse. The reintroduction of Schubert's melody in the chorus of "Shoeboot's Serenade" only makes sense

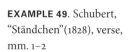

EXAMPLE 49. Schubert, "Ständchen"(1828), verse, mm. 1–2

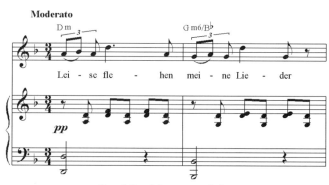

Translation: *My songs gently flow*

EXAMPLE 50. Handy, "Shoeboot's Serenade" (1915), verse, mm. 1–4

with reference to its earlier appearances in the verse, particularly as it is so stylistically at odds with the down-home lyrics and music used elsewhere in the chorus. Thus the chorus makes little sense on its own. This is a shame, as the work overall is not only coherent but contains much of merit. Besides, one can only admire the chutzpah of an imagination that attempted to weave two totally disparate music cultures—twentieth-century African American folk and nineteenth-century Viennese classical—into the fabric of a popular song.

"Hesitating Blues"

With this experiment behind him, Handy returned to safer ground with "Hesitating Blues," copyrighted in July 1915. This work uses the successful approach of "Yellow Dog Blues," combining twelve-bar blues with popular song form. Unlike the earlier work, however—unlike, in fact, any of Handy's earlier blues except "Shoeboot's Serenade," if one calls that a blues—"Hesitating Blues" uses just two melodic themes, both twelve-bar, one for the verse, the other for the chorus. Each is repeated, so that both sections are twenty-four bars in length. To compensate for the lack of contrasting material, Handy puts the chorus in the subdominant, B♭ major (he probably took this idea from the song version of "The Memphis Blues," which had used precisely this key change at the same moment).

The core of the song is contained in the verse, which is an ingenious adaptation of the folk blues song-type usually known as "Hesitation Blues." This song, which has been recorded by numerous folk singers, black and white, since the 1920s, is in its folk form simply a succession of twelve-bar blues stanzas, each stanza subdivided into a four-bar verse and an eight-bar refrain. For example, the second stanza of the version by black songster Jim Jackson recorded for Vocalion in 1930 runs:

> *Verse:* I'm going to the river with a rope and rock,
>   And the way you treat me I'm going to jump over the dock.
> *Refrain:* Tell me how long will I have to wait:
>   Will I get you now or must I hesitate?[43]

The four-bar verse, eight-bar refrain structure of "Hesitation Blues" is shared by many other blues. In fact, the form was to become extremely popular in the 1920s, when it produced some of the greatest race record hits of the era, such as like Papa Charlie Jackson's "Shake that Thing" and Tampa Red and Georgia Tom's "It's Tight Like That." However, "Hesitation Blues" was one of the earliest examples of this type (the folk singer Leadbelly dated it between 1907 and 1910), perhaps even its progenitor.[44] It is at any rate certainly the first example to appear in print.

Handy's version keeps its characteristic verse-refrain structure intact, but constantly tinkers with the lyrics of the refrain to give greater variety, adding internal rhymes in the process. The refrain of Handy's first stanza, for instance, runs "Tell me how long will I have to *wait*? / Please give me 298, why do you hesi*tate*?" The theme of the folk version of "The Hesitation Blues" is the frustration the singer feels as he or she is made to "hesitate," due to the unwillingness of his/her lover to commit. While this is also the basic theme of Handy's version, the song opens with a different scenario: the female protagonist tries to contact her lover by telephone and becomes frustrated with the operator who "hesitates" in making the connection (hence the above-quoted refrain). It is a witty, sophisticated transformation of the original idea.

The most distinctive feature of Handy's chorus lies in the harmony. It uses a twelve-bar blues sequence that is entirely regular except for one striking change: in the seventh measure, it prolongs the subdominant (IV) harmony instead of returning to the tonic (I) chord (table 9). This change, which might on the surface seem quite arbitrary, is actually of great significance, for it is associated with proto-blues rather than blues, particularly blues ballads like "Frankie and Johnnie" that flourished in folk culture from the turn of the century (these will be examined in detail in chapter 6 of this book). By 1915, the "Frankie and Johnnie" sequence was rare in published music, having been almost entirely supplanted by the regular blues sequence. In other words, Handy is deliberately using an archaic style in the chorus of "Hesitating Blues." This chimes with the fact that the inspiration behind the chorus was, according to Abbe Niles, the style of a blind black Memphis pianist called Seymour Abernathy.[45] Presumably Abernathy played in a somewhat passé proto-blues style.

Handy's reworking of "Hesitation Blues" was not the first to appear in print. Five weeks earlier, the white Kentucky-based songwriting team of Billy Smythe and Scott Middleton copyrighted a version titled simply "Hesitation Blues."[46] While I suspect that Handy was prompted to produce his version after seeing or hearing the Smythe-Middleton version, the fact that the marketplace was able to bear two published versions of the same song simultaneously (for both were commercially successful) attests to the general popularity of the song in folk culture. This is confirmed

Table 9. Harmonic Analysis of "Hesitating Blues," Chorus, Main Theme

Measure	1	2	3	4	5	6	7	8	9	10	11	12
Chord	B♭	B♭	B♭	B♭7	E♭	E♭	E♭	B♭	F7	F7	B♭	B♭
Numeric	I	I	I	I	IV	IV	IV	I	V	V	I	I
Prototype Blues	I	I	I	I	IV	IV	I	I	V	V	I	I

by a spate of field transcriptions from the period.[47] It is further corroborated by its reappearance in another popular blues from the following year, Perry Bradford's "Lonesome Blues."[48]

Smythe and Middleton's version is quite different from Handy's. Whereas Handy uses the hesitation theme in his verse and a separate twelve-bar theme for his chorus, Smythe and Middleton reverse this sequence: their verse uses an independent blues theme, while their chorus consists of four traditional stanzas of the hesitation theme, beginning "I'll go down to the levee, take a rocking chair, / If the blues doesn't leave me, babe, I'll rock away from here." Also unlike Handy, they quote the text and music very literally, and while their version is quite haunting, they make no attempt to add a new dimension to the folk version of the song, as Handy does with the inclusion of his telephone operator, for example.

"Joe Turner Blues"

Handy's next blues, "Joe Turner Blues," has the same overall structure as "Hesitating Blues": a verse and chorus, each with a double twelve-bar blues structure and with the chorus in the subdominant (IV). Also like "Hesitating Blues," "Joe Turner Blues" draws heavily on folk sources, both in its text and music. In fact, the melody of its chorus appears to be one of the oldest of all blues melodies. The blues singer William "Big Bill" Broonzy dated it to the early 1890s,[49] while the folklorist Abbe Niles suggested it was "perhaps the prototype of all blues."[50]

In terms of its eponymous central character, Joe Turner, there are conflicting accounts. Handy believed the original song to have been inspired by Joe Turney, the brother of Pete Turney, a governor of Tennessee in the 1890s. Joe was notorious for providing the state with free labor: he would trick black laborers into committing minor misdemeanors, have them arrested, tried in a kangaroo court, and placed on a chain-gang.[51] The earliest field transcription of the song, made around 1907, refers to Turner's "fohty links o' chain."[52] According to Handy, these were used to bind eighty prisoners at a time into a chain gang.[53] In contrast, Big Bill Broonzy's Joe Turner is someone of opposite character: a benevolent slave owner who arranged for anonymous deliveries of food and other essentials to his slaves when times were hard (note, however, that while these two characters are quite different from one another, they are both authoritarian white men).[54] Handy's own version of the song ignores both these identities and recasts the central character into a generic blues-ridden lover, warning his girl at the song's opening, "You'll never miss the water till your well runs dry / . . . You'll never miss Joe Turner till he says good-bye," and complaining in time-honored fashion "[I] spent all my money [on you], now you call Joe Turner cheap."

One major difference of "Joe Turner Blues" from Handy's earlier blues is that there is little attempt to add sophistication to the original folk style with sassy lyrics (the telephone operator in "Hesitating Blues") or exotic rhythms (the tango section in "St. Louis Blues"). The work uses a straight twelve-bar sequence throughout, and the lyrics, as can be seen from the examples I have just quoted, are down-to-earth and consistently somber in tone. The stanzas are in the traditional AAB blues format, and the lines apparently mostly derive from traditional sources

EXAMPLE 51. Handy, "Joe Turner Blues" (1915), chorus, melody and text, mm. 1–3

(or at least are of venerable antiquity). The song's first line, for example, is almost identical to the title of a successful popular song from the early 1870s, "You'll Never Miss the Water Till the Well Runs Dry."[55] In short, "Joe Turner Blues" is much closer to an unmediated traditional twelve-bar blues than anything Handy had produced earlier. Indeed, it is arguably the closest he ever came to the style of pure folk blues. The only obvious concessions to Tin Pan Alley are the standard introduction and vamp, the key change in the chorus, and occasional musical devices like the four-note chromatic motif that begins the chorus (example 51). Like its counterpart in "Yellow Dog Blues" (example 47), this seems to have been inspired by the song version of "The Memphis Blues," which uses the same device at precisely the same point (example 35b).

"Beale Street Blues"

Handy's next blues was originally called "Beale Street" but quickly retitled "Beale Street Blues."[56] It appeared almost a year later and is in stark contrast to the traditionalism of "Joe Turner Blues."[57] It is quintessential Handy, drawing simultaneously from popular song and folk traditions to create a unique work that is much too individual to be regarded as belonging comfortably to either genre. It is, in fact, one of Handy's greatest achievements, perhaps his greatest. Indeed I would argue that it is one of the most original and inventive vernacular songs ever composed by anyone.

"Beale Street Blues" is unique in Handy's blues output in that its subject matter is not the plight of individual people. Instead the song is a celebration of, and a tribute to, the thoroughfare that symbolized the heart of Memphis's black district—a neighborhood that Handy had been closely associated with since his arrival in the city in about 1905. This in itself was a remarkably original conception for 1916. Although songs celebrating urban environments had been quite common in popular music since the 1890s, they were almost always about New York, including the best known example, the 1894 hit "The Sidewalks of New York."[58] Handy's "Beale Street Blues" was the first popular song—at least the first to have any degree of commercial success—whose prime focus was the celebration of a southern city.[59] In producing this work, Handy at one stroke upended the popular song tradition dating back to before the Civil War, which glorified the South exclusively as a place of rural idyll, most famously in songs by Stephen Foster like "My Old Kentucky Home." By challenging this tradition, Handy paved the way for a slew of Tin Pan Alley successes from the 1920s and 1930s, particularly two jazz standards by fellow African Americans, Creamer and Layton's "Way Down Yonder in New Orleans"

(1922) and Spencer Williams's "Basin Street Blues" (1928). Even before we get to its musical content, therefore, "Beale Street Blues" is already exceptional simply because of its subject matter. However, I suspect that it is this subject matter, so at odds with the archetypal blues theme of relationship turmoil, that has ultimately limited the appeal of "Beale Street Blues" and ensured, popular though the work has been, that it has never had the universal appeal of "St. Louis Blues," even though it is hardly its musical inferior.[60]

In its original edition, the work was subtitled "Another Memphis 'Blues,'" a tag that not only referred to the song's subject matter but that also apparently was intended to encourage sales by linking the work to "The Memphis Blues"—by far Handy's best-known composition at the time—in the mind of the sheet-music-buying public. However, this was more than just a sales ploy, for the two works show strong structural similarities. Like "The Memphis Blues," "Beale Street Blues" has three sections, the outer two of which use a twelve-bar blues format and the last of which is in the subdominant (here E♭). Also like "The Memphis Blues," the work started life as an instrumental composition and was only later reconceived as a song (the original copyright deposit, made in December 1916, was for piano only; the song version was not copyrighted till March of the following year). But whereas Norton's song version of "The Memphis Blues" changed the original considerably in order to make it conform to the verse-chorus format of popular song, "Beale Street Blues" was changed not at all. One consequence of this is that its form is most unusual, making for a song, with three genuinely independent sections, that is structurally quite different from a regular popular song. This was also the case with "St. Louis Blues," but here the first two sections are even more autonomous than in the earlier work.

The first section of the work is a double twelve-bar blues strain in which the singer introduces his topic by telling his audience that he is a worldly person who has visited many places (New York's Broadway, San Francisco's Market Street) and done many things ("strolled the Prado"—Madrid's famous art museum—and "gambled on the Bourse"—i.e., the French stock market). His recommendation, after all this experience, is for the traveler to "see Beale Street first." The second section of the song is a vivid account of what you will find on Beale Street, beginning with the people ("pretty Browns in beautiful gowns" along with "honest men and pickpockets skilled"), continuing with the venues ("Hog-nose restaurants and Chitlin' Cafes," "places, once places, now just a sham," and "Golden Balls [i.e., pawnbrokers] enough to pave the New Jerusalem") and the visitors ("men who rank the first in the nation / Who come to Beale for inspiration"), before finally summing up with the memorable lines:

If Beale Street could talk,
If Beale Street could talk,
Married men would have to take their beds and walk,
Except one or two,
Who never drank booze,
And the blind man on the corner who sings the Beale Street Blues.

All this is set to an eight-bar melody (played four times straight) which is one of Handy's most effervescent creations, beautifully encapsulating the vitality of the urban experience evoked by his lyric (example 52).

The third and final part of the work is the Beale Street Blues itself, the plaint of "the blind man on the corner" who was introduced to us at the end of the previous section. Both the music and lyric of the final section are closely modeled on traditional folk blues: it consists of two stanzas of standard twelve-bar blues, using a typical rural-type blues melody, while the lyrics employ the standard AAB construction for the first stanza (the first four measures are given in example 53). The only unconventional aspect of this section is that it is based on a tango rhythm. Handy's most famous use of this device, of course, is in the B-section of "St. Louis Blues," but he used it elsewhere in his work, especially in his blues compositions. As discussed earlier, Handy's use of Latin rhythms worked at two levels, connecting both with his mainstream

EXAMPLE 52. Handy, "Beale Street Blues" (1916), B section

EXAMPLE 53. Handy, "Beale Street Blues" (1916), chorus, mm. 1–4

audience, with whom such rhythms were all the rage, and with a deep expressive element in black folk music. And nowhere in Handy's work is the device used with greater power than here, its effect enhanced by the unprepared key change from the previous section.

In fact, the use of rhythm in "Beale Street Blues" is one of its most striking features, each of its three sections adopting a different style. In addition to the "Spanish tinge" in the final section, the first, with its use of "swung" dotted rhythms, is in the up-to-date fox-trot/jazz style, while the second, using even eighths and melodic syncopation, harkens back to the older style of ragtime, then in the process of being supplanted by jazz. In short, the work is a kind of summing up of the last twenty years of African American folk-derived vernacular culture, drawing simultaneously from established styles like ragtime and the tango and from forward-looking genres like jazz and blues. Handy uses these disparate styles to create effective contrasts between the work's sections, and it is entirely to his credit that he does this while at the same time managing to give the piece a strong sense of overall cohesion.

BLUES AFTER THE MOVE TO NEW YORK (1917–1953)

The Move North

"Beale Street Blues" was written at a seminal time in Handy's life, for it was in 1917 that he made the decision to move away from the South, relocating initially in Chicago for a year before settling permanently in New York in 1918. There is a sense, then, in which "Beale Street Blues" is Handy's farewell to the South, an affectionate appreciation of the city that had been his home for more than a decade, and in which he had flourished professionally and creatively.

There were several reasons for the move. Disenchantment with the Memphis music scene was one. One of Handy's main professional activities had been the booking of bands, and it was poorly paid and increasingly unrewarding work, especially when many of his most loyal musicians were called up in the First World War draft.[61] Second, Handy had had enough of the inherent racism of southern culture, with its lynch mobs and anti-black environment that had affected his life in so many ways.[62] The most important reason for the move, however, was his increasing success as a composer and publisher—success that had encouraged Handy to make a bid for national prominence by establishing himself in the northern cities that were the centers of the music industry. He had therefore not only the personal desire to move, but also the economic incentive.

Indeed, from both the personal and economic viewpoints, the move was a remarkable success. Handy and his family flourished in the cultural climate of New York, where he quickly became associated with the burgeoning Harlem Renaissance. And although economically the ride was much less stable—a particularly rocky patch in the early 1920s was almost to ruin him—his business affairs ultimately prospered.

What about the music that Handy composed after the move? This question is more difficult to answer. In the period following the move up till the end of 1920, Handy produced only two works that were blues-related: the humorous war-themed pop song "The Kaiser's Got the Blues" (1918), co-written with Domer C. Browne, and "Aunt Hagar's Blues," which appeared in 1920.[63] The charming lyric of the former, which was discussed briefly in chapter 2, portrays the German commander Kaiser Wilhelm getting the blues due to problems caused by his enemies. Musically, the work's most obvious connection with blues is its verse, which uses the standard twelve-bar blues format. Despite the song's wit and musical integrity, it made little impression in the marketplace, all but disappearing amid hundreds of war-related songs that were coming out of Tin Pan Alley at this time.

"Aunt Hagar's Blues"

"Aunt Hagar's Blues," on the other hand, proved to have considerable staying power and is still played by jazz bands today. As with many of Handy's earlier blues, this started out as a three-strain instrumental work, in which form it was originally published in November 1920 as "Aunt Hagar's Children." The title is a phrase by which African Americans spoke of their race, referring to the story in Genesis where Hagar, a slave of Sarah, had a child, Ishmael, with Sarah's husband Abraham, and then was subsequently banished.[64] The main theme of "Aunt Hagar's Children" is the sixteen-bar melody used in the first strain, which, according to Abbe Niles, was based on a snatch of black folk song with the words "I wonder where's my good ole use to be," which Handy had heard many years before.[65] We know that Handy's reworking of the theme predates his move to New York, for he had already interpolated it into his 1917 band recording of Douglass Williams's "Hooking Cow Blues" (Columbia A-2420). The other two strains of "Aunt Hagar's Children" use standard twelve-bar blues structures. Handy published a vocal version of the song in 1921 titled "Aunt Hagar's Children Blues" in standard verse-chorus format but with an added patter chorus (an optional extra section tagged on the end of the chorus that was often used if the work needed to be extended in performance). When Handy ran into serious financial problems in 1922, he sold the work to the New York publisher Richmond-Robbins, who produced a "New Revised Edition" of the song, this time titled "Aunt

Hagar's Blues," with slightly altered lyrics and the patter chorus incorporated into the verse. It is this version of the song that has been the most popular over the years.

The lyrics of the song are by Tim Brymn, the African American bandleader and song-writer who had composed the very first popular blues in 1912 with Chris Smith. They concern an incident at a black church, where a preacher rails against the immorality of ragtime. Aunt Hagar, a congregation member, stands up and shouts that the power of blues (here presumably synonymous with ragtime) is irresistible and by implication a positive thing, and that there is no use preaching against it. The chorus describes the power of Aunt Hagar's children singing the blues "like a choir from on high broke loose."

Brymn's lyric is engaging and lighthearted. However, it does not quite make sense at a surface level, for blues were not usually sung in churches: indeed, they were traditionally regarded as "the Devil's music." Bearing in mind, however, that the phrase "Aunt Hagar's Children" refers not to a particular person but to the black race in general, it is possible to read a symbolic meaning into this lyric, according to which the blues, as the essence of all black vernacular music, triumphs despite the attempts of mainstream (white) society to suppress it. This interpretation is confirmed by an interview Handy gave to Dorothy Scarborough, in which he said "Aunt Hagar's Blues" "shows something of the inequality of justice as between the black and the white."[66] In essence, then, "Aunt Hagar's Blues" is a song of racial uplift, stressing the triumphant power of black music, and, by implication, black culture in general, in the face of white suppression. As such, the work clearly shows the influence of the Harlem Renaissance, with which Handy (and Brymn) had by 1920 become strongly associated. While Handy had been preoccupied with the racial uplift issue before the move to the North, as is shown by the "Aframerican Hymn" he composed in 1916 while still in Memphis, the sophistication of "Aunt Hagar's Blues" seems to me to reflect thoroughly the influence of New York.

Other Handy Blues of the 1920s

The sophisticated northern approach of "Aunt Hagar's Blues" increasingly predominates in Handy's blues of the 1920s. Evidence for this is found in the subjects of his some of his blues-related works, most obviously "Harlem Blues" (1923) and "Wall Street Blues" (1929), which are clearly related to New York, while "Southside" (1922) and "The Gouge of Armour Avenue" (1924) are inspired by Handy's experiences in Chicago. In "Golden Brown Blues" (1926), Handy collaborated with the black poet Langston Hughes, the leading light of the Harlem Renaissance, whose work was the quintessence of African American sophistication (Handy and Hughes collaborated again in 1942 on "Go and Get the Enemy Blues"). Several of Handy's 1920s blues are filled with witty, urbane references. "The Basement Blues" (1924), for example, has been described by Elliott Hurwitt as containing "a riotous catalog of puns, corny jokes, and period slang, much of it commenting on race and caste distinctions within black society in Handy's era."[67]

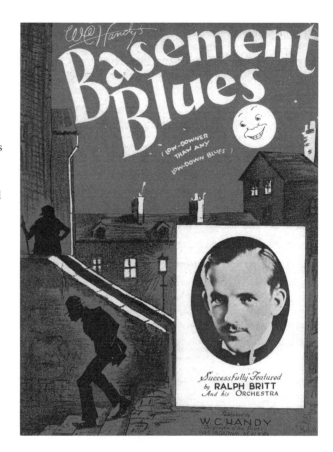

FIGURE 22. "Basement Blues" (1924), musically intricate and with sophisticated lyrics, is typical of Handy's blues productions after his move to New York. However, like most of his work from this era, it was not a commercial success. (Author's collection)

The problem with all these blues was that they failed to sell. In fact, the only Handy works from the 1920s to enjoy commercial success were those heavily based on folk material, especially "Loveless Love" (1921), a relatively simple reworking of the folk song "Careless Love," and "Atlanta Blues" (1923), a version of the proto-blues "Make Me a Pallet on the Floor." These numbers aside, Handy was never again to compose a work that met with serious commercial success after "Aunt Hagar's Blues," even though he continued writing regularly and publishing his music well into the 1930s.

So why did the blues of the 1920s generally not catch on like his earlier work? For one thing, the marketplace was by this time becoming saturated with blues. Handy's earlier blues had appeared when there was far less competition. For example, "The Memphis Blues" was only the fourth published blues to appear while "St. Louis Blues" was the sixteenth. These blues, therefore, along with their inherent merits, had the added enormous benefit of maximum exposure in an undersupplied market. In comparison, 140 blues were published in 1920 alone, and while there is no precise data for subsequent years, the number must surely have increased significantly as the genre continued to gain momentum into the decade, thanks to a revolution in popular taste that Handy himself had been instrumental in bringing about.

Another reason for Handy's comparative failure as a blues composer in the 1920s was generational. Born in 1873, he was one of the earliest of all bluesmen, of the same generation as pioneer black songsters like Ragtime Henry Thomas (b. 1874), Gus Cannon (b. 1883), and "Papa" Charlie Jackson (b. ca. 1880), who were among the first to perform (and record) blues. Like the blues recorded by these musicians, Handy's were essentially ragtime-based, and he never really comfortably made the transition into jazz. This is clearly shown by his recorded legacy. In 1917, Handy made an important series of recordings for Columbia. Although it is possible to excuse the recordings as being not up his regular standard—the performances were apparently somewhat underrehearsed—it is telling that they are closer in style to ragtime than jazz, even though they were apparently intended by Columbia to be jazz recordings in the manner of the Original Dixieland Jazz Band (in fact, one of the numbers the band recorded was the ODJB's hit "Livery Stable Blues"). Later recordings by Handy have much the same character. Particularly revealing are his last band recordings, which were made for the Varsity label in 1939. Accompanied by a group consisting of top New York jazzmen of the day, including J. C. Higginbotham on trombone, Luis Russell on piano, and Pops Foster on bass, Handy barely holds his own. This is clearly evident on his singing on "Way Down South Where the Blues Began," a Handy original from 1933, and "Loveless Love." While quite charming, Handy's vocals have a much older and straighter rhythmic feel than his backing. It would seem that he was simply unable or unwilling to make the shift into the full jazz idiom, and by the 1920s he was competing against other much younger African American blues composers like Clarence Williams, who had a more natural grasp of the new style.

Beyond all this, however, there was a deeper reason for Handy's lack of success: his relocation to the North. After the move, his only blues to have commercial viability were "Aunt Hagar's Blues," whose main theme was composed before the move, and folk-based material like "Loveless Love" and "Atlanta Blues," which are closer to arrangements (or at least simple reworkings) of pre-existent material than the more personal and thoroughgoing achievements of Handy's earlier blues. In short, his creativity diminished significantly after the move, at least as far as his blues were concerned. The result was that, while the later blues have much to recommend them, they lack the freshness, experimentation, and sheer unabashed exuberance that characterizes even the less successful works of the 1910s like "Jogo Blues" and "Shoeboot's Serenade." As to whether this loss was due to Handy being physically removed from his southern roots, or his changed social milieu, or because of the responsibilities of running a major publishing house, or some combination of these, one can only speculate.

It is not surprising, then, that Handy cut his losses and in 1926, spurred on by the encouragement of his friend Abbe Niles, combined all his earlier blues, along with arrangements of relevant folk material and popular blues by others, into *Blues: An Anthology.* The anthology, which was simultaneously a celebration and a history of its subject, has from the time of its appearance been justly regarded as a classic, a starting point for any serious study of early blues. Just as important, it cemented Handy's status, first established in 1913 by George Norton's lyric to "The Memphis Blues," as the preeminent living authority on the genre. This is ironic given that he was never again significantly to add to it.

Not, however, that he was idle. He focused his energies on numerous compositions, ranging from jazz songs like "Who's That Man?" (1928, co-composed with Spencer Williams) to art songs such as his thoroughly effective setting of Walter Malone's poem "Opportunity" (1932). There are a large number of arrangements of spirituals, resulting in 1938 in the appearance of *W. C. Handy's Collection of Negro Spirituals*. His interest in patriotic and racially uplifting material culminated in the fascinating 1944 collection, *Unsung Americans Sung*. Meanwhile, under his aegis, his firm published a continuous stream of compositions and arrangements by others, ranging from the popular to the arty, and penned by everyone from top professionals to comparative unknowns. I suspect that much of this activity was altruistically or ideologically based, for it must have generally netted quite modest returns, if not outright losses.

There were, however, two striking exceptions to this trend: hit songs written by others but published by Handy, such as Eddie Green's "A Good Man is Hard to Find" (1918) and Maceo Pinkard's "Sugar" (1927); and Handy's own blues from the 1910s. These blues, in fact, have a most unusual reception history. Back in the 1910s, as is the case today, if a new popular song was to become a hit, it normally did so quickly. However, Handy's blues had comparatively little impact at first, except for "The Memphis Blues," which was the work that he was primarily associated with throughout much of the 1910s. However, as his music gradually became known through an accumulation of recordings and performances, that situation changed. In particular, hit recordings of Handy blues—such as Earl Fuller's 1917 version of "Beale Street" for Victor (the first royalty payment for which netted Handy a remarkable $1857);[68] Ben Selvin's 1920 rendition of "Yellow Dog Blues" for Emerson; and the Original Dixieland Jazz Band's performance of "St. Louis Blues" for Victor the following year—showed to an ever-increasing public that Handy was far more than a one-hit wonder.[69]

The slow growth in the popularity of Handy's blues reflects a number of factors. First, it shows the difficulty of a regional publisher trying to reach a national audience, especially if that publisher happened to be black. It also reflects the public's unfamiliarity with the new genre of blues. But most of all, it demonstrates the extraordinary originality and quality of Handy's work, which like a fine wine, needed time to mature in the public's consciousness before it was ready to be fully savored. And savored it was. For although Handy's creativity with blues rapidly diminished after the move north, the unique body of work he produced in the preceding six years, from 1912 to 1917, sustained him financially for the rest of his life and kept his publishing firm solvent long after his death.

• • •

So what ultimately is Handy's contribution to popular blues of the 1910s? Of his compositions, "The Memphis Blues" was seminal in its influence: more than any other blues, it catalyzed popular blues culture in the period 1913–15. And while Handy's subsequent blues were not nearly as well known in the 1910s as they were later to become, nevertheless a majority of them acquired a relatively solid commercial footing soon after their inception, particularly in the black entertainment world.[70] Furthermore, Handy's output was unique for its quantity: altogether he published nine blues and blues-related works in the 1910s, more than any other individual at the time. On the other hand, the sheer originality of Handy's blues songs—their unusual three-section forms, their flirtation with Latin rhythms and unfashionable key changes—meant that they were too far removed from the formulas of Tin Pan Alley to be widely imitated within the mainstream. Even so, the large number of his blues, combined with the growing success of most of them, gradually established Handy as the dominant voice of popular blues during the 1910s.

Handy consolidated this reputation in three ways: through recordings, through publishing, and through proselytizing. The 1917 recordings for Columbia gave the mainstream public a chance to actually hear the band whose power had been so graphically depicted by George Norton in the lyric to "The Memphis Blues." They were not disappointed. For although the performances were scarcely authentic jazz, they stood out from straight ragtime performances, particularly due to the novelty of being played by a black band, at that time a rarity on record. Helped by a vigorous publicity campaign by Columbia, which declared a "Handy week" to launch the records, they quickly became bestsellers.[71]

The second way that Handy enhanced his status was through his work as a publisher. His publishing business expanded rapidly in the second half of the 1910s, especially after the move to New York, and central to this activity was the publication of a number of important early blues works by others. In the 1910s, for instance, Handy issued Will Nash's "Snakey Blues" (1915, example 5), "Florida Blues" by William King Philips (1916), and "Big Chief Blues" by Al Bernard (1919). Promoting the work of others in this way confirmed Handy's importance as a major force in popular blues culture.

Third, Handy consolidated his reputation through what might loosely be termed proselytizing, particularly through interviews for newspapers and other publications. Throughout his life, he was a tireless promoter of black culture. He was articulate and well-spoken, and he had a holistic understanding of blues from its folk roots to its commercial derivatives that was unmatched, especially in the 1910s. Furthermore, the fact that he was middle-aged rather than of a younger generation gave his statements an implicit authority. It is not surprising, then, that when the folklorist Dorothy Scarborough included a chapter on blues—the first serious folkloristic exploration of the subject—in her 1925 book *On the Trail of Negro Folk-Songs,* she turned to Handy as her main informant.[72] Both his 1926 *Blues: An Anthology* and his 1941 autobiography *Father of the Blues* can be considered parts of this drive to proselytize.

Handy's compositions, recordings, publishing, and public relations activities had all combined by the end of the 1910s to give Handy patriarchal authority in the newly emerging field of blues. It was but a short step from there to the "Father of the Blues" image that has dominated his reputation since.

To be sure, the epithet has been problematic, for while it may have been good for Handy's image with the general public, it aroused the indignation of both colleagues and historians who regarded it as misleading and presumptuous. The most famous attack was by Jelly Roll Morton, who fought a bitter media battle with Handy in 1938, arguing that he, Morton, was the originator of jazz, and openly accusing Handy of plagiarism.[73] I do not blame Morton for his attack. By 1938, Handy had become one of the most famous living African Americans and a cultural icon. Morton, in contrast, was for various reasons comparatively neglected at that time, and his career was at low ebb. While his resentment of Handy is therefore understandable, it was misplaced. Handy had always acknowledged the folk roots of blues, and the "Father of the Blues" label was essentially a show business tag: it was not intended to be taken literally as a claim that he had actually invented the genre. Yet the issue of Handy's plagiarism, as raised by Morton's attacks, has haunted Handy's reputation. For instance, writing in 2005 in the booklet accompanying the reissue of Morton's Library of Congress recordings, John Szwed dismisses Handy as not "having any remarkable creativity," apparently considering such an opinion uncontroversial enough as not to require a further explanation.[74]

So what about the question of Handy's creativity? Is it really fair to describe Handy as a composer when he was so reliant on folk sources? Would a label like "arranger" be more accurate? Well, that is certainly so in some instances. Handy's arrangements of black spirituals are just that, and they are so described by him on the sheet music. Certain of his blues from the 1920s, such as "Loveless Love," which stayed quite close to the folk original, might also be regarded as little more than arrangements . However, Handy's creativity played a decisive part in most of the blues examined in this chapter. As such, his role is very much that of a composer, not an arranger. He rarely copied blindly from his sources but constantly transformed them in a multitude of ways, imaginatively combining them with each other or grafting them onto ideas that were entirely his own. The result was a powerful alloy, a unique blend of folk and commercial culture that was crucial in establishing the genre of popular blues. In doing so, it changed the course of American music.

CHAPTER 5

The Creativity of Early Southern Published Blues

The most creative and original in early published blues are those written by composers based, or at any rate raised, in the South. The obvious reason for this is that southern composers were geographically and culturally closer to the folk sources of blues: indeed, some were actually part of the folk blues tradition as performers. Northern blues composers, in contrast, tended to be closer in style to mainstream popular music of the day. Their work therefore tends to be less distinctive.[1]

The most celebrated example of a blues composer within the period is, of course, W. C. Handy, a southerner, born in Alabama, whose most important work was created in Memphis between 1909 and 1917. But there were many other southern-based composers producing blues before 1921. Their blues are not only historically interesting but also display a remarkably high creative standard. Few are well-known today, and a number, including some of the most interesting examples, are almost entirely unknown. Between them, they constitute a woefully neglected body of work that, in addition to being valuable in its own right, has much to tell us about the development of early blues.

These blues, then, are the subject of this chapter. I begin with a chronological examination of the earliest published southern blues (1912–1914) before considering the work of three com-posers who produced some of the most interesting blues of the period: Euday Bowman, George Thomas, and Perry Bradford. The chapter concludes with the development of southern blues in the second half of the 1910s. I should stress that few of these works were influential or well-known in their day: my choice of material is concerned with stylistic individuality, not popularity, and these two factors coincide only rarely, as in the case of Perry Bradford's "Crazy Blues," which was both compositionally unorthodox and a historic milestone due to its considerable influence.

SOUTHERN PUBLISHED BLUES OF 1912–1914

It is no exaggeration to say that the early blues industry was dominated by the South. Between 1912 and 1914, the first three years of the industry, no fewer than fifteen of the twenty-one blues to appear were published there; and of the six that were not published in the South, at least three were composed by southern writers. Turning first to the blues of 1912, of the five blues copyrighted in that year (see table 1.1, in chapter 1), three have already been discussed: Chris Smith and Tim Brymn's "The Blues" in chapter 1, Leroy "Lasses" White's "Nigger Blues" in chapter 2, and Handy's "The Memphis Blues" in chapter 4. This leaves Franklin Seals's "Baby Seals' Blues" and Hart Wand's "Dallas Blues" for immediate attention. Of the pair, "Baby Seals Blues" was the first to be copyrighted (though only by a matter of days) and so will be considered first.[2]

"Baby Seals Blues"

"Baby Seals Blues" is one of the most intriguing and original of early published blues, offering us a rare, comparatively unmediated glimpse of early blues as it emerges from its folk origins into black vaudeville. The song's composer, H. Franklin "Baby" Seals, was a pianist, singer, and comedian from Mobile, Alabama, who was a major entertainer in southern black vaudeville, where he is known to have been active from at least 1909 until his untimely death in 1915.[3] "Baby Seals Blues" is superficially in the form of a popular song, with a conventional introduction and vamp followed by two verses and a chorus (the first verse and chorus are quoted in example 54). Beyond this superficial level, however, the song is thoroughly at odds with the Tin Pan Alley prototype. For one thing, it is published as a vocal duet, reflecting the fact that it was originally so performed by Seals and his female stage partner, Floyd Fisher. While many songs of the era in both black and mainstream vaudeville were performed as duets, "Baby Seals Blues" is the only one that I know—and certainly the only blues—to be published in that form, the text being clearly divided between the male and female characters.[4] The scenario of the text is familiar enough. In the verse (mm. 1–20), the man sings of how he has the blues because his lover has abandoned him. In the chorus (mm. 21ff.), the two characters dialogue, and she comforts him, telling him she loves him (mm. 21–27) and promising to return (mm. 42–43). Throughout the text, the theme of having and singing the blues is central, beginning and ending the song, and occurring four times altogether (mm. 1–8, 19–20, 29–32, and 45–48). Of these, the opening phrase (mm. 1–4) is particularly striking, setting the familiar, folk-derived trope "I got the blues / can't be satisfied today" with a dramatic melodic sweep, culminating in the high F at the beginning of m. 3 and colored by blue notes in mm. 1 (C♯) and 4 (A♭). The music of the phrase returns with great effect at the climax of the song (mm. 41–45), linking verse and chorus in a most satisfying manner, one reminiscent of Handy's recurring use of motifs in songs such as "Yellow Dog Blues" (example 46). No less effective is the opening of the chorus (mm. 21–23), where the female character bursts in with "Honey baby, mamma do she do she double do love you," a curiously distorted amorous declaration that is also found in recordings of folk

EXAMPLE 54. Seals, "Baby Seals' Blues" (1912), verse and chorus

EXAMPLE 54. Continued

EXAMPLE 54. Continued

blues from the 1920s, such as Blind Lemon Jefferson's "Long Lonesome Blues" ("Doggone my side, papa, do your mama papa do double do love you").[5]

Perhaps the most individual feature of "Baby Seals Blues" is the structure. The twenty-bar verse has a standard sixteen-bar form (subdivided into two eight-measure periods, mm. 1–8 and 9–16), ending with a four-bar passage linking to the chorus (mm. 17–20). This is actually quite a common structure for verses in songs of the period. What is most unusual, however—particularly for 1912—is that it simultaneously incorporates a twelve-bar blues structure (mm. 1–12). The 28–bar chorus is even more distinctive, consisting of a twelve-bar blues (mm. 21–32), followed by two eight-bar periods (mm. 33–40, 41–48). The overall effect of all this is unpredictability: the song never settles down into a conventional sixteen-measure—or even twelve-measure—formula. In the hands of a less creative composer than Seals, this could result in the song losing its focus. Instead, it is used by Seals to build a powerful dramatic intensity.

This points to one of the most fascinating cultural influences on "Baby Seals Blues": the notion of blues as "colored folks' opera." According to research by historians Lynn Abbott and Doug Seroff, this was a hot-button issue in the black press between 1910 and 1920, and it fed into a wider cultural debate, deriving ultimately from a famous remark made by the Czech composer Anton Dvořák on a visit to America in 1893: that the future of American music lay in combining black folk music with the European art tradition.[6] Looking at "Baby Seals Blues" as a transmogrified operatic love duet helps us understand not only its dramatic intensity, but also what one contemporary critic referred to as its "clever nature," that is, its sophisticated, arty structure.[7] Certainly the operatic side comes across strongly in the only recording of the song from the period, by Seals's colleague Charles Anderson, a black vaudevillian who had been performing the work since 1913.[8] Anderson, who specialized in female impersonation, sings it in what Abbott and Seroff refer to as a "folk-operatic tenor voice." They add: "this record survives to demonstrate an unabashedly comical resolution of 'high' and 'low' art, a positive realization of 'colored folks' opera.'"[9]

"Dallas Blues"

"Dallas Blues" was composed and published by a white violinist and small-time bandleader from Oklahoma City named Hart A. Wand. Unlike "Baby Seals Blues," which enjoyed only limited appeal and was only recorded once, "Dallas Blues" has become a jazz standard: Tom Lord's jazz discography, for example, lists 105 recordings of the song.[10] In fact, aside from Handy's "The Memphis Blues," it was to be the most commercially successful of the first wave of published blues.

The familiar version of "Dallas Blues," a song with lyrics by professional wordsmith Lloyd Garrett, was in fact the third edition of the work, published in 1918 by Frank K. Root in Chicago. The first two editions, published earlier by Wand in Oklahoma, are for piano only and have mostly been ignored; the first version, for instance, was recorded only once, on an 88–note piano roll.[11] I would argue that this neglect is unfair, for both of the earlier versions have considerable musical and historical interest as examples of ragtime-influenced folk blues.

The 1912 original consists of a single strain (example 55), an attractively quirky twenty-bar melody that is, in effect, a twelve-bar blues with the last eight measures repeated. The strain is first stated straight and then repeated in an embellished form, of which the first eight measures are given in example 56. The second edition of the work uses the same theme but precedes it with a standard twelve-bar melody (example 57), so that the work now has two strains.[12] The song (i.e., third) version keeps both themes of the second edition. However, it truncates and adapts the original twenty-bar theme, used for the chorus, to make a conventional twelve-bar blues sequence.

As a result of this cut and other less dramatic changes, the Chicago song edition is considerably more conventional than the original Oklahoma version. This kind of conventionalizing is typical of blues as it moved from its southern roots to the North. Exactly the same thing happens,

EXAMPLE 55. Wand, "Dallas Blues" (1912), first version, A strain

EXAMPLE 56. Wand, "Dallas Blues" (1912), first version, A¹ strain, mm. 1–8

EXAMPLE 57. Wand, "Dallas Blues" (1912), second version, A strain, melody

for instance, with George Thomas's "New Orleans Hop Scop Blues," which is far less idiosyncratic in the New York edition of 1923 than in its original New Orleans edition of 1916. The purpose of this, of course, was to make the work more acceptable to the mass market. However, I would argue that in the process these blues lose some of their individuality and charm.

One of the most attractive elements of the original version is its raw folksiness. This is most evident on the repeat of the strain, where the melody is given an out-and-out ragtime treatment with dense chords in the right hand (example 56). This in turn brings up the issue of Wand's role in the work: was he really the composer, or was this basically folk music that he heard and decided to adapt for commercial purposes? In his interview with blues historian Samuel Charters, Wand maintained that "Dallas Blues" was composed by him, though he admitted the title for the work was given to him by a "colored porter" who overheard him playing it and who remarked, "That gives me the blues to go back to Dallas."[13] I am skeptical of this anecdote. The use of the blues sequence, the quirky asymmetric twenty-bar structure, and the folk-ragtime realization of the piano arrangement all strongly suggest that the porter had a considerably greater role in "Dallas Blues" than just providing its title. The suspicion that "Dallas Blues" is in fact an early folk blues is also suggested by the fact that a number of early field transcriptions are known, along with another version that, though never published, was recorded by white vaudeville artist Marie Cahill for Victor in 1917 (see also example 62 for a further manifestation of the theme of the "Dallas Blues" in published blues).[14] The clincher is that, for the original copyright deposit at the Library of Congress, the composer is listed as anonymous: Wand's role is confined to that of publisher.

"1913 Medley Blues"

The four works titled blues published in America in 1913 were: "1913 Medley Blues" by Alex M. Valentine, "Blues" by Edna M. Burrows and Jack Stanley, W. C. Handy's "Jogo Blues," and "I've Got the Blues" by Philip Baxter. Of these, "Jogo Blues" was discussed in chapter 4; Burrows and Stanley's "Blues" is a conventional parlor song in waltz time; while "I've Got the Blues," despite its promising title and the fact that its composer was located in Carthage, Texas, is a comic ragtime song with no apparent reference to blues culture in either its musical idiom or its text, save for the title phrase, which crops up at the beginning of the chorus. This leaves "1913 Medley Blues," a four-strain rag for piano that, in contrast to these other works, is of profound historical significance.

Perhaps the most surprising thing about the work is that it has been entirely ignored: I can find no mention of it anywhere, which is little short of astonishing, given its importance. The composer, Alex M. Valentine, is a shadowy figure who seems to have been Memphis-based, at least during the 1910s. He is known to have set up his own publishing firm, the Bluff City Music Company, in the Palace Theatre Building in Memphis around 1920. Among the company's publications were Valentine's "Four O'Clock Blues" and Juanita Butler's "Moline." However, when he wrote "1913 Medley Blues," Valentine was not self-publishing and instead contracted the work's publication to the H. Kirkus Dugdale Company of Washington, D. C., one of the largest vanity publishers in America.[15] In addition to being a composer, Valentine was apparently an arranger and bandleader. In fact, the original copyright deposit of "1913 Medley Blues" in the Library of Congress is in the form of a band arrangement: the published piano version was only copyrighted eight months later.[16]

Of the four strains of "1913 Medley Blues," the first two are twelve-bars each and closely related to blues, while the last two both have conventional sixteen-measure lengths. The first strain, quoted in example 58, takes what is to my knowledge a unique approach to blues harmony, hanging on to the subdominant (IV) chord until the end of m. 8 instead of resolving it to the tonic (I) chord in m. 7. The effect is quite unusual. The melody of this strain makes prominent use of blue notes (for instance, the thirds C♯ in mm. 0 and 12 and sevenths such as the A♭s in mm. 3–4 and the D♭s in mm. 5 and 6–7) as it does elsewhere in this work. One curious characteristic of this strain is its density: there are no breaks in the melody whatsoever, which gives it a curiously breathless feeling.

EXAMPLE 58. Valentine, "1913 Medley Blues" (1913), A strain, melody

EXAMPLE 59. Valentine, "1913 Medley Blues" (1913), D strain, melody, mm. 1–8

EXAMPLE 60. a. Valentine, "1913 Medley Blues" (1913), D strain, melody, mm. 1–3;
b. Handy, "Jogo Blues" (1913), A strain, melody, mm. 1–3 (original G major)

One of the most interesting passages in the work occurs in the last strain, the first half of whose melody is quoted in example 59. The passages indicated in the score (mm. 0–2, 4–6) bear remarkable similarity to the beginning of Handy's "Jogo Blues," later to be recycled by him as the chorus to "St. Louis Blues": the two are compared in example 60. This similarity is particularly interesting since Valentine and Handy were both Memphis-based bandleaders at this time.[17] "Jogo Blues" was in fact registered for copyright at the end of July 1913, four months after "1913 Medley Blues," which suggests that the influence between the two works, if indeed there was any direct influence, may have been more from Valentine to Handy than vice versa. In my analysis of "St. Louis Blues" in the previous chapter, I pointed out that Handy's theme was almost certainly influenced, albeit unconsciously, by Maggio's "I Got the Blues" of 1908. In any case, the basic three-note cell from which both Handy's and Valentine's themes derive (example 37) was a common element of African American musical expression. Neither of these facts, however, rules out the possibility that Handy could also have been influenced by "1913 Blues Medley." Indeed the specific stimulus for his creating the "Jogo Blues" theme, which presumably was composed sometime in the spring or early summer of 1913, could easily have been hearing a performance of Valentine's work.

Blues of 1914

As mentioned in chapter 1, twelve blues were published in 1914, a substantial increase from earlier years (see table 1.2). Like the blues produced during the first two years of published blues, most were of southern origin. Of these, two by W. C. Handy, "St. Louis Blues" and "Yellow Dog Blues," have already been examined, and two more, by Euday L. Bowman, are discussed later in this chapter. Of the remainder, five are of particular interest and are discussed here: William King Phillip's "Florida Blues," Ted Barron's "Original Blues," William Spiller's "New York Tango Blues," J. Paul Wyer's "Long Lost Blues," and an unpublished song by Billie House and Pat Patterson simply called "Blues."

The first of the five to appear was William King Phillips's instrumental "Florida Blues," registered for copyright in April. Originally self-published by Phillips in Jacksonville Florida, the work was republished by W. C. Handy in Memphis in 1916. Phillips was a colleague of Handy's, having played clarinet and saxophone in Handy's Memphis band from around 1910.[18] Under Handy's aegis, the work did well. It was recorded by the bands of Charles Prince (Columbia A-5920, 1917), Ford Dabney (Aoelian Vocalion 12211, 1919) and Lemuel Fowler (Columbia 14111–D, 1925), the last of these being a hot jazz version; a vocal edition of the song, with words by Dave Hoffman and Arthur Neale, was included in Handy's *Blues: An Anthology* in 1926.

"Florida Blues" is an ebullient, highly pianistic work that uses a twelve-bar structure for each of its three strains and incorporates unexpected breaks and quirky dotted rhythms. In chapter 2, I suggested that the use of dotted rhythms in published blues and related genres of the 1910s was related to the emergence of jazz, and indeed this work seems very jazzy. Example 61 shows the second strain.

EXAMPLE 61. Phillips, "Florida Blues" (1914), B strain, mm. 1–12

Ted S. Barron's "Original Blues: A Real Southern Rag," published by the obscure New York firm of Metropolitan Music, is, like "Florida Blues," a three-strain piano blues, with each strain based on the twelve-bar blues sequence. Unlike "Florida Blues," however, it had little commercial success and was never recorded. The composer, Ted S. Barron (1879–1943), was an active, if now largely forgotten, Tin Pan Alley tunesmith who composed many popular songs and instrumental numbers, though he never had a major hit.[19] Despite the fact that Barron was both a northerner (he was born in Queens) and white, "Original Blues" shows a strong grasp of the early southern blues-ragtime idiom, and one wonders how he familiarized himself with it at a comparatively early date. The final strain is a straightforward reworking of the main theme of Wand's "Dallas Blues," though this was probably not out-and-out plagiarism because, as I suggested earlier, this melody is most likely of folk origin (example 62; compare with example 55).

The next blues to be registered for copyright in 1914 was also published in New York and is in fact named for the city. Written and published by William Spiller, it is titled "New York Tango Blues." Spiller was a black musician from Virginia who gained wide renown in mainstream vaudeville with his band, the Six Musical Spillers.[20] According to the first page of the

EXAMPLE 62. Barron, "Original Blues" (1914), D strain

music, the group performed the work, which is quite surprising in that it is particularly well suited to solo piano: its opening strain, for instance, is based on a wistful, syncopated motif, stated in the right hand in m. 1, that lies very naturally under the hand (the first eight measures are given in example 63). The work has a complex structure: there are four strains arranged as AABBACDD if all indicated repeats are performed. Surprising for a published blues of this vintage written by an African American, none of the strains use any sort of twelve-bar format: all are sixteen measures long. In other respects, however, the work is very bluesy. The tempo is slow and the mood melancholic throughout, and there is the frequent use of blue notes in the melody, for instance, the evocative use of sevenths and thirds in mm. 1–4 of example 63 (the E♭ and A♭ in mm. 1–2, and the B♭ and E♭ in mm 3–4). Perhaps the most interesting feature of this piece historically is the linking of blues to the tango, thereby preempting Handy's "St. Louis Blues," which was not registered for copyright till almost four months later. However, unlike Handy's work, "New York Tango Blues" does not make use of the defining quality of the tango: the bass line consisting of dotted eighth and sixteenth notes, followed by two eighths. Instead, its bass line is built on a conventional even-eighths feel (as in example 63). In fact, there is nothing in this piece stylistically to define it as anything other than blues-tinged ragtime or perhaps proto-jazz (there is some use of "swung" dotted rhythms in the second strain). The title is therefore a mystery. Did the Spillers dance the tango to it as part of their stage act? Or was it performed by them with a more explicit Latin feel?

Of the six vocal blues published in 1914, by far the most integrated, aside from Handy's contributions, is "Long Lost Blues." The music for this was composed by J. Paul Wyer, a clarinetist and violinist from Pensacola, Florida, who had been performing blues since at least 1909, when, as a member of W. C. Handy's Memphis band, he had a star role in popularizing "The Memphis Blues." "Long Lost Blues" was published by the Chicago Music Bureau, a firm set up

EXAMPLE 63. Spiller, "New York Tango Blues" (1914), A strain, mm. 1–8

in 1912 by the African American William H. Dorsey, musical director at the Monogram Theater, who is credited on the sheet music as the work's arranger. The song's lyricist was H. Alf Kelley, a pianist and staff arranger at the firm.[21] It is in the form of a popular song, with the standard verse and chorus of sixteen bars each. In a prototypical scenario, the singer longs for her lover, who has deserted her. The individual spin in the song is that he was not only her lover but also a blues musician: she misses both him and his "loving long lost blues." The chorus is based on a repeated eight-bar folk melody, given in example 64, that is closely related to the eight-bar folk blues "Bucket's Got a Hole in it," recorded by such luminaries as Louis Armstrong, Hank Williams Jr., Kid Ory, and Washboard Sam. What is particularly interesting about this melody is its chord sequence. Reduced to its simplest form, it consists of the harmonies IV–I–V[7]–I, with each chord lasting two measures. The same chord sequence was used as the first (example 63) and fourth strains of "New York Tango Blues." In fact, this sequence, a regular twelve-bar blues sequence less its first four measures, was often used in early folk blues and proto-blues as a substitute for the regular twelve-bar sequence, or even alongside it (as was the case with "Dallas Blues," example 55).[22]

The blues considered so far have all been *published* blues. There exists, however, deep in the bowels of the Library of Congress, the manuscript of another blues from 1914, sent in for copyright registration but never published. And it is one of the most interesting of all early blues. It is a song simply titled "Blues," with words by Billie House and music by Pat Patterson, about whom nothing is known except their location at the time when the song was copyrighted: Dallas, Texas.[23] This was also the location of Leroy "Lasses" White's "Nigger Blues," copyrighted almost two years earlier, and the two have in common that they are the only blues songs copyrighted before 1915 that exclusively contain twelve-bar stanzas in the manner of a traditional blues. Unlike "Nigger Blues," however, which is simply a non-narrative compilation of floating folk stanzas,

EXAMPLE 64. Kelley and Wyer, "Long Lost Blues" (1914), chorus, melody and text, mm. 1–8

House and Patterson's blues has a narrative—or at least part of one: the singer has the "bluest blues a man ever had" because his "gal done left me for old Jimmy Blye." When he learns this, he takes his automatic and goes out "on a hunting trip." He finds the lovers at the porters' ball dancing to the "Porter's Rag," an unpublished instrumental work by the same writers, registered for copyright at the same time as "Blues."[24] At this point—after five stanzas—the narrative breaks off and the work abruptly ends with an eight-measure piano coda. My suspicion is that this is not the whole work: when originally performed, the story probably reached a gory climax, but the composers just notated the first part of the song because that was all that was needed for copyright purposes. Either way, the narrative aspect of the lyric, along with its "badman" and vengeful subject matter, is highly suggestive of a blues ballad, the style of folk song that was the immediate predecessor of blues. The most well-known blues ballad, then as now, is "Frankie and Johnnie," which is likewise a tale of bloody revenge caused by amorous infidelity. One particular connection between the two songs is that the object of Johnnie's fickle attentions is usually named Nelly (sometimes Alice) Bly; here the equivalent role is played by a Jimmy Blye.

If the lyric for House and Patterson's "Blues" is in a not-yet-fully-evolved blues style, the same cannot be said of the music, which is strongly in the early folk blues idiom. This is particularly true of the piano accompaniment, a fully scored example of the early Texas barrelhouse style. Example 65 gives the first eight measures of the second stanza. The piano part in the first four measures is especially striking: a complex descending line of octaves in the right hand accompanied by a powerful "oompah" bass pattern broken only in the fourth measure as the

EXAMPLE 65. House and Patterson, "Blues" (1914), verse 2, mm. 1–8

octave line submerges into the bass clef. All this occurs over a voice part written literally on a monotone. The combination of the two is electric. In the final stanza, the left hand breaks out into a boogie-woogie figuration, while the right hand maintains a very bluesy riff (example 66). This kind of writing was not to reach the mainstream for another twenty years. In sum, this work is a paradox, musically advanced yet showing an old-fashioned approach to its lyrics. It is, in short, a unique survival in the evolution of blues.

EUDAY L. BOWMAN

Discussion of early Texas piano blues leads naturally to the topic of Euday Louis Bowman. Bowman (1886–1949) was a white ragtime pianist and composer from Forth Worth, Texas, best known for his "Twelfth Street Rag" (1914), one of the most recorded and commercially successful rags of all time. The reason that he is included for discussion here is that over a period of less than a year and a half, from May 1914 to October 1915, he published four piano blues: "Forth Worth Blues," "Colorado Blues," "Kansas City Blues," and "Tipperary Blues."[25] A fifth, "Rosary Blues," was registered for copyright in January 1916 but never published during Bowman's lifetime, only appearing in print in 1996.[26] One of Bowman's blues, "Kansas City Blues" (1914), was a comparative success, garnering two major recordings in the 1910s, by the Victor Military Band (Victor 18163, 1916) and Wilbur Sweatman's Jazz Band (Columbia A-2768).[27] A

EXAMPLE 66. House and Patterson, "Blues" (1914), verse 5, mm. 1–5

FIGURE 23. Wilbur Sweatman's best-selling recording of Euday Bowman's "Kansas City Blues." (Author's collection)

song version with words by George H. Bowles found its way into Handy's *Blues: An Anthology* in 1926. Unfortunately, Bowman's three other published blues were failures in his lifetime, with minimal sheet music sales and recordings. However, this is in no way indicative of their quality: they are consistently fine, idiosyncratic examples of the genre and, like House and Patterson's "Blues," a historically invaluable record of early Texas folk blues.

Bowman's blues are stylistically linked with his rags, which is not surprising given how closely the two genres were related at this stage in their development. Thus, Bowman's blues consist of several strains and use the basic ragtime idiom of "oompah" bass and syncopated right hand. One particular characteristic of both his blues and his rags is the irregular lengths of some of the strains. The first strain of "Shamrock Rag" (1916), for instance, has fourteen measures, the second of "Petticoat Lane" (1915) has twenty-five (twelve plus thirteen), while the first strains of "Colorado Blues" (1914) and "Tenth Street Rag" (1914) are both sixteen and a half measures long. In fact, almost every one of his works includes at least one such asymmetric strain. This approach is most unusual. Nearly all published ragtime is confined to neatly ordered eight-, sixteen-, or thirty-two-bar strains: the asymmetric structure found in Bowman's works shows his folk-derived approach—a point to be explored further below—and gives them a refreshing unpredictability. Another folk-derived characteristic shared by Bowman's ragtime and blues compositions is that they do not change key, aside from a single blues and two rags. Again this is quite unorthodox. A majority of instrumental blues of the era, such as those by Handy, and including nearly all published rags, employ at least one key change to create variety. It is a tribute to the creativity of Bowman's work that it rarely sounds monotonous despite the lack of modulations.

Although Bowman's blues have much in common with his rags, there is one crucial difference between them: the twelve-bar blues sequence.[28] In fact, Bowman shows remarkable flexibility with the sequence, lengthening or contracting it according to his whim. For instance, the main strain of "Rosary Blues" (example 67) is eleven bars long, the initial I chord (D♭) lasting three measures rather than the usual four, so that the move to the IV chord (G♭) is on m. 4 rather than the expected m. 5. One of Bowman's favorite devices, found in all his blues except "Tipperary Blues," is to extend the twelve-bar blues sequence to sixteen bars by repeating mm. 5–8 before moving on to mm. 9–12. An instance is given in example 68, the first strain of "Kansas City Blues," where precisely this happens: having behaved as a regular blues sequence till m. 8, m. 9–12 repeat mm. 5–8; mm. 13–16 then conclude the blues in the normal way.

This adaptation of the standard twelve-bar blues sequence was not invented by Bowman but derived from folk sources. For instance, the early blues-related folk song "Sweet Petunia," which survives in a number of recordings by African Americans from the 1920s and 1930s, used a similar sixteen-bar expanded blues structure.[29] Incidentally, the chromatic ♭VI chord (D♭), used in mm. 6 and 10, a substitute for the expected IV chord (B♭), is a favorite coloring

EXAMPLE 67. Bowman, "Rosary Blues" (1916), A strain

EXAMPLE 68. Bowman, "Kansas City Blues" (1914), A strain

for Bowman, and is found in several of his other blues and rags. One other thing to note about this theme is that it is closely related to the chorus of Handy's "Yellow Dog Blues," which had appeared in print the previous year (compare examples 68 and 47).

Another feature of Bowman's writing is his habit of reprising back material in constantly varied forms. He was, in fact, a master of this approach, which must have been inspired by his improvisatory skills as a pianist. The most spectacular use of the device is in his "Twelfth Street Rag," which, uniquely for a work of published ragtime, consists of just one basic strain with two variations. He uses a similar technique to a lesser extent in four of his five blues. Probably the most inspired example is the second strain of "Colorado Blues" (1914). In its initial appearance this is a regular twelve-bar blues (example 69a). It is then repeated with the melody considerably varied (example 69b; note that, as the left hand part is essentially the same for both versions, I have for ease of comparison given it only for example 69b). The clincher is that on the repeat the first measure is simply omitted so that the strain is now eleven bars long.

EXAMPLE 69. a. Bowman, "Colorado Blues" (1914), B strain, right hand only;
b. Same, B¹ strain, both hands

This kind of freedom in handling the twelve-bar structure is directly derived from folk blues. In the work of artists like Blind Lemon Jefferson, for example, very few blues performances are strictly twelve-bar: elongated or contracted structures, such as eleven, fourteen, or fifteen and a half bars, are more common.[30] It is, however, exceedingly rare for such lopsidedness to makes its way into print, at least in this era. When blues composers like W. C. Handy were adapting their folk sources, they almost always did so in a way that evened out these irregularities. The fact that Bowman does not follow this convention shows the commercially unmediated nature of his work.

Altogether, Bowman's voice is one of outstanding originality, and it is to be regretted that his legacy was not more extensive. In the five blues that have survived, the earthy nature of his folk-derived approach combines with the pianistic sophistication of his writing to produce a style of remarkable distinctiveness. They are never less than inventive, hardly ever predictable, and marked by a raw creativity. In short, they must be considered one of the most significant achievements in the early history of the blues.

GEORGE W. THOMAS

George Washington Thomas (c. 1885–1937) was a black pianist, composer, publisher, arranger, and recording artist who produced three of the most interesting blues of the pre-1921 period: "New Orleans Hop Scop Blues" (1916), "Houston Blues" (1918), and "Muscle Shoals Blues" (1919).[31] Thomas was born in central Arkansas and moved with his family to Houston in his early teens. He then began working as an itinerant musician, settling in New Orleans around 1914.[32] There he became active as a publisher, beginning in 1915 with his song "It's Hard to Find a Lovin' Man That's True." Thomas was prolific: he is known to have composed or co-composed twenty works between 1915 and 1920 in a wide range of styles, including blues, ragtime, jazz

FIGURE 24. George W. Thomas (Courtesy Montgomery Archive)

songs, and waltzes. After relocating to Chicago in 1920, he became even more active, composing around sixty works during the decade, many of them blues-related.

In addition to this creative legacy, Thomas is also important for being the driving force behind a whole family of blues musicians. His younger brother Hersal was a notable pianist who made important recordings for Okeh before his untimely death at around eighteen years of age. His daughter Hociel also recorded for Okeh, as did the most famous member of the clan, George's younger sister Sippie Wallace, who has long been regarded as one of the major performers of vaudeville blues.

Thomas's first published blues, "New Orleans Hop Scop Blues," was also one of his most successful. According to the historian Michael Montgomery, who has untangled the complex history of this work, it originally appeared in 1916, published by the composer. Thomas then brought out a further three editions between 1917 and 1919, with sales propelled in part by a front cover that is one of the most eye-catching in all published blues. A singer on stage tells her blues-playing pianist to "drive 'em down, big boy." He memorably replies, "I'll do that same thing." A fifth version of the song is known exclusively from a piano roll (Kimball 10070), while a sixth—the best known—appeared in 1923 in a New York edition produced by Clarence

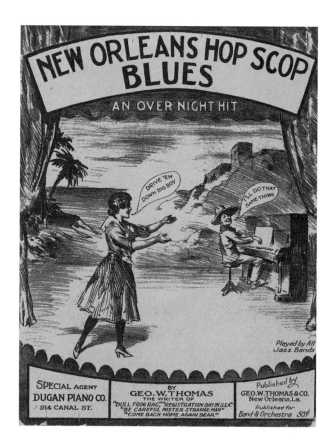

FIGURE 25. The striking cover to the original 1916 edition of George Thomas's first published blues. (Courtesy Montgomery Archive)

Williams, the pioneering black music entrepreneur, whom Thomas had originally known in New Orleans.[33] While all six editions of the song have clear musical and textual differences, they share the same basic structure of verse and chorus preceded by a four-bar introduction.[34] It was the New York edition of the song that was to be the most important. Under Williams's aegis, it received recordings by various jazz bands and blues singers, the most celebrated being by Bessie Smith in 1930. The song eventually achieved the status of a minor standard among traditional jazz bands. Tom Lord's jazz discography, for example, lists thirty-eight recordings, and the work is still occasionally performed by revivalists.

The focus of the lyric is the "Hop Scop Blues" of the title, apparently a type of blues dance popular in New Orleans. The text is clearly influenced by George Norton's lyric to Handy's "The Memphis Blues," which, after all, was in 1916 still the best known published blues. Both songs begin by celebrating southern cities—New Orleans and Memphis, respectively—in language focusing on the concept of hospitality: New Orleans is described in Thomas's lyric as "a great big old southern town / where hospitality you will surely find," while Norton mentions Memphis residents' "hospitality, / they were good to me." The parallel continues as both songs then celebrate the performance of blues. Norton's lyric eulogizes a blues rendition by Handy's band focusing on the cathartic effect of the music on the listener, while Thomas's is concerned with the Hop Scop Blues dance, his chorus loosely describing both the movements associated with it ("Glide, slide, dance, prance, hop, stop"—see example 70) and, like Norton's lyric, the physical and emotional effects of the music ("the Hop Scop Blues will make / You do a lovely shake, / It will make you feel so grand").

However, the close relationship between the lyrics of the two works is not reflected in their music. Unlike Handy, Thomas uses a twelve-bar sequence throughout the entire work, the verse originally consisting of three blues stanzas (shortened to two in later editions), and the chorus consisting of two. The three-stanza verse is particularly interesting in that its second stanza is truncated by a measure, so that it is eleven measures long (example 71), an approach derived from folk blues and one found very rarely in published blues of the era (although compare with Euday Bowman's "Rosary Blues" (example 67), which uses the same device in its first strain). The folksiness of Thomas's verse is reinforced by raw voicings in the accompaniment, such as those seen in m. 2 of example 71. Both these features—the eleven-measure blues sequence and the unusual voicings—were ironed out in later editions as the work moved into the commercial mainstream. However, I would argue that, in the course of being conventionalized, the song lost some of its individuality.

Probably the most striking moment in the work is the beginning of the chorus (Example 70), where, as mentioned, the voice calls out the movements associated with the dance (spoken in the first edition, sung in later editions). It is accompanied by a dramatic change of texture in the piano, which up till now has been continuous and full: the right hand plays stopped chords, while the left plays octave figurations outlining the harmony, strongly suggestive of boogie-woogie. Later editions made this feel even more explicit by notating the figurations as even eighths (example 72). As boogie-woogie historian Peter Silvester points out, "New Orleans Hop Scop Blues" is the first published blues to use boogie-woogie figurations (indeed, there is a suggestion that the term "Hop Scop" is an onomatopoeia-like evocation of the bass riff).[35] Its importance in this regard is underlined by the fact that, as late as 1940, the work was reissued in a boogie-woogie piano folio.[36] In fact, Thomas seems to have been an early pioneer of boogie-woogie, and it is an essential ingredient in many of his other blues compositions, such as "The Fives," a song from 1922 that was apparently a major influence on important boogie-woogie performers like Jimmy Yancey, Albert Ammons, and Meade Lux Lewis.[37]

Thomas's two other published blues from before 1921 are also interesting and effective works. "Houston Blues" from 1918 has much in common with "New Orleans Hop Scop Blues"; both

EXAMPLE 70. Thomas, "New Orleans Hop Scop Blues" (1916 version), chorus, mm. 1–12

EXAMPLE 71. Thomas, "New Orleans Hop Scop Blues" (1916 version), verse, mm. 13–23

EXAMPLE 72. Thomas, "New Orleans Hop Scop Blues" (1917 version), chorus, mm. 1–4, bass-line

songs are essentially celebrations of blues performances in the respective southern towns of their titles. The verse of "Houston Blues," which uses a double twelve-bar blues stanza, states how the blues in Houston "is just the blues for me," and dwells on how "The music is sweet / I can't help from shaking my feet." The chorus, using a non-blues sixteen-measure structure, is stylistically a slow drag with a strong ragtime feel, its soulful effect undermined by the rather prosaic lyric, a description of Houston girls dancing the blues and of the jazz band playing it (the first four measures are given in example 73).

Thomas's final pre-1921 published blues is "Muscle Shoals Blues," like its two predecessors named for a southern town, this one in Colbert County, Alabama. The work, copyrighted in 1919, was originally composed for piano, though as far as I am aware it was never published in that form. The song version appeared two years later. Musically, the two versions share the same basic material, but with considerable differences in the details. This is another example of Thomas's habit of tinkering with his compositions, a trait already seen in the various re-workings of "New Orleans Hop Scop Blues." The song is in standard verse-chorus format, with both sections using a double-stanza blues structure of twenty-four measures (in the original instrumental version, the chorus uses the same melody expanded to thirty-two measures). The chorus (example 74) is a particularly striking example of Thomas's down-home piano style, with boogie-woogie riffs in the left hand of the accompaniment in mm. 7–8 and 12. The work received several recordings in the 1920s, including versions by vaudeville blues singers Lizzie Miles and Edith Wilson, and band versions by W. C. Handy, Fletcher Henderson, Bennie Moten, and Ladd's Black Aces. One of the most striking renditions was a 1922 solo piano version that marked the recording debut of Thomas "Fats" Waller (Okeh 4757).[38]

EXAMPLE 73. Thomas, "Houston Blues" (1918), chorus, mm. 1–4

EXAMPLE 74. Thomas, "Muscle Shoals Blues" (1921 song version), chorus, mm. 1–12

PERRY BRADFORD

Perry Bradford (1893–1970) was a black music entrepreneur who is almost exclusively remembered in blues history for his role in instigating the "Crazy Blues" recording session for Okeh in August 1920.[39] As mentioned in the introduction, the session was crucial in that it was the first to feature a black female blues singer (Mamie Smith) and, even more important, led to the development of the race record industry. While Bradford's role in the event is undeniable, the attention it has drawn from commentators has overshadowed his more directly creative achievements elsewhere.[40] He was a gifted vocalist, bandleader, and pianist whose artistic talents resulted in a series of recordings in the 1920s—under such names as Perry Bradford's Jazz Phools and the Georgia Strutters—that are widely admired by connoisseurs. He was also a

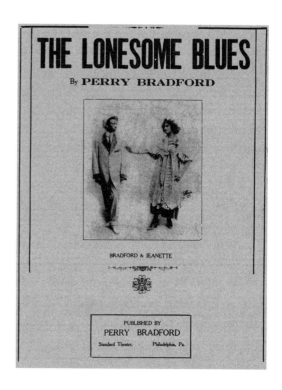

FIGURE 26. The cover to the original 1916 version of Perry Bradford's "Lonesome Blues," showing him with his vaudeville partner Jeannette Taylor. (Courtesy Montgomery Archive)

fluent composer, copyrighting dozens of works from the mid-1910s till the 1940s. In particular, Bradford created a series of blues between 1916 and 1921 that is one of the most interesting bodies of work in the early development of the genre. Altogether there are six blues by him that are known to have been published before 1921, all of them songs: "Lonesome Blues" (two versions, from 1916 and 1918, respectively), "Harlem Blues" (1917), "Broken Hearted Blues" (1918), "Don't Care Blues" (1919), "Crazy Blues" (1920), and "Fare Thee Honey Blues" (1920). In addition, there is an unpublished blues from 1918, "Nervous Blues," which exists as a copyright deposit in the Library of Congress.[41]

Although his major success was achieved in the North, Bradford, like all the major blues composers of the era, was a southerner. Born in Montgomery, Alabama, his family moved to Atlanta when he was around six. By the age of sixteen, Bradford, after a stint as a minstrel, was performing regularly in black vaudeville in a comic double-act with his professional partner, Jeannette Taylor. Billed as "Bradford and Jeannette," their act combined music, dance, and cross-talk in a manner typical of male-female acts in black vaudeville at the time, such as those of Baby Seals and Floyd Fisher, and Stringbeans and Sweetie May. And, as with these other stars, Bradford featured blues, beginning in 1916. By 1918, his act consisted of "nothing but the blues."[42] It is safe to assume, therefore, that Bradford's published blues stem directly from his experiences in vaudeville.

Taken as a group, Bradford's early blues are relatively consistent in approach. They are all of the type I termed *homeopathic* in chapter 3, that is, slow and cathartic in mood, and their lyrics are all variations on the standard theme of the singer having the blues due to the desertion of a lover. Of course, many vocal blues of the era, particularly those written by black composers, share these characteristics. Where Bradford's early blues are unique is in their complexity. Whereas most published vocal blues use two themes, Bradford's use three or four. "Harlem Blues," for instance, has four themes, and "Fare Thee Honey Blues" has three; "Crazy Blues" uses four themes in the original version recorded by Mamie Smith, and three in the simplified sheet version that appeared in its wake. Bradford's approach is demonstrated by example 75, the complete score of the first version of "Lonesome Blues," one of the most original published blues of the pre-1921 era.

Like almost all of Bradford's blues, "Lonesome Blues" is loosely cast in a standard popular song form, with verse (mm. 8–46) and chorus (mm. 47–62) preceded by a conventional introduction (mm. 1–4) and vamp (mm. 5–6). However, the verse is unusually dense, having three distinct sections: a sixteen-measure theme (mm. 7–22), followed by two separate twelve-bar blues passages (mm. 23–34 and 35–46). Including the sixteen-measure chorus (mm. 47–63), therefore, the song as a whole has four separate musical sections. Normally in a work with this number of ideas, a composer will use various kinds of repetition in order to give a sense of coherence. W. C. Handy's "Yellow Dog Blues," for instance, also has four sections, but the second uses the same music as the first, and there is a subtle but important motivic relationship between the verse and chorus (see example 46). Bradford, by contrast, makes little attempt to make the different sections of his blues cohere musically, the tendency being to simply present one unrelated idea after the other. In "Lonesome Blues," for instance, the only musical connection between the different sections is the opening two measures of the first section (mm. 7–8), which return at the end of the verse, buried in the accompaniment and at double the speed (mm. 45–46). However, the material in these passages is so generic to the blues idiom that it fails to make a strong impression in the way the reprise of a more distinctive motif would (the pitches of the melody, B♭–A–A♭–G form a four-note falling chromatic motif, and the harmonies form what I term a *barber shop ending*: both these devices are widely used in early popular blues).

In addition to a lack of repetition *between* sections, Bradford's blues tend to lack repetition *within* each section. For instance, in the opening section of "Lonesome Blues" (mm. 7–22), a different melody is used for each of the four-bar subdivisions (mm. 7–10, 11–14, 15–18, and 19–22). One could argue for a faint relationship between mm. 11–13 and 19–21; apart from that, the material of this section is through-worked with minimal repetition in much the same way as the work as a whole.

The sheer number of ideas in Bradford's early blues—combined with the fact that there is little relationship between them and minimal repetition within each section—makes the songs unusually dense. It could be argued that this was the result of compositional inexperience—

EXAMPLE 75. Bradford, "Lonesome Blues" (1916), complete

EXAMPLE 75. Continued

EXAMPLE 75. Continued

EXAMPLE 75. Continued

fledgling composers have a tendency to overpack their works with ideas. However, the fact that the non-blues songs that Bradford was composing over the same period are essentially conventional Tin Pan Alley numbers, with none of the musical density of his blues, suggests that this feature of his blues writing is entirely deliberate. I would speculate that Bradford's inspiration for this musical complexity is derived from the lyrics of traditional folk blues. In that style, the text typically lacks a superficial coherence, being just a succession of unrelated floating strains, as for example in "Nigger Blues" (example 5). In "Lonesome Blues" and similar works, Bradford simply applies the same principle to the music, stringing one idea after the other with relatively little concern for overt musical narrative.[43]

Whatever its origin, the complexity of Bradford's blues shows the experimentalism and creativity of the genre in black vaudeville at the time, and its effect, as evidenced, for instance, in Mamie Smith's recordings, is impressive, creating an intense experience for the listener, and encouraging a focused engagement in a manner much more typical of art music than of vernacular music.

Indeed, I would argue that Bradford's blues style is a highly original manifestation of the notion of blues as "colored folks' opera" that was prevalent in black vaudeville in the 1910s. The constant shift of musical ideas and the cathartic style of his blues convey an overwrought emotionalism that is a loose analogue of the experience of listening to opera. Much the same thing was found with Baby Seals's eponymous blues, although in that instance there was somewhat more musical interconnectedness within the work.

One must be careful, however, not to push the opera analogy too far. As with Seals, Bradford's basic frame of reference is low culture, not high. For instance, one characteristic of his blues is the frequent use of preexistent folk material. Thus, in "Lonesome Blues" the two twelve-bar sections in the verse are both borrowed from folk blues: the first (mm. 23–34) is Bradford's take on the well-known "Hesitation Blues," while the second (mm. 35–46) is the melody "I'll See You When Yo' Troubles All 'll be Like Mine," a proto-blues that W. C. Handy had earlier used for the final strain of his "Jogo Blues" (1913). Other folk blues material in Bradford's blues of this period include "Make Me a Pallet on the Floor" (found in "Don't Care Blues," "Broken Hearted Blues," "Fare Thee Honey Blues," and the published version of "Nervous Blues" [1922]), "Frankie and Johnnie" ("Frankie Blues" [1921]), and "Fare Thee, Honey, Fare Thee Well" ("Fare Thee Blues" and "Evil Blues" [1923]).

Perhaps surprisingly, Bradford's best-known blues, "Crazy Blues," does not borrow overtly from folk material. Instead, it borrows extensively from his earlier blues. Thus, of the four sections of the work as it was performed by Mamie Smith on her Okeh recording, the first had already been used as the opening of "Harlem Blues" and the unpublished "Nervous Blues," the second is taken from "Nervous Blues," while the fourth is the chorus of "Broken Hearted Blues." Only the third section of the "Crazy Blues" recording—the chorus of the published version— uses at least some material that was apparently not used in earlier works. Even here, however, there is a clear musical relationship with the choruses of "Nervous Blues" and "Harlem Blues," and a portion of the lyrics were transplanted as well.[44] It is remarkable that such a cut-and-paste job should have produced Bradford's greatest success, especially as the work is as complex as any of his earlier blues. And lest it be argued that the sole reason for the work's popularity is that it happened to be chosen for Mamie Smith's historic blues recording debut, it should be mentioned that, while the Okeh recording obviously helped the work become famous, "Crazy Blues" caught on more than did the record's flipside, an orthodox pop song by Bradford titled "It's Right Here for You."[45]

Having said this, it is possible to exaggerate the popularity of "Crazy Blues." A work this intricate was not going to gain enduring and widespread popularity in the manner of a more conventional Tin Pan Alley bestseller. Bradford was well aware of this fact, and when writing for a more general audience he simplified his blues style considerably. A typical case is "Lonesome Blues." The original edition of the work, published by Bradford from the Standard Theatre in Philadelphia, where he was appearing at the time, was aimed mainly at black audiences who had heard him perform it in his vaudeville act. In 1918, however, two years after its original appearance, Bradford revised the song for New York publication by the firm of Frederick Bowers. Presumably thinking of a more mainstream public, Bradford simplified the chorus and replaced the intricate three-theme, forty-measure verse with a straightlaced twelve-bar non-blues theme. The result is a charming, but thoroughly conventional, popular song with only a tangential musical relationship to the blues idiom.

The dumbing down of "Lonesome Blues" was to foreshadow a more general stylistic shift in Bradford's blues writing as his name began to be more widely known after the success of "Crazy Blues." For instance, "If You Don't Want Me Blues" (1921), which was also recorded by Mamie Smith for Okeh, is close to a regular Tin Pan Alley song, with a straightforward verse and thirty-two bar chorus. His subsequent blues, with only a few exceptions, are consistently less intricate than his earlier work.

Unfortunately for Bradford, this obvious adaptation to public taste did him only limited good. After the success of "Crazy Blues" he became one of the busiest African Americans on the New York music scene of the 1920s, composing, publishing, performing, and recording prolifically. Nonetheless, he tragically never became successful enough at any one activity to secure an enduring artistic legacy. As a performer, his vocal and pianistic work were excellent but lacked the star quality of an Armstrong, Morton, or Bessie Smith. Moreover, as Jasen and Jones remark, "his songs had no staying power, and when their original recordings were forgotten, their day was over."[46]

Given the exceptional sophistication of his early blues, it is tempting to condemn Bradford for the later watering-down of his style. To do so, however, would obscure the fact that even his later blues are highly competent, and that the stylistic shift he made was largely necessary as he moved away from an audience in black vaudeville to a more general public. It is wiser, instead, to hold up his early work not only as products of a very fine individual talent, but also (and perhaps more important) as striking examples of the creative richness and imaginative daring of black vaudeville blues during the 1910s.

SOUTHERN PUBLISHED BLUES OF 1915–1920

As blues began to gain nationwide popularity and became increasingly established in the entertainment centers of New York and Chicago, many southern-based composers and lyricists upped their roots and moved to the North. Thus, in the second half of the 1910s southern blues led two increasingly separate lives. The first was a transplanted one in the North, where it assimilated elements of popular music. The other was in the South, where it continued to have close links to its folk origins. I will first discuss the work of those who moved to the North.

Of the four major blues composers examined in the last two chapters—W. C. Handy, Perry Bradford, George Thomas, and Euday Bowman—all except Bowman moved north: Handy relocated to Chicago in 1918 (and thence to New York), Bradford settled in New York at around the same time, and Thomas arrived in Chicago in 1920. As the composers moved north, their styles inevitably became more mainstream. Perhaps the most dramatic example of this trend is Perry Bradford, whose originally intricate blues style simplified drastically in the early 1920s. But it also happened with the others in a more subtle way. For example, there is the case of George Thomas, whose "New Orleans Hop Scop Blues," originally published in New Orleans in 1916, had many of its musical idiosyncrasies ironed out by the time it appeared in its New York edition a few years later.

The challenge, therefore, once blues moved to the North and its composers were writing for an established mass market, was to strike a balance: they needed to create music sufficiently individual to catch the attention of consumers, while at the same time they needed to conform closely enough to consumers' expectations of the genre that they would not be alienated and baffled by the work (indeed, one could argue that this balance is required for much successful popular culture). From this point of view, the work of the composers discussed here had only partial success. W. C. Handy, as was mentioned in the chapter 4, never had a blues hit once he moved north, while Perry Bradford and George W. Thomas had limited impact with their blues, which formed only a part of their total musical activities.

Other southern migrants fared better. The African American composer Spencer Williams (1889–1965), who moved from New Orleans to Chicago in 1907, produced an impressive series of blues and jazz songs. Some of these became standards, among them "I Ain't Got Nobody" (1915),[47] "Tishomingo Blues" (1916, example 17), "Everybody Loves My Baby" (1924), and "Basin Street Blues" (1928). His outstanding blues composition, however, and one of the most commercially successful from the period, is "Royal Garden Blues" (1919). The work was co-authored with its publisher, Clarence Williams (1898–1965, no relation), also from New Orleans, who was to become the single most important African American in the popular blues industry in the 1920s, publishing, composing, recording, and broadcasting with unrivalled success. "Royal Garden Blues," named for a Chicago nightclub, is cast in the mold of Handy successes like "St. Louis Blues" and "Beale Street Blues," with two themes for the verse and one for the chorus. Unlike these Handy works, however, "Royal Garden Blues" uses a twelve-bar blues sequence throughout. The most striking section is the chorus (example 76), whose melody is built almost entirely on a simple two-bar riff played five times in succession, three times straight (mm. 1–2, 3–4, and 5–6), the last two times (mm. 7–8 and 9–10) with small differences of pitch. This riff-based approach to melody was entirely new to blues at the time, although it was to become standard in later blues-derived genres such as boogie-woogie and rock and roll.[48] "Royal Garden Blues," then, is the quintessential example of a successful late 1910s popular blues written by a relocated southerner, combining the familiar (the Handy-esque three-theme blues song) with the novel and catchy (the riff approach to the chorus). It is not surprising that the song became so popular.

What, then, of blues left behind in the South? There are two basic trends. Some southern-published blues of the late 1910s are strongly influenced by developments in the North and move stylistically closer to mainstream popular music. For instance, a 1918 Prohibition blues, "The Bone Dry Blues" by June Bauer and self-published in Judsonia, Arkansas, is essentially a popular song, the only thing distinguishing it as a blues being the "I've got the blues" trope that pervades the chorus (example 77).

This example, however, is atypical, for a large majority of southern-published blues from later in the 1910s clearly reflect folk influences just as they did earlier in the decade. For blues

EXAMPLE 76. Williams and Williams, "Royal Garden Blues" (1919), chorus, mm. 13–24

EXAMPLE 77. Bauer, "The Bone Dry Blues" (1918), chorus, mm. 1–8

was continuing throughout this period to develop as orally transmitted folk music in the South, and doing so relatively independent of the styles emerging from the North. Folk-influenced published blues from the late 1910s therefore play an important role in documenting the development of folk blues before their emergence on record in the late 1920s. For instance, the chorus of a 1916 blues with the unpromising title "The German Blues: It's Neutral," published in Kentucky by its "composer" Louis E. Zoeller, turns out to be an unusually accurate transcription of five verses of a bawdy folk blues that was later recorded by Ivy Smith in 1930 ("Milkman Blues," Gennett 7251) and Charles "Cow Cow" Davenport in 1938 ("I Ain't No Ice Man," Decca 7462), among others (example 78; note the truncated fourth measure in the example, reflecting folk blues performance style).

An even more remarkable example of folk-influenced southern blues is "Louisiana Blues" (1916), composed and published by the otherwise unknown R. T. Dooley from Gainsville, Texas. It is, quite simply, one of the most idiosyncratic adaptations of folk blues I have seen. Example 79 gives the last part of the verse. The vocal line consists of a series of anguished phrases punctuated by wide leaps (for example, the mid-phrase rising octave leap on "to turn," mm. 2–3, and the subsequent drop of an eleventh over the next two notes), the frequent use of pauses to draw phrases out in a most emotive manner (mm. 3, 5, 7), and a whole series of blue notes (for instance the blue seventh Ab/G♯ in m. 1). Note also the disjointed lyrics ("I'd like to turn to / to my home / my lonely home / Louisiana Blues / yes the blues") and the accompaniment, which uses raw voicings in the left hand throughout and some obtrusive dissonances (for instance, the A in the right hand at the beginning of m. 3, clashing with the Ab in the left on the second beat). All these factors combine to make a powerfully cathartic effect. This is, in short, one of the most compelling homeopathic blues ever to appear in print. Whether or not "Louisiana Blues" is genuinely the creation of Dooley, or whether it is, like "The German Blues," just a recreation of something encountered in the field, is unclear. Either way, the influence of folk blues is pervasive.

• • •

Drawing all this together, the storyline of blues in the first two decades of the twentieth century is as follows. First, as discussed in chapter 1, folk blues spreads and takes root in southern black vaudeville by 1910, where its popularity leads to the creation of the published blues industry in 1912. That industry is initially largely confined to the South but, once established, rapidly

EXAMPLE 78. Zoeller, "The German Blues: Its Neutral" (1916), chorus 1, melody and text

EXAMPLE 79. Dooley, "Louisiana Blues" (1916), verse, mm. 16–23

moves northwards, until by the end of the decade production is located mainly in the North, fueled creatively by a number of African American southern composers like Perry Bradford, Spencer Williams, and Clarence Williams, who have moved to New York and Chicago, the northern centers of production. In the process of transplantation, however, blues loses some of its southern folk flavor, acquiring elements of mainstream popular music, and at times becoming indistinguishable from it. Northern blues eventually becomes part of the mainstream popular music industry, just as ragtime had done when it emerged from its folk roots in the late 1890s. Blues produced in the South, meanwhile, remains largely folk-based. It continues to develop semi-independently from the commercial mainstream. Southern-published blues have slowed to a trickle by the end of the decade, and orally transmitted folk blues remains a geographically and racially localized phenomenon, only gaining acceptance in the North through the release of race records of black folk blues artists in the late 1920s.

One question that arises from this narrative is the prehistory of published blues. If the published blues industry starts up in 1912, is there any precedent for it in the commercial sector? In other words, are there published and/or recorded compositions from before 1912 that bear significant traits of blues? And if so, do they tell us anything about the development of the blues genre as a whole? The answer to these questions is resoundingly in the affirmative, and these published proto-blues form the subject of my final chapter.

CHAPTER 6

Published Proto-Blues and the Evolution of the Twelve-Bar Sequence

In this final chapter, I examine proto-blues, that is, compositions published before the 1912 start-up of the blues industry that show a clear musical and/or textual relationship to blues. Such proto-blues are important for three reasons. First, they broaden our understanding of the emergence of blues in American culture, for they show both the development of the basic elements of blues and the integration of those elements into a coherent genre. Second, since published proto-blues are often folk-derived, they provide invaluable, and at times quite detailed, musical testimony to the early development of the genre in the folk sector. This is particularly important, because such evidence is otherwise lacking.[1] Third, many proto-blues have aesthetic worth independent of their historical import.

The field of published proto-blues has been almost entirely neglected by blues scholarship. Indeed, much of the music I discuss in this chapter is known only to a handful of pioneering scholars. Even the better-known compositions are mostly famous as pop songs: their connection to blues culture has generally not been recognized. Despite this, such is the quantity and significance of published proto-blues that I believe an entire book could be devoted to the subject. In the limited space devoted to the topic here, I will focus on what I consider the two single most important and revealing issues, one textual, the other musical. The textual element is the development of the blues song, that is, a song whose text is centrally concerned with the protagonist, usually the singer, "having the blues." This is the focus of the first part of the chapter. In the second and more substantial part, I deal with the musical element, the development of the twelve-bar blues sequence. I begin, then, with the development of the blues song.

DEVELOPMENT OF THE BLUES SONG

The history of Western music, both art and folk, is littered with examples of songs of lament or loss, particularly concerning a lover. I explored this notion in chapter 3, pointing out, for instance, the similarities between blues and a dirge like John Dowland's "In Darkness Let Me Dwell." However, such songs are obviously not blues, and their texts could not be mistaken for such. The basic characteristic of a blues song lyric, as the genre developed in the early decades of the twentieth century, is much more specific: its text centralizes the specific concept of the singer (or less typically, a third party) having the blues. Thus, the analysis of the early popular blues idiom in chapter 2 showed that over four-fifths of blues songs published before 1921 used the phrase "I've got the blues," or some variant thereof.

By this definition, the first known published blues song is from 1850: "I Have Got the Blues To Day!" with music by Gustave Blessner and words by Sarah M. Graham.[2] Blessner was a prolific composer of waltzes, polkas, and the like; nothing is known of Graham. Despite the work's early date, the circumstances of the song are remarkably similar to later blues: the male singer-narrator has been deserted by his lover, Fannie, and he consequently has the blues. However, in all other respects, the song is far removed from regular blues, as is demonstrated by the first verse, quoted in example 80. This is, in fact, a thoroughly conventional sentimental parlor song, using characteristically lofty language ("Life was a rosy dream I vow, / It seems a horrid nightmare now!") and a musical idiom loosely derived—and considerably watered down—from romantic European art song (notice, for instance, the twist to the minor in m. 11, which is reminiscent of the style of Franz Schubert's art songs).

The next known blues song, from 1871, is also a sentimental parlor composition. Titled "Oh, Ain't I Got the Blues!" with words and music by A. A. Chapman, the musical style is again unexceptional.[3] The text, however, is of considerable interest. Like Blessner and Graham's "I Have Got the Blues To Day!" the basis of the song is that the singer has the blues. There are four verses, each giving a different cause for his blues. In the first, the cause is social: the singer has no friends, and he has fallen in with an "awful set." In the second, it is his general life circumstances that have caused his blues. In the third, he has the blues because a wealthy uncle leaves his inheritance to his cousins rather than himself. And in the fourth, the cause is the opposite sex: all the "prettiest girls / My hand do refuse / . . . And leave me with 'the blues.'" The song is bound together by an eight-measure chorus (example 81). The fact that the singer lists multiple causes for the blues in the verses in a seemingly random fashion suggests a general sense of complaint with little overall coherence. It thus makes a fascinating parallel with traditional country blues texts like that found in "Nigger Blues" (example 5), which are simply non-narrative compilations of floating folk strains. However, Chapman's work, in contrast to a typical blues, is comic in intent, the various reasons for the singer's blues being rather extreme.

"Oh, Ain't I Got the Blues!" is a minstrel song: the front cover tells us that it was performed by Welch and Hughes of White's Minstrels. The minstrel background is interesting in terms of

EXAMPLE 80. Blessner, "I Have Got the Blues To Day" (1850), verse 1

the connection to the blues, because it immediately places the work within the context of African American culture, however indirectly. In fact, the earliest known connection between African Americans and the blues pre-dates this song by several decades. In an article from 1839 titled "A Negro with the Blues," which appeared originally in the black newspaper the *New Orleans Picayune*, Sam complains to his friend Pete Gumbo that he has "what de white folks calls de

EXAMPLE 81. Chapman, "Oh, Ain't I Got the Blues" (1871), chorus

bloos . . . de raal indigo bloos." When Pete asks Sam what he means by the phrase, the latter gives the following eloquent reply: "Woll, you see, when a man's got de bloos he looks forard into de commin footoority jest as though he was gwine to draw a blank in de big lottery—he feels like as if all de delightsum prizes in dis low down scene hadn't a single number on 'em. Wen he gets in de mornin he feels bad, and wen he goes to bed at night he feels wusser. He tinks dat his body is made ob ice cream, all 'cept his heart, and dat—dat's a piece ob lead in de middle. All sorts ob sights are hubbering around, and red monkeys is buzzing about his ears. Dar, dem's what I got now, and dem's what I calls de bloos."[4]

Sam's insistence that he has what "de white folks" call blues suggests that in 1839 the term had not yet gained widespread currency in the African American community. However, some of the phraseology used here is so strongly prescient of the later blues idiom that it is impossible to believe that the notion of a black man having the blues had not already started to permeate the cultural consciousness of this time—at any rate in New Orleans. In particular, images like indigo blues, the name of a 1918 published blues composition by Isham Jones, and a heart full of lead are familiar textual associations of mature blues culture.[5] And, as Dale Cockrell has remarked, "one would love to hear what Bessie Smith . . . would have done with the 'red monkeys . . . buzzing about his ears.'"[6]

Given the early date of this article, it is perhaps surprising that the earliest known song to link the notion of having the blues with African Americans does not appear until the end of the century: "Oh Susie! Dis Coon Has Got the Blues," by J. W. Murray and F. C. Mock, published in 1897 by the major New York firm of Witmark and Sons. As is implied by the title and confirmed by the parodic use of dialect in the lyrics, the singer is African American. The first verse and chorus run:

Verse 1
Susie is de gal o'mine dat doesn't let me sleep,
Oh! Susie I feel blue.
Lub you more'n I can tell,
Lub you good and deep,
Oh! Susie, yes I do,
When I get some money,
Don't I blow it all for you?
Susie, you know I do,
Susie, come be mine,
I will treat you fine
Or dis coon will turn blue.

Chorus
Oh! Susie, I hope you'll neber lose me,
Oh! Susie, do tell me, will you choose me?
Susie, come break loose,
Don't act like a goose,
Susie, dis coon has got de blues.

As with Chapman's "Oh! Ain't I Got the Blues!" there is no real narrative here. Instead, the text is centrally concerned with the emotional state of the singer, amplifying his frustration about his lover's unwillingness to commit to the relationship. From this point of view, the song is reminiscent of mature blues. However, as with the two earlier songs, its satirical use of dialect clearly suggests that it is intended humorously. In fact, this is a coon song: its use of dialect and the word "coon" in its title and elsewhere are typical of the genre.

The next blues song to appear is also a coon song. Dating from 1901, "I've Got de Blues" was composed by the successful black vaudeville team of Chris Smith and Elmer Bowman (this is the same Chris Smith who, with Tim Brymn, started the entire popular blues industry in January 1912 with "The Blues").[7] The most striking part of the song is its chorus, the first half of which is quoted in example 82, where the protagonist sings the blues, complaining that his "head is aching" and his "heart is breaking." As in "Oh Susie! Dis Coon Has Got the Blues," there is use of black dialect, but here it is very mild (just the substitution of "the" with "de"), so that it clearly establishes the protagonist as black but without being denigrating. This song is the first to be examined here that uses some features of the musical idiom of blues. These include the slow drag feel of the extract (a result of the slow tempo combined with the intricate ragtime figurations of the accompaniment); the move to the IV chord (E♭) from the I chord (B♭) at m. 5, perhaps relating to the use of the same progression at the same point in a regular twelve-bar blues sequence; and the use of the device I call a four-note chromatic motif in the right hand of

EXAMPLE 82. Smith and Bowman, "I've Got de Blues" (1901), chorus, mm. 1–8

the piano part at mm. 4–5, which I showed in chapter 2 to be a common expressive feature of published blues. It is certainly possible, therefore, that the chorus is based on folk-type material that is a very early form of blues; I discussed in chapter 1 how this is the case with another of Smith's compositions, the 1912 "The Blues," co-composed with Brymn (example 1).

In fact, one could make a case that "I've Got de Blues" is in some ways the most advanced blues song to be published until Smith and Brymn's "The Blues" eleven years later, in that it is the only one whose text combines the notion of an African American having the blues with at least some elements of the musical idiom of popular blues. In contrast, a 1909 song by J. R. Shannon, titled "Gee, But I've Got the Blues," uses the old-fashioned elevated language of the parlor ballad rather than the racy black dialect of the coon song, and its musical idiom is similarly archaic.[8]

Nonetheless, there are two blues songs produced in the first decade of the twentieth century that represent a considerable evolutionary advance on "I've Got de Blues." The first of these is Antonio Maggio's "I Got the Blues," published in New Orleans in 1908, which was examined in chapter 4 in connection with Handy's "St. Louis Blues"—on which, I argued, it was an important influence. In terms of the development of blues, its significance lies in the fact that it is the first example in print linking the notion of having the blues to the twelve-bar sequence. The work was published as a piano solo, not a song, but I would suspect from its title that the blues theme in it must have originated as a folk song: I certainly know no other example of a bona fide ragtime instrumental composition that uses the first person singular in its title.

The other blues song of the 1900s that moves beyond Smith and Bowman's "I've Got de Blues" is also a New Orleans composition: Robert Hoffman's "I'm Alabama Bound," first published in 1909, and which in its first edition was subtitled "The Alabama Blues." As discussed in chapter 1, this was the first time that a published composition was titled using the formula "The X Blues." This fact is of tremendous importance, for it symbolically marks the beginning of blues as a reified genre. The interest of the work, however, does not just reside with the title. Two of the three themes used in the original instrumental version are important black folk proto-blues songs: the title theme, "I'm Alabama Bound," which, under various different titles, was recorded by such pioneering blues artists as Papa Charlie Jackson, Jelly Roll Morton, Blind Lemon Jefferson, and Charlie Patton;[9] and the melody usually called "Fare Thee, Honey" or, more fully, "Fare Thee, Honey, Fare Thee Well," which is first known from a published coon song version from 1901, and which has been recorded and published numerous times since, including as the final strain of Will Nash's "Snakey Blues" (example 6).[10] In 1910, Hoffman published a song version of "I'm Alabama Bound" with words by John J. Puderer, which uses the "I'm Alabama Bound" theme for the verse and the "Fare Thee, Honey" melody for the chorus: the first half of each is given in examples 83 and 84. The references to "low down measly coon" in the verse and "low down nigger" in the chorus, and the ragtime accompaniment, show that this is, like Smith and Bowman's "I Got de Blues," a coon song, although by 1910 the vogue for coon songs had passed. It is therefore not surprising that the work achieved its greatest success with an instrumental recording rather than a vocal one, by the band of Charles Prince (Columbia A-901, 1911).

In sum, there are a number of songs published throughout the second half of the nineteenth century that can be regarded as blues songs, since their texts are centered round the notion of the protagonist having the blues. Some of these have surprising parallels to later blues texts. However, it is only in the first decade of the twentieth century that such songs acquire the musical characteristics of blues. Thus, I turn now to the question of the musical development of the blues idiom, and specifically to its most distinctive feature, the twelve-bar sequence.

THE EVOLUTION OF THE TWELVE-BAR BLUES SEQUENCE

The Proto-Blues of Hughie Cannon

There are altogether two dozen known compositions published before the start-up of the blues industry that use chord sequences that are clearly related to the twelve-bar blues form. Overall, this body of work—the earliest publication of which dates from 1895—is quite diverse, and it embraces a wide variety of coon songs, popular songs, and ragtime instrumentals published in the South, Midwest, and North by both white and black composers, with material ranging from regionally produced obscurities to some of the top hits of the era. However, within this

EXAMPLE 83. Hoffman and Puderer, "I'm Alabama Bound" (1910 song version), verse, mm. 1–8

EXAMPLE 84. Hoffman and Puderer, "I'm Alabama Bound" (1910 song version), chorus, mm. 1–8

diverse field, one particular name is dominant: that of Hughie Cannon (1877–1912). He is associated, directly or indirectly, with over half (thirteen) of these works, ten of which he wrote himself, plus another three, composed by others, that relate to his 1902 smash hit "Bill Bailey, Won't You Please Come Home?"[11] It is with Cannon, then, that I begin.

Cannon was a white ragtime pianist, minstrel performer, and composer who is now remembered solely for the aforementioned "Bill Bailey," which has become one of the best-loved songs of the era. The son of two actors, he was born in Detroit, grew up in Connellsville, Pennsylvania, and began working as a performer sometime in the 1890s. He was apparently a fine pianist who, in the words of an acquaintance, "could really play ragtime."[12] He also excelled at soft shoe dancing.[13] The first of his twenty-five known songs, a coon song titled "I Don't Want No Jonah Hangin' Round," appeared in 1899, issued by the New York firm of Howley, Haviland, & Co., which was to be his publisher for the next four years. The following year saw the publication of his first proto-blues, "Just Because She Made Dem Goo-Goo Eyes," co-written with John Queen. Although long forgotten today, the song was a major commercial success at the time, becoming the ninth best-selling song of the year, according to Gardner.[14] Cannon's last known publications date from 1905, by which time he had relocated to the Midwest, where he spent

FIGURE 27. The only known photograph of Hughie Cannon (left) with fellow proto-bluesman John Queen, taken ca. 1901, a year before Queen's death. (Courtesy Montgomery Archive)

the remaining seven years of his life working as an itinerant piano player. By all accounts, Cannon's life was not a happy one. He suffered from acute alcoholism, of which he died "alone and penniless" in the Lucas County Hospital in Ohio at the age of thirty-five. By a cruel irony, the divorce that ended his only marriage was granted the same day as his death, June 17, 1912.[15]

In total, there are ten surviving proto-blues written by Cannon that make use of the twelve-bar form. All these are coon songs, and all except one use the sequence in the verse—in a double-stanza, twenty-four bar form.[16] Perhaps the most impressive of these songs is "You Needn't Come Home" (1901), which uses the sequence for both verse and chorus, making it unique for a proto-blues of the period. Example 85 gives the first of three verses and choruses. The work is typical of the humorous subject matter of a coon song: a wife turns her husband out of the house—we are never told exactly why—and despite his pleas, refuses to yield, repeatedly telling him "well, you needn't come home." The use of the twelve-bar sequence throughout makes it similar to a folk blues. Indeed, one can view Cannon's song as based on a single melody, just as a folk blues would be, for the melody Cannon uses in the chorus is really just a variation of that of the verse.

The chord sequence of the song is identical to a regular blues sequence, with only one difference. In a regular blues, the harmony returns in m. 7 to the I chord (D) from the IV chord

FIGURE 28. Cannon's first proto-blues, co-written with John Queen: "Just Because She Made Dem Goo-Goo Eyes," one of the major hits of 1900. (Author's collection)

EXAMPLE 85. Cannon, "You Needn't Come Home" (1901), melody and text of verse 1 and chorus 1

(G), but here the return is delayed by a measure. This may not seem significant, but it is, for folk blues hardly ever use this variant, and even in printed blues it is extremely rare. However, while the variant is essentially unknown in fully developed folk blues songs, it is used for the well-known pre-blues folk song "Frankie and Johnny."

This fact is not coincidental. Consider example 86. It compares the standard melody and text of "Frankie and Johnny" with the second half of the first verse of a 1904 song by Cannon titled "He Done Me Wrong": the chord sequences are identical, the melodies closely related, and there is even the textual parallel of "he done me/her wrong" at the end of the stanza. The "Frankie and Johnnie" chord sequence was a favorite of Cannon's. All told, six out of his ten songs using the twelve-bar sequence employ it as the harmonic basis of their verses, although none of their melodies is as closely related to that of "Frankie and Johnnie" as "You Done Me Wrong." Indeed, some of Cannon's ventures into the twelve-bar form are seemingly a long way removed harmonically and melodically from "Frankie and Johnny." Take, for instance,

EXAMPLE 86. **a.** "Frankie and Johnny," melody and text of verse 1;
    b. Cannon, "He Done Me Wrong" (1904), melody and text of verse 1, mm. 1–12 (original D major)

the verse of Cannon's most successful song, "Bill Bailey, Won't You Please Come Home?" (1902; the first half is given in example 87). The melody superficially bears little relationship to "Frankie"—for instance, the first four measures of "Bill Bailey" consist of one repeated pitch as opposed to the gracious melodic arches that characterize the opening of "Frankie." In addition, the chords diverge considerably, especially at mm. 5–8. How then can one explain that some of his twelve-bar songs, such as "He Done Me Wrong," are closely related to "Frankie" both harmonically and melodically; while others, such as "You Needn't Come Home," are closely related harmonically but less so melodically; and certain songs such as "Bill Bailey" seem quite unrelated either harmonically or melodically?

The solution to this problem lies in the fact that "Frankie" is not a song that stands in isolation. In fact, it is a member of a large and complex family of folk songs of which it is but the best-known example. Another member is "The Ballad of the Boll Weevil," a longtime favorite of folk revivalists, given in typical form in example 88. It has approximately the same relationship to "Frankie" as does the verse of "Bill Bailey" examined in the previous example: a shared twelve-bar structure, but with a different melody, and a significantly divergent chord sequence (like "Bill Bailey," "Boll Weevil" stays on the I chord at m. 5 rather than moving to IV, an important departure from the "Frankie" prototype).

EXAMPLE 87. Cannon, "Bill Bailey, Won't You Please Come Home?" (1902), melody and text of verse 1, mm. 1–12 (original G major)

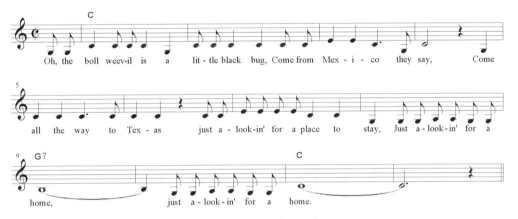

EXAMPLE 88. "The Ballad of the Boll Weevil," melody and text of verse 1

This suggests that Cannon was familiar not just with the specific song "Frankie and Johnny," but also with the family of songs of which "Frankie" was a member. This would remain just a theory if it were not for the fact that there is a certain property shared by members of the "Frankie" song family and all of Cannon's twelve-bar songs, but which is not found in any other folk material of the era. That property has to do with the phrasing of the melody. To illustrate it, I will use "Frankie." Each stanza of "Frankie" has three lines, each of which is split into two phrases. There are thus six half-line phrases per verse, each of which is approximately two measures, as can be seen by examining example 86a. I shall label these six phrases *a* through *f*:

Line 1: *a.* Frankie and Johnny were lovers,   *b.* O, Lordy, how they could love!
Line 2: *c.* They swore to be true to each other,   *d.* just as true as the stars above:
Line 3: *e.* he was her man,   *f.* but he done her wrong.[17]

The first four phrases, *a–d*, begin on, or just before, an odd-numbered measure. Thus, *a*, "Frankie and Johnnie were lovers," starts at m. 1; *b*, "O, Lordy, how they could love!" at m. 3; *c*, "they swore to be true to each other," just before m. 5; and *d*, "just as true as the stars above," just before m. 7. However, the last two phrases, *e* and *f*, do the opposite, starting on even numbered measures: *e*, "he was her man," starts just into m. 8, while *f*, "but he done her wrong," starts just into m. 10.

This might seem a purely theoretical notion, but it is of real musical significance, for this simple rhythmic shift occurring two-thirds of the way through the stanza heightens tension and creates a sense of rhythmic urgency, especially at the moment that the shift occurs in m. 8 ("the stars above / He was her man"). This feature—the three-line, six-phrase stanza with the phrases shifting from odd to even measures on the fifth phrase—is one generally shared by members of the "Frankie" family. For instance, "Boll Weevil" (example 88) is divided as follows:

Line 1: *a.* Oh, the boll weevil is a little black bug   *b.* come from Mexico they say.
Line 2: *c.* Come all the way to Texas   *d.* just a-lookin' for a place to stay,
Line 3: *e.* just a-lookin' for a home   *f.* just a-lookin' for a home.

Just as in "Frankie," phrases *a–d* start on, or just before, odd-numbered measures (1, 3, 5, 7), while *e–f* start just into even measures (8, 10). The fact that no other known folk song group from this era uses this particular phrase pattern means that it effectively becomes a genetic marker for the family. A comparison with the verse of any of the Cannon songs quoted above shows that they use exactly this phrase structure. For example, the verse to "Bill Bailey" (example 87) breaks down as follows:

Line 1: *a.* On one summer's day   *b.* sun was shining fine,
Line 2: *c.* the lady love of old Bill Bailey   *d.* was hanging clothes on de line
Line 3: *e.* in her back yard   *f.* and weeping hard.

Once again, the six phrases begin on, or just before, mm. 1, 3, 5, 7 and just after mm. 8 and 10. So, even though the verse to "Bill Bailey" departs melodically and harmonically from "Frankie," its phrase structure links it with the "Frankie" song family. And all nine of Cannon's songs that use the twelve-bar sequence employ this structure.

Another feature of songs of the "Frankie" family is that the last line (two phrases) of each stanza is a refrain. Thus, in "Frankie and Johnny," "He was her man / but he done her wrong" occurs at the end of every stanza, as does the repeated line "just a-lookin' for a home" at the end of each stanza of "Boll Weevil." The refrain idea is also taken up by Cannon in over half of his twelve-bar songs. For instance, "Well, You Needn't Come Home" (example 85) uses its title as a refrain for each twelve-bar stanza (and the similarity between this refrain and that of "Boll Weevil" just quoted is presumably not coincidental).

Songs of the "Frankie" family are assumed to be of black origin, and because most of them are based on actual events (usually violent crimes committed in the black underworld), it is possible to date a number of the songs. The inspiration for "Frankie and Johnny," for instance, was the murder of one Allen Britt, a black ragtime pianist, by his lover, Frankie Baker, in St. Louis in October 1899.[18] Another member of the song family, "Sta(c)kolee" (also known as "Stack Lee," Stagolee," etc.),[19] was also based on a St. Louis underworld homicide, this one in

December 1895.[20] Similarly, "Delia," another member, was based on a 1900 murder in Savannah.[21] "Boll Weevil," on the other hand, is not based on a single incident, but was inspired instead by the gradual devastation caused by the cotton-eating insect, which crossed the Texas-Mexico border in 1892: presumably the folk song emerged shortly afterwards.[22] The evidence, therefore, consistently suggests that the "Frankie" song-type became widespread from about the mid-1890s, just a few years before Cannon begun to use it in print, beginning with "Just Because She Made Dem Goo-Goo Eyes" in 1900 (of course, he may well have been incorporating it into his minstrel act at an earlier date).

Proto-Blues by Other Members of the Cannon Circle

Although Cannon's involvement with the "Frankie" song family was far more extensive than anyone else's, he was not the only person in the commercial sector to make use of it. There are, in fact, three other relevant songs known from before 1910, and between them they do much to flesh out our understanding of pre-blues culture in both the folk and commercial sectors. The three songs all relate in their subject matter to Cannon's song "Bill Bailey." They are: "Ain't Dat a Shame?" (1901), by Walter Wilson and John Queen; "Since Bill Bailey Came Home" (1902), by Billy Johnson and Seymour Furth; and "Bill, You Done Me Wrong" (1908), by the Leighton Brothers, Bert and Frank. These three songs, taken together with Cannon's "Bill Bailey, Won't You Please Come Home?" and "He Done Me Wrong" (1904), connect in a loose narrative. In the first of the series, "Ain't Dat a Shame?" Bill angrily leaves the home of his "ladyfriend" and then begs in vain to be allowed back. In "Bill Bailey, Won't You Please Come Home?" the woman has a change of heart and begs him to return. In "Since Bill Bailey Came Home," he actually returns. The remaining two songs in the series, Cannon's "He Done Me Wrong" and the Leighton brothers' "Bill, You Done Me Wrong," are closely related, both dealing with the lamentations of the grief-stricken Mrs. Bailey after Bill's death (from cholera, or in a railroad accident, according to the different songs).[23] All these five songs share the same basic structure of a Frankie-related, twenty-four measure verse followed by a conventional chorus of either sixteen or thirty-two bars.

There are a number of issues that arise from the "Bill Bailey" series of songs. The first concerns the question of the protagonist himself. Legend has it that the songs were inspired by a musician acquaintance of Cannon's named Willard Godfrey Bailey. However, the evidence is strongly against this interpretation, if for no other reason than that Cannon probably did not become acquainted with Bailey until after most of the series had appeared in print.[24] Another possibility is that the character was simply a fiction created by Queen and Wilson in "Ain't Dat a Shame?"—the first installment of the series. According to this theory, Cannon wrote "Bill Bailey, Won't You Please Come Home?" as a response, partly inspired by his relationship with Queen (this is the same John Queen who partnered with Cannon on "Just Because She Made Dem Goo-Goo Eyes" in 1900). The other songs in the series were responses to these first two songs, which were both substantial hits in their day.[25]

While this explanation is plausible, it is tempting to suggest that the Bill Bailey character was somehow derived from oral tradition, given the influence of the "Frankie" family on all five songs. The strongest piece of evidence in support of this claim is a transcription of a folk ballad called "I Went to the Hop-Joint," which appears in Scarborough's *On the Trail of Negro Folk-Songs*.[26] The twelve-bar melody is unmistakably a member of the "Frankie" family, being closely related to "Frankie and Johnny," and each stanza of the text having the typical structure of two-line verse and one-line refrain. However, the hero is Bill Bailey; the first stanza, for instance, runs:

> I went to the hop-joint and thought I'd have some fun.
> In walked Bill Bailey with his forty-one!
> Oh, baby darlin', why don't you come home?

Notice, too, that the "why don't you come home?" refrain is similar to that of Cannon's "Bill Bailey," namely, "won't you come home?" It is very possible, therefore, that "I Went to the Hop-Joint" is exactly the kind of folk song that was the direct inspiration for Cannon and his colleagues in their Bill Bailey songs.[27]

A second issue arising out of the Bill Bailey series involves the close ties between a quintet of authors and composers: Cannon, Queen, Wilson, and Bert and Frank Leighton. These relationships influenced their works as both songwriters and minstrel performers. All five were active in minstrel companies around the turn of the century. Cannon was a member of Barlow's minstrels during the 1898–99 season, and perhaps through 1900, where he specialized in what was described as a "negro oddity," an intriguing phrase that suggests at least a coon song—and perhaps one with a proto-blues connection.[28] Bert Leighton and Walter Wilson joined the same company in August 1899, staying till June of the following year.[29] This presumably means that they were working alongside Cannon for a time and hence came to know him personally. The most successful and enduring professional partnership among the five men arose between Bert Leighton and his brother Frank, who began working together in minstrelsy at the end of 1900. By 1904 they had worked their way up to Lew Dockstader's Minstrels, one of the top companies of the era.[30] In 1905 they moved permanently into vaudeville, where they continued to perform into the 1910s, and perhaps into the 1920s.

In terms of song-writing, the central figure seems to have been John Queen, for he is the only one of the group known to have collaborated with all the others. He worked with Cannon on three songs published in 1900 and 1901 ("Goo-Goo Eyes" being much the most successful);[31] he also collaborated with Walter Wilson not only on "Ain't Dat a Shame?" but also on "Fare Thee, Honey, Fare Thee Well" (1901), the first appearance in print of the African American folk song of that title, which was to have various manifestations in popular blues culture up to the 1930s. There was also a creative association between Queen and Bert Leighton; on the original copyright title for "Ain't Dat a Shame?" filed in the Library of Congress by the publisher, they

FIGURE 29. Proto-blues composer Bert Leighton, minstrel and vaudevillian. (New York Public Library, Billy Rose Theatre Collection)

are given as the composers, not Queen and Wilson.[32] Queen (c. 1860–1902), originally from New Orleans,[33] was the first of the group to publish a proto-blues, an 1899 coon song called "All Alone."[34] While it does not use a twelve-bar structure, "All Alone" does seem to be related to the "Frankie" prototype: each stanza follows the standard model of two-line verse with one-line refrain, and, unlike most turn-of-the-century coon songs, it is fully stanzaic, that is, it lacks a chorus. These factors point to a folk connection, and the subject-matter of the song—the loneliness of the singer—hints at something quite bluesy (even though, because of the minstrel context, the mood is lampooned rather than conveyed straight). The first of its ten stanzas is given in example 89.

Queen's extensive role in the publication of proto-blues should not lead to the conclusion that it was he who was solely responsible for bringing the genre to the group. A 1922 article by the Leighton brothers describes their circle as "a group of American minstrels, most of whom died young after going down into strange places to bring up the songs of Negro outcasts, of cowboy, miner and gambler."[35] This suggests that the group's members drew their material

EXAMPLE 89. Queen, "All Alone" (1899), melody and text of verse 1

directly from black (or, at least, folk) sources as much as from each other. Certainly the itinerant lifestyle of a minstrel would have presented ample opportunities for contact with folk proto-blues musicians. Barlow's minstrels, the company that employed Cannon, Wilson, and Bert Leighton, toured extensively in the South. In December 1898, for instance, when Cannon was probably with the troupe, it toured Mississippi, visiting such soon-to-be blues hot-spots as Vicksburg (on the 9th) and Greenville (on the 13th).[36] Not that proto-blues was only to be heard in the South. In their 1922 article, the Leightons describe how they encountered the black folk song "Fare Thee, Honey, Fare Thee Well" in Montana, performed by a black female pianist in a saloon, "reeking and rattling with crude revelry."

The picture that emerges, then, is of a circle of enterprising white minstrel performers who appropriated extensively from black folk culture as it existed at the turn of the century, incorporating it into their acts, and in some instances adapting it for publication. Of these men, Cannon's achievement is much the most substantial. He was, of course, the most prolific, with his numerous published songs using "Frankie"-related twelve-bar sequences. In addition, some of his compositions are surprisingly suggestive of blues. In "He Done Me Wrong," for instance, there is a tragic undertone, caused not only by the singer bemoaning the death of her husband from cholera, but also owing to the ambivalent nature of their relationship: from the verse quoted in example 86b, it is clear she loved him (as she has been "weeping hard" since his death) even though he "done me wrong." The sense of emotional outpouring is very similar to blues, and it is reinforced in the music not only by the twelve-bar form but also by the expressive use of blue notes (for instance, the blues thirds in mm. 8–9 of example 86b) and the appearance of the barbershop cadence in the accompaniment at the end of the verse (example 90).[37] Although I suspect in Cannon's day the song would have mainly been performed allopathically (i.e., quite fast and humorously) in the minstrel/coon song tradition, the inherent bluesy qualities of the song were brought out in a soulful recording by the white blues singer Marion Harris in 1920.[38] When performed in this fashion, "He Done Me Wrong" is as close as a published proto-blues gets to fully evolved homeopathic blues culture.

EXAMPLE 90. Cannon, "He Done Me Wrong" (1904), verse, mm. 22–24

Blues Ballads and the Emergence of the Twelve-Bar Form

So what do the proto-blues of Cannon, Queen, and their associates tell us about the early development of blues? As a corollary to that, why was the "Frankie" song family central to published proto-blues of this period?

Songs of the "Frankie" family—such as "Stagolee," "Delia," and of course "Frankie and Johnny"—belong to a category of folk song known as *blues ballads.* Blues ballads are defined by David Evans as "narrative folksongs that tell a story in a very loose, subjective manner and tend to 'celebrate' events rather than relate them chronologically and objectively in the manner of other American folk ballads."[39] As already discussed, blues ballads are mostly, if not entirely, based on actual events and characters, and most seem to be of black origin. The genre probably dates from the 1860s, reaches its height in the 1890s, and appears to die out by the mid-1920s.[40]

Blues ballads have long been acknowledged as the immediate precursor of blues. An influential theory of Paul Oliver's, taken up by Evans and others, argues that blues were formed by the fusion of field hollers and the twelve-bar harmonic structure of blues ballads of the "Frankie" type.[41] This is supported by other evidence. For example, W. C. Handy, who was intimately versed in turn-of-the-century proto-blues culture, stated that the earliest blues were what he referred to as "a *kind* of song," and he cited "Frankie and Johnny," "Stack O' Lee," and other blues ballads as examples.[42]

However, blues ballads of the "Frankie" family vary in closeness to the fully evolved blues genre. For instance, a song like "Boll Weevil," although typically twelve-bars in length, is somewhat removed from a standard blues sequence, while "Frankie and Johnny" has, as discussed, only one relatively minor divergence, the prolonging of the IV chord in the seventh measure. Presumably, then, the variety of twelve-bar "Frankie"-related chord sequences and melodies found in the work of Cannon and his colleagues reflects the diversity of the "Frankie" song family. It provides important documentation for the evolution of blues at this stage in its development, giving us a taste of the twelve-bar melodies and harmonic approaches out of which blues was to emerge.

The question then arises about the extent to which published proto-blues document the subsequent emergence of the straight twelve-bar blues form. As there is very little surviving field documentation of black folk music from the period—a small number of transcriptions of lyrics, almost no transcribed music, and no recordings whatever—we do not know for sure the precise path along which the blues sequence emerged from the "Frankie" song family. Indeed, it seems simplistic to suggest that it did so using a single path rather than a number of interrelated paths: evolutionary processes are not usually that straightforward. The basic progression of events, however, is clear, at least in overview. The "Frankie and Johnny" chord sequence, indeed the entire blues ballad genre, was at its height at around the turn of the century, at which time the twelve-bar blues sequence had yet to emerge. By the 1920s, this situation had reversed: the blues sequence was omnipresent, while the "Frankie and Johnny" sequence, along with the blues ballad generally, was in terminal decline.[43]

This basic narrative is substantiated in much published proto-blues and blues. Thus, the "Frankie and Johnny" sequence is overwhelmingly the most common twelve-bar sequence found in published proto-blues from before 1913. In addition to Cannon's six songs that use it, there is also the Leightons' "Bill, You Done Me Wrong" (1908) and a quartet of songs from 1912: "All Night Long," by Shelton Brooks (Chicago: Will Rossiter); "You're My Baby," by Arthur Seymour and Nat D. Ayer (New York: Remick); "I'm a Do-Right Woman," by Edgar Leslie and Lewis F. Muir (New York: F. A. Mills); and "Frankie and Johnnie," by the Leighton Brothers and Ren Shields (Chicago: Tell Taylor) (this being the first published version of the folk song). All these songs, like the earlier songs of Cannon's circle, have a standard verse-chorus format and use the "Frankie" sequence for their verses.[44]

After 1912, the "Frankie" sequence suddenly disappears from view in the commercial sector. Despite the much larger number of twelve-bar songs published in the period 1912–1920—most of them blues, of course—hardly any use the "Frankie and Johnny" sequence. The only exceptions I have been able to find are the chorus of Handy's "Hesitating Blues" (1915) and the verses of two obscure blues from 1918: "Love-Sick Blues," by Shelton Brooks (New York: Joseph Stern); and "Baltimore Blues," by Eubie Blake and Noble Sissle (New York: Witmark). Interestingly, all of these artists were African American, providing clear evidence that, despite the increasing importance of the straight blues sequence, the "Frankie and Johnny" sequence still had at least some currency in African American culture at the time (Handy, as already noted, remarked that the chorus of "Hesitating Blues" was suggested by the playing of a Memphis pianist of his acquaintance named Seymour Abernathy). In the 1920s, the use of the sequence is rarer still. I have found just two examples: "Jackass Blues," by white bandleaders Art Kassel and Mel Sitzel (Chicago, Melrose Brothers, 1925); and Duke Ellington's well-known "Creole Love Call" (Victor 21137, 1927).

Now let us examine the rise of the straight twelve-bar blues sequence in published proto-blues. There is only one known example from before 1910, the first strain of Maggio's "I Got the

EXAMPLE 91. Chapman and Smith, "One o' Them Things!" (1904), A strain

Blues" (1908, example 40). Other examples are known, but they are all modified in some way. An instance is the first strain of an obscure St. Louis ragtime composition from 1904 titled "One o' Them Things!" by James Chapman and Leroy Smith (example 91).[45] The strain has a double twelve-bar structure. While its second half is a blues sequence, the first half differs from the standard model in that it cadences on chord V (G, mm. 11a–12a), rather than resolving to chord I (C). In other words, this is really a twenty-four bar sequence whose second half is identical to a twelve-bar blues sequence. Its melody is almost certainly folk-derived, for it resurfaces a decade later in an early published folk-influenced blues, Will Nash's "Snakey Blues," copyrighted in 1915 (example 6, mm. 1–12).

Another example of a modified blues sequence is found in the third strain of a 1905 rag, "Texas Rag" by Callis Jackson, published in Dallas (example 92), and which expands the sequence to sixteen bars. Thus, the first twelve bars of the strain correspond to the standard blues

EXAMPLE 92. Jackson, "Texas Rag" (1905), C strain

pattern. There follow two different four-bar extensions, the first landing on V (B♭, m. 15a), the second on I (E♭, m. 15b).[46]

The divergences from the twelve-bar blues sequence in these and similar examples from the first decade of the twentieth century most likely represent genuine variants in folk culture.[47] This, combined with the fact only once is the sequence presented straight in printed music before 1911, seems to reflect its relative scarcity during this period (as opposed to the "Frankie" sequence, which has a comparatively strong presence in published music).

That situation was, however, about to change dramatically. In terms of published music, the rise of the sequence came not as one would expect in 1912 with the start-up of the popular blues industry, but the year before. In 1911, there suddenly appeared four Tin Pan Alley songs using the straight twelve-bar blues themes. All the songs use the sequence in the same way, as a double twelve-bar structure for their verses. The songs in question are: "Let's Go to Savannah G.A.," by L. Wolfe Gilbert, Lewis F. Muir, and Maurice Abraham (New York: F. A. Mills); "When Ragtime Rosie Ragged the Rosary," by Edgar Leslie and Lewis F. Muir (New York: F. A. Mills); the runaway success "Oh, You Beautiful Doll," by A. Seymour Brown and Nat D. Ayer (New York: Remich), whose (non-blues influenced) chorus remains a sing-a-long favorite even today; and "(Honky Tonky) Monkey Rag," by Chris Smith (Chicago: Thompson).[48]

How are we to interpret all this evidence? Put simply, the "Frankie and Johnnie" sequence predominates before 1911, the straight blues sequence after 1912. The eight popular songs from 1911 and 1912 that use a twelve-bar sequence—four of the straight blues type, four of the "Frankie and Johnny" type—must therefore reflect a crossover period that was happening in folk culture, presumably at around the same time.

This sense of transition is reflected in the work of the white ragtime composer Lewis F. Muir, who composed (or co-composed) three of the songs with twelve-bar verses listed above: "Let's Go to Savannah G. A." and "When Ragtime Rosie Ragged the Rosary," which both use the straight blues sequence, and "I'm a Do-Right Woman," which uses the "Frankie and Johnny" sequence. Similarly, Antonio Maggio, whose "I Got the Blues" of 1908 uses a regular blues sequence, wrote another piano rag, titled "Bad-Rag," which, while never published, exists as a copyright deposit in the Library of Congress from 1910, and whose first strain is based on the "Frankie and Johnny" sequence.[49] The work of these two men shows the interchangeability of the two sequences within this critical change-over period.

An important point about the twelve-bar proto-blues of 1911 and 1912 is their popularity. Chris Smith's "Monkey Rag" was the thirty-eighth bestselling song of its year; Shelton Brooks's "All Night Long" was the thirty-third; "You're My Baby" was the nineteenth; and "Oh, You Beautiful Doll" was the second.[50] The four songs thus facilitated the development of blues in popular culture in two ways. First, they proved the commercial viability of the blues-related twelve-bar sequence in the musical marketplace of the 1910s—a time when the conventional wisdom was that only inherently symmetrical structures of sixteen- and thirty-two-bar structures were readily sellable on Tin Pan Alley. Second, the songs, especially the verse of the extremely popular "Oh! You Beautiful Doll," familiarized the ear of the general public to the sound of the twelve-bar blues sequence, preparing for the reception of the new genre.

Why Did the Blues Sequence Evolve?

If, as all the evidence shows, the blues sequence developed from the "Frankie and Johnny" sequence, there must have been a good reason for it to do so. So, why did the blues sequence evolve? What was unsuitable about the "Frankie and Johnny" chord sequence for the needs of the new genre? As already mentioned, the difference between the two sequences is slight, consisting of the prolongation of the IV chord by a single measure in the second line of text. How can a difference so slight be so crucial?

The answer is quite simple and lies in the characteristic phrasing of the melodies of the two song-types. This is demonstrated in example 93, which compares the text and harmony of the first stanza of "Frankie and Johnny" with that of Handy's "St. Louis Blues" (given here as a typical example of fully evolved blues). As already noted, blues ballads of the "Frankie and Johnny" type have three lines per stanza. Each line is subdivided, for instance, the first line of "Frankie and Johnny" runs: "Frankie and Johnny were lovers / O Lordy, how they could love." Blues share this three-line, two phrases-per-line approach, as, for instance, the first line of Handy's "St. Louis Blues": "I hate to see / de evening sun go down."

There is, however, a major difference between the two genres. In a blues ballad, the first two lines (four phrases) of the stanza tend to be longer than the first two lines of a blues. For

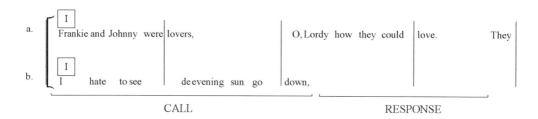

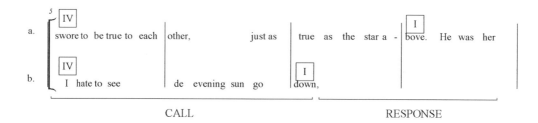

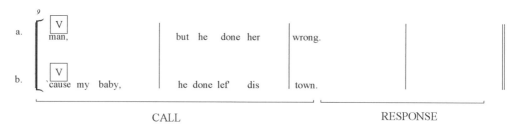

EXAMPLE 93. a. "Frankie and Johnny," text and harmony of verse 1;
   b. Handy, "St. Louis Blues" (1914), text and harmony of verse 1

example, the first line of "Frankie" has fifteen syllables, while the first line of "St. Louis Blues" has ten. Consequently the line concludes later in a blues ballad than it would in a blues. Thus, the first line (mm. 1–4) of "Frankie and Johnny" concludes at the beginning of the fourth measure, while that of "St. Louis Blues" concludes at the beginning of the third. Similarly, the second lines finish at the beginning of the eighth and seventh bars, respectively. The third lines of the two songs, however, run parallel, both ending at the beginning of the eleventh measure (the reason for this convergence is due to the characteristic rhythmic shift in the "Frankie"-type blues ballad at m. 8, discussed earlier, and also because the last line of the blues ballad, the refrain, is closer in length to a typical blues line, being shorter than its first two lines).

A feature shared by both "Frankie"-type blues ballads and regular blues is that the melody of each of their three lines come to rest on the tonic (I) chord. Although the first lines of "Frankie and Johnny" and "St. Louis Blues" end at different times, this makes no difference to the harmony, for typically the entire first line is harmonized by a I chord. It also does not affect the third line, because the first and third lines run in parallel, both ending—and thus arriving on the I chord—at the beginning of m. 11. The issue, then, is with the second line. In both songs, the line starts (m. 5) with a IV chord. As the lines end at different points, they therefore move back to the tonic chord at different times. Thus in a blues, the return to I is at m.7, in "Frankie" it is at m. 8: hence the difference between the two chord sequences.

All this is confirmed by looking at the examples given in this chapter. The blues ballads and verses of the Cannon songs (examples 85–88) all have the melody of their second lines ending at the beginning of m. 8 of their respective twelve-bar stanzas, whereas in proto-blues using a straight twelve-bar form—for instance, "Texas Rag" (example 92), or the first strain of Maggio's "I Got the Blues" (example 40)—the melodic phrase clearly ends at the beginning of m. 7.

Now if the reason the blues chord sequence evolved from the "Frankie" sequence was because of a changed approach to phrasing, this in turn raises the issue of what caused that change. The decisive factor seems to be that the revised phrasing allowed for the inclusion of call and response patterns. Call and response is defined as "the performance of musical phrases or longer passages in alternation by different voices or distinct groups, used in opposition in such a way as to suggest that they answer one another."[51] The use of call and response is integral to blues, where each vocal line of the stanza is responded to by an instrument, as indicated in example 93b. A specific instance is given in example 94: the beginning of the first stanza of Bessie Smith's famous 1925 Columbia recording of Handy's " St. Louis Blues." Smith sings the call (mm. 1–2), and the response is given by Louis Armstrong on cornet (mm. 3–4). Note that Armstrong's response is as long as Smith's call—two measures—and while this is not always the case, the call-response format is at its most typical when there is plenty of room for the response. Because the first two lines of a blues ballad like "Frankie" are typically longer than that of a blues, they allow no time for a real response. Hence, as the new genre evolved, the lines needed to shorten in order to free up the necessary space.

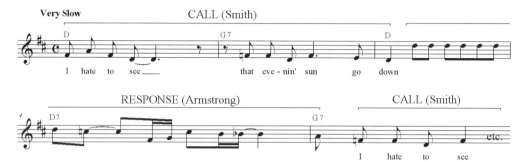

EXAMPLE 94. Bessie Smith's 1925 recording of Handy's "St. Louis Blues" (Columbia 14064–D), melody and text of verse 1, mm. 1–5

Again, though, we face the question "Why?": why did blues adopt call and response as part of its idiom, whereas the blues ballad did not? There are two factors to consider.

One is the different expressive nature of the two genres. The blues ballad is external: it celebrates particular events or tells a story with no direct relationship to the singer, and consequently it is usually sung in the third person. Blues, on the other hand, is internal: it describes, or at least is generated by, the singer's inner turmoil, and it is typically sung in the first person. Blues ballads are therefore impersonal, whereas blues are personal.

The other relevant factor is race. While the blues ballad is clearly African American, it seems to have evolved in part from the Anglo-American folk ballad. I shall be discussing this evolution in more detail later in the chapter, but for now it suffices to say that the blues ballad is, as it were, whiter than fully evolved blues.

Blues is therefore a genre that is both blacker and more personally expressive than its predecessor. It follows that, as the new style emerged from the old, it incorporated emotive aspects of the black musical idiom. One of these was call and response, a device carried over from Africa into African American slave society and manifested in a variety of cathartic genres, such as the field holler, ring shout, and spiritual.

These earlier genres, however, were ensemble music: the call was typically given by a soloist or a small group, and the response was made by a larger group. Blues was different in that it usually involved individual voices or instruments for both call and response (as in the Bessie Smith-Louis Armstrong exchange quoted in example 94). This emphasis on individual rather than collective expression greatly increased the sense of personal statement. Indeed, in its most essential form, in the country blues of artists like Robert Johnson and Blind Lemon Jefferson, the blues is a solo genre, the singer playing the response on his own guitar. The sense of interior dialogue in such solo performances seems to be at the heart of blues expression, and it is an important part of its therapeutic process, as discussed in chapter 3.

Putting this together, it is possible to provide a fairly clear-cut explanation of the chain of events that led to the metamorphosis of the "Frankie" sequence into the straight blues sequence. It begins with the sociological factors discussed in chapter 3: the desire for a new musical style devised for the purpose of "curing the blues." This in turn created the need for the development of a strongly personal and expressive idiom, which led to the incorporation of clear call and response patterns into the "Frankie"-type song. As a result, the first and second lines of each stanza were shortened, which in turn required the tonic chord at the end of the second line to arrive a bar earlier in the new style than in the old. Such a chain of cause and effect provides a nice example of how a sociological need for a new musical genre can result in very specific changes to a pre-existent idiom.

"I Natur'ly Loves That Yaller Man"

The systematic use of call and response is very rare in published music before the start-up of the blues industry; given that the twelve-bar sequence is equally rare, it is little short of astounding to find a published work that uses both elements dating from as early as 1898. The work in question is an obscure coon song entitled "I Natur'ly Loves That Yaller Man," with words and music by the black songwriting and vaudeville partnership of Lawrence Deas and Jack "The Bear" Wilson.[52] The part of the song relevant to this discussion is the music of the first twenty measures of the thirty-two measure verse (the last twelve measures are in a much more conventional style); the complete verse in quoted example 95. The first twenty measures consist of five four-bar phrases, each of which has the identical call and response pattern of a blues: the vocal phrase—the call—begins in the first measure and ends at the beginning of the third, and is immediately followed by an intricate, syncopated response of similar length in the melody line of the piano accompaniment. Though the melody of the call varies, the response is identical every time.

The harmony is unmistakably blues-related: the first twelve measures use a standard blues sequence, of which the last eight bars are repeated (mm. 13–20). A very similar scheme is found in some early published blues, such as the first version of Wand's "Dallas Blues" (example 55). However, this structure is partially undercut by the lyric, which instead parcels the verse as a whole into regular eight-bar chunks—that being the length of time filled by each couplet (e.g., "White folks all say, and think they're right, / That all coons, to them, they look alike!"). Nevertheless, the use of elements such as the twelve-bar sequence, call and response, the slow tempo, and the frequent and emphatic use of the blues third in both the call (mm. 2, 10, 18) and each of the instrumental responses gives this passage a remarkably bluesy feeling. An additional element is the frequent use of falling contours in both the call and the response. Melodic phrases that fall (i.e., end with a lower pitch than they began) are an important feature of blues, lending the music a doleful quality, and while this pattern is also found in regular popular songs, its prevalence here contributes to the bluesy atmosphere. Especially striking is the precise pattern used: in each case, the line first rises above its starting note before falling. This particular shape was selected—out of a possible fifteen—by Titon in his survey of country blues as being the most typical of the genre.[53] The wide range of these lines adds to the effect: they all span an octave or just under.

EXAMPLE 95. Deas and Wilson, "I Cert'ly Loves My Yaller Man" (1898), verse 1

EXAMPLE 95. Continued

Musically, then, the first part of "I Natur'ly Loves That Yaller Man" is remarkably suggestive of the integrated blues idiom. But what does it tell us of the early development of the blues?

As already mentioned, according to mainstream blues historiography, blues were formed when the twelve-bar structure of the blues ballad fused with other black folk genres like the field holler. What elements came from the field holler and related styles? First, there was the call and response element. Second came the cathartic/therapeutic approach, which, as discussed in chapter 3, was integral to slave music, but which was comparatively absent in the more mildly expressive and less emotionally wrought blues ballad. Third is the question of tempo: the evidence suggests that blues ballads were performed quite fast, while folk blues—at least the homeopathic variety—were typically slow.[54] Fourth, is the use of descending vocal phrases, which are common in the field holler but not a notable characteristic of blues ballads.

These four features are present in "I Natur'ly Loves That Yaller Man," which implies that its style is one that evolved from the field holler and related genres rather than the blues ballad, though whether it is an example of the style that was to graft with the blues ballad to create fully evolved blues, or whether this is just a random piece of jetsam in the evolution of the genre, is unclear. Either way, the song provides a fascinating sample of a particular proto-blues idiom that is unique in published music.

"The Bully Song"

Before I conclude, I have one other published proto-blues to examine. It is "The Bully Song," one of the most revealing of all proto-blues and also the earliest, predating even "I Natur'ly Loves That Yaller Man."

"The Bully Song" is a coon song of black folk origin first encountered in a reference in a black Kansas City newspaper in 1894.[55] However, it was allegedly heard somewhat earlier by W. C. Handy in St. Louis.[56] There are other reports of it being performed in St. Louis at the same time, or perhaps even earlier, by a black singer named Mama Lou in Babe Connor's brothel.[57] The song was first published in 1895, and by the end of the following year no fewer than six different published versions were in circulation, a testament to its enormous popularity in the mainstream.[58] While these versions are closely related, the best known is that of Charles E. Trevathan, as this was the one performed by the white ragtime singer May Irwin, who featured it in a successful 1895 show, *The Widow Jones,* and did more than anyone to popularize the number.[59] Trevathan was a southern sports writer who picked up the song either from his "colored boy" Cooley or from blacks in Tennessee, depending on whose account you believe.[60] His version is not only the best known, but it is also the longest and most interesting. It will therefore form the basis for this discussion.

Like almost all other published proto-blues songs, the importance of "The Bully Song" centers on the verse, which uses a twelve-bar melody sung twice.[61] That melody is given in example 96, along with the text of the first of no fewer than seven verses. Although the song

FIGURE 30. A poster for *The Widow Jones*, an 1895 comedy featuring May Irwin (center), in which she popularized "The Bully Song." (Library of Congress, Prints & Photographs Division)

was published with a conventional sixteen-measure chorus, the evidence suggests that the folk original had no chorus, but that it was simply stanzaic in the manner of a folk blues.[62]

The song has a loose narrative. It tells about the hunting down of a "bully," a "red-eyed river roustabout," in an unnamed black community by the protagonist, a "Tennessee nigger," who at one point is referred to as "Mr. Johnsing" (presumably dialect for *Johnson,* a stereotypical black name in coon songs). He succeeds in his purpose ("a cyclone couldn't have torn him up much worse," he proudly remarks). At the end of the narrative, the protagonist is triumphant: "Dere's [now] only one boss bully, and dat one is me."

With its loose narrative, violent "bad man" theme, and its setting in the black underworld, "The Bully Song" has the aspect of a blues ballad, and it is usually classified in this manner by folklorists.[63] The connection is reinforced by the fact that structurally the song uses the "Frankie" stereotype of a three-line stanza, consisting of a two-line verse ("Have you heard about the Bully dat's just come to town? / He's 'round among de niggers a-layin' their bodies down") and one-line refrain ("I'm a looking for dat bully, and he must be found"). In addition, that refrain is a measure

EXAMPLE 96. Trevathan, "May Irwin's Bully Song" (1896), melody and text of verse 1

shorter than the preceding two lines of the verse, as in songs of the "Frankie" family. There is, in addition, a specific textual parallel between the "Bully Song" refrain and that of "The Ballad of the Boll Weevil," one of the most famous songs of the "Frankie" family: compare "I'm *a-lookin' for* dat bully" (example 96, mm. 9–10) with "just *a-lookin' for* a home" (example 88, mm. 9–10).

Yet despite these connections, "The Bully Song" differs from the "Frankie" prototype in important ways. Although the third line of "The Bully Song" is *musically* shorter than the first two, *textually* it is the same length, all three lines having either thirteen or fourteen syllables. It is therefore different from the "Frankie"-type stanza, whose third line is usually several syllables shorter than the preceding pair (in "The Bully Song," the shorter musical length of the third line is achieved by rhythmic compression, squeezing into three measures [mm. 9–11] the same amount of text that occupied four measures for both of the first two lines [mm. 1–4, 5–8]).

The phrasing of "The Bully Song" also diverges from the "Frankie" model. Whereas songs of the "Frankie" type, as we have seen, have a crucial rhythmic shift at the beginning of the third line (the refrain), no such shift happens in the "Bully Song." For this shift to occur, the phrase "I'm a lookin' for dat bully" would have to begin on the second eighth note of m. 8, as I have indicated in the purely hypothetical example 97.[64] In actuality, the refrain begins on the last eighth before m. 9, in parallel with the first two lines of the stanza.

"The Bully Song," then, offers subtle, but significant, divergences from the "Frankie" prototype. How, then, should one understand its place in the development of the twelve-bar blues form? Peter Van der Merwe has suggested that the origins of the twelve-bar structure of the "Frankie" song family derive from a standard British ballad type of two-line verse plus one-line refrain.[65] According to this theory, African Americans would have encountered songs with this structure through crosscultural contact with Anglo-American colonists. They then applied the structure to their own ballads, which in turn led to the development of the "Frankie" song family.

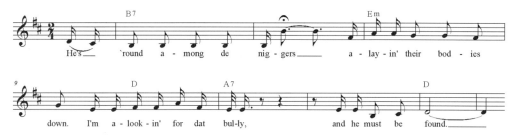

EXAMPLE 97. Trevathan, "May Irwin's Bully Song" (1896), melody and text of verse 1, mm. 5–12, with the rhythm shifted in m. 8 to conform to the "Frankie" song family stereotype.

This theory is an attractive one, for the Anglo-American influence would explain why the blues ballad is a rather more detached and less emotionally expressive genre than "purer," more cathartic African American styles (particularly blues) that developed out of it, or slave music (e.g., field hollers) that preceded it. Support for this theory is presented in example 98, an American version of the celebrated English folk song "Mister Frog Went A-Courting," titled "A Frog He Would A-Wooing Go," which was published in Boston around 1860.[66] This song, a British ballad that has been traced to the sixteenth century, is known from numerous versions.[67] This particular one has the identical structure of the "Frankie" family, that is, a twelve-bar structure consisting of eight-bar verse plus four-bar refrain, which is repeated in each of its fourteen stanzas. The example therefore represents a plausible link between the "Frankie" song-type and its British ancestors. Ballads like "Mister Frog Went A-Courting" are known to have been popular among blacks.[68] Indeed, this particular song is known to have evolved into the black folk song "Sweet Thing" sometime in the 1880s or early 1890s.[69]

In the process of becoming African Americanized, so to speak, such songs became more rhythmic. Van der Merwe demonstrates this by quoting four examples using the "Frankie" structure, starting with "Tattie Jock," an eighteenth-century Scottish folk song and ending up with Mississippi John Hurt's recording of "Frankie," each song becoming more rhythmically vital as the African American influence becomes more pervasive.[70] The phrase-shift at the beginning of the refrain of "Frankie" family songs is an example of this rhythmic vitality, giving each stanza an important push forward at a structurally crucial moment. It is therefore not surprising that the phrase-shift is found only in the fully evolved African American blues ballads of the "Frankie" family, not in their less rhythmically charged Anglo-American ancestors.

It would seem, therefore, that the "The Bully Song" represents a slightly earlier evolutionary manifestation of the "Frankie"-type blues ballad, for it shares the characteristic twelve-bar structure of a two-line verse and single-line refrain, yet lacks the hallmark shift in phrasing between the verse and refrain. This hypothesis is supported by the chronology: "The Bully Song" is known from the early 1890s, whereas the earliest known reference to another member of the "Frankie" family is not until 1897.[71]

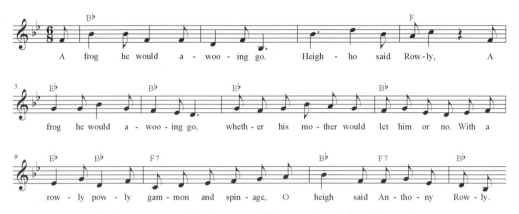

EXAMPLE 98. Smith, "A Frog He Would A Wooing Go" (ca. 1860), melody and text of verse 1

• • •

From the evidence presented in this chapter, it is possible to put together a more detailed and coherent picture of the emergence of blues than has hitherto been available. First, the notion of a blues song, that is, of a song centered around the singer having the blues, exists in mainstream American culture in the nineteenth century. It is, however, rare and, furthermore, is purely a textual conceit, lacking any significant musical aspect of the blues idiom. This situation only begins to change in the first decade of the twentieth century with Smith and Bowman's "I've Got de Blues" of 1901. Following this, there is more overlap between the textual and musical elements of blues, especially in Maggio's "I Got the Blues," the first work to combine the notion of having the blues with the twelve-bar sequence, and Hoffman's "I'm Alabama Bound," subtitled "The Alabama Blues" in its first edition, the first song to be titled using the formula "The X Blues." Maggio's work appears in 1908 and Hoffman's in 1909; 1910 is the year of the first known reference to someone performing the blues, ventriloquist "Johnnie" Woods in the Airdome Theater in Jacksonville, Florida. These three elements combine to give clear evidence of the emergence of a reified genre at around this time.

A relatively coherent narrative tracks the evolution of the twelve-bar blues sequence. The narrative begins with British ballads of the type where each stanza consists of a couplet verse and single-line refrain. These were then brought to America by Anglo-American settlers ("A Frog He Would A Wooing Go," example 97). Ballads using this structure were taken up by African Americans and adapted by them for their "bad man" ballads, perhaps as early as the 1880s (though the earliest surviving example, "The Bully Song," is traceable only to the early 1890s). As "bad man" ballads became increasingly popular in the late 1890s, the structural formula was used more and more often, and it acquired the standardized phrasing of songs of the "Frankie and Johnny" type.

In terms of harmony, the early twelve-bar blues ballads used widely differing chord sequences. This diversity is reflected in the published works of Hughie Cannon and his colleagues between 1900 and 1905 (and also in "The Bully Song" of the previous decade), which show a wide variety of harmonic approaches. Eventually, however, the "Frankie and Johnny" sequence came to predominate; indeed, the fact that it is the only sequence used more than once in the work of Cannon and others suggests that it was already becoming standard by the turn of the century. Over the same period, the "straight" blues sequence was starting to acquire a foothold in folk music. Evolving from the "Frankie" sequence, it was better suited to handle the greater emotional demands of the emerging blues genre. Its status was at first tentative, as is reflected in its rarity and lack of standardization in published music in the first decade of the century. However, that situation changed rapidly in the 1910s. In the first two or three years of the decade, both sequences appeared equally often in print, and after the start-up of the blues industry in 1912, the straight sequence suddenly became far more common. By the end the end of the decade, if not before, the "Frankie" sequence had all but died out in published sheet music. While the printed record presumably does not exactly mirror orally based folk culture, the narrative it provides is too coherent and too supportive of mainstream theories of the emergence of blues for it to be regarded as anything other than a highly revealing, if hitherto unrecognized, primary source of documentation tracing the early evolution of the genre.

My final point concerns the fundamental importance of ragtime to this evolution. Almost all proto-blues, whether songs or instrumentals, are based on ragtime. This is, perhaps, unsurprising. Ragtime was, after all, the medium for the dissemination of African American secular music in the mainstream before the rise of popular blues in 1912. Less obvious is the fact that the relationship between ragtime and proto-blues was two-way. A number of twelve-bar proto-blues, such as "The Bully Song," "Bill Bailey," "Ain't Dat a Shame," and "Just Because She Made Dem Goo-Goo Eyes," were among the most popular songs of their era. As thoroughly as any other compositions, they fanned the flames of the ragtime craze that swept America in the late 1890s and early 1900s.

• • •

Blues today are everywhere, their influence universal and undeniable. Almost every kind of Western vernacular music, from jazz to rock, from country to rap, Sinatra to Metallica, has been in part shaped by the genre. As Willie Dixon has so eloquently expressed it: "The blues are roots; everything else is the fruits."[72] The musicologist Susan McClary has expanded on this idea, describing the mainstream of all twentieth century Western music as a "mighty river . . . cut by a force known as the blues."[73] This chapter, then, has been a brief exploration of some of the streams that combined to create that river. In the process much has been revealed, I hope, that is of historical and musical interest. Beyond this, perhaps the greatest significance of this material—in fact of all the material examined in this book—is that it marks the first joyous celebration in American culture of an entirely new and uniquely potent genre—the blues. More than a century on, we are still celebrating.

APPENDIX: TITULAR BLUES, 1912–1915

Scope and Definition

This chronological appendix lists all known titular blues compositions published as sheet music in the United States from 1912 to the end of 1915. Titular blues are works that were originally titled using either the formula "(The) X Blues" (examples: "The Memphis Blues," "New York Tango Blues") or the formula "I've got the X blues" (examples: "I've Got the Blues," "I've Got the Weary Blues and Don't Know What to Do"). The listing shows all known versions of a composition to appear before 1921, a different version being defined as a change in one or more of the following: the title, the composer, the author, the copyright holder, the publisher, or the published status (i.e., when a work initially copyrighted in unpublished form is finally published). Items are listed in chronological order of copyright date as recorded in the copyright archives of the Library of Congress. Later versions of a composition are listed immediately below the initial version of the work regardless of the date when later versions were copyrighted. A bracket ({) in the left-hand margin connects two or more different versions of the same composition. A much more extensive version of this appendix appears on the book's website (longlostblues.com), listing all known titular blues up to 1921.

Explanation of Column Headings

COLUMN 1: © DATE. The copyright date of the composition presented according to the formula Month/Day/Year (for example, "12/4/14" means December 4, 1914). When a composition was not copyrighted, the fact is footnoted, and the date given is the date of publication as accurately as can be determined. This is usually to the nearest year, in which case the item is placed after the exactly dated entries for the year in question. An asterisk (*) placed before the date means that the version in question was unpublished.

COLUMN 2: TITLE. The full title of the composition as it appears on the Library of Congress copyright entry. Where the work was published but not registered for copyright, the title is taken from the printed sheet music. Where the composition is only known from recordings and/or piano rolls, the title is taken from the relevant labels; if it was not possible to consult these, the title is taken from a company catalog.

COLUMNS 3–4: WORDS AND MUSIC. Column 3 indicates the lyricist(s) (if any), and column 4 indicates the composer(s). All items originally appeared either as songs for voice and piano or as instrumentals for piano only, except where noted. If the item is an instrumental, column 3 is blank.

COLUMN 5: NAME & LOCATION OF © HOLDER. The name of the copyright holder along with its location. In the case of a published work, the copyright holder is usually the publisher. Where the two are different, the name of the copyright holder appears in column 5, and the publisher's name and location is identified in a footnote. When the work is published but not copyrighted, column 5 gives the name and location of the publisher.

1. © Date	2. Title	3. Words	4. Music	5. Name & Location of © Holder
1912				
01/12/12	Blues (The)[1]	Chris Smith	James T. Brymn (arr. Eugene Platzmann)	Shapiro Mus., New York
08/03/12	Baby Seals Blues: Sing 'Em— They Sound Good to Me	Franklin Seals	Franklin Seals (arr. Artie Matthews)	Seals & Fisher, St. Louis
08/06/12	Dallas Blues[2]		Hart A. Wand[3] (arr. M. Annabel Robbins)	Wand Pub., Oklahoma City, Okla.
—/—/12	Dallas Blues[4]		Hart A. Wand	Wand Pub., Oklahoma City, Okla.
—/—/18[5]	Dallas Blues	Lloyd Garrett	Hart A. Wand	Frank K. Root, Chicago
09/27/12[6]	Memphis Blues (The), or Mister Crump		W. C. Handy	W. C. Handy, Memphis[7]
11/10/13	Memphis Blues (The)	George A. Norton	W. C. Handy	Theron Bennett, New York
*11/09/12	Negro Blues	Le Roy "Lasses" White	Le Roy "Lasses" White	Le Roy "Lasses" White, Dallas
—/—/13	Nigger Blues	Le Roy "Lasses" White	Le Roy "Lasses" White	Le Roy "Lasses" White, Dallas[8]
1913				
*03/29/13	1913 Medley Blues		Alex M. Valentine, Jr.	Alex M. Valentine, Jr., Memphis [9]
12/01/13	1913 Medley Blues		Alex M. Valentine, Jr.	Hayworth Mus., Washington D.C.
06/06/13	Blues	Edna M. Burrows	Jack Stanley	E. M. Barrows, Little York, Ill.[10]
07/26/13	Jogo Blues (The)		W. C. Handy	Pace & Handy, Memphis.
09/08/13	I've Got the Blues	Philip Baxter	Philip Baxter	Philip Baxter, Carthage, Tex.[11]
1914				
*04/07/14	Florida Blues (The)		William K. Phillips	William K. Phillips, Jacksonville, Fla.
09/15/15	Florida Blues (The)		William K. Phillips	Florida Mus. Pub., Jacksonville, Fla.
—/—/16	Florida Blues (The)		William K. Phillips	Pace & Handy, Memphis
—/—/17	Florida Blues (The)		William K. Phillips	Florida Mus. Pub., Jacksonville, Fla.
01/04/17	Florida Blues (The)	Hezekiah Jenkins / Charles A. Jones	William K. Phillips	Pace & Handy, Memphis
05/11/14	Original Blues (The): A Real Southern Rag	Hezekiah Jenkins / Charles A. Jones	Ted S. Barron	Metropolis Mus., New York
05/23/14	New York Tango Blues		Willliam N. Spiller	Willliam N. Spiller, New York
07/24/14	Alamo Blues		Philip L. Eubank	Philip L. Eubank, San Antonio, Tex.
07/31/14	Long Lost Blues (The)	H. Alf Kelley	J. Paul Wyer (arr. W. H. Dorsey)	H. A. Kelley / J. P. Wyer, Chicago[12]
08/18/14	I've Got the Weary Blues and Don't Know What To Do	Johnnie Anderson / Jesse Smith	Johnnie Anderson / Jesse Smith	Hatch & Loveland, Los Angeles

1. © Date	2. Title	3. Words	4. Music	5. Name & Location of © Holder
09/11/14	St. Louis Blues	W. C. Handy	W. C. Handy	W. C. Handy, Memphis[13]
*10/06/14	Kansas City Blues		Euday L. Bowman	Euday L. Bowman, Fort Worth, Tex.
08/14/15	Kansas City Blues		Euday L. Bowman	Euday L. Bowman, Fort Worth, Tex.
—/—/15[14]	Kansas City Blues	George H. Bowles	Euday L. Bowman	J. W. Jenkins, Kansas City
10/12/14	Railroad Blues	Westbrook H. Carr	Westbrook H. Carr	Bush & Gerte, Dallas
*10/22/14	Colorado Blues		Euday L. Bowman	Euday L. Bowman, Fort Worth, Tex.
08/14/15	Colorado Blues		Euday L. Bowman	Euday L. Bowman, Fort Worth, Tex.
12/02/14	Yellow Dog Rag	W. C. Handy	W. C. Handy	W. C. Handy, Memphis[15]
—/—/19	Yellow Dog Blues[16]	W. C. Handy	W. C. Handy	W. C. Handy, New York[17]
—/—/14[18]	I Got the Blues	John C. McKinnon	John C. McKinnon	Syndicate Mus., St. Louis
1915				
01/18/15	Broadway Blues (The)	J. Brandon Walsh	Terry Sherman	Will Rossiter, Chicago
01/30/15	Bernard Hall Blues; or, Oh You Tutts Johnson		Morris Victor / Benjamin H. Homer	M. Victor, Baton Rouge, La.
02/18/15	Chinese Blues	Fred D. Moore	Oscar Gardner	Tell Taylor, Chicago
03/08/15	Original Chicago Blues (The)		James White	Frank K. Root, Chicago
05/04/15	Fort Worth Blues		Euday L. Bowman	Euday L. Bowman, Fort Worth, Tex.
05/05/15	Hesitating Blues (The)	W. C. Handy	W. C. Handy	Pace & Handy, Memphis
05/05/15	Hesitation Blues, or Oh! Baby Must I Hesitate	Scott Middleton / Billy Smythe	Scott Middleton / Billy Smythe	B. Smythe, Louisville, Ky
—/—/15	Hesitation Blues: One Step		Scott Middleton / Billy Smythe	B. Smythe, Louisville, Ky.
05/25/15	Tar-Heel Blues (The)[19]		J. Tim Brymn	Shapiro Bernstein, New York
06/18/15	Just Blues		Dorothy Harris	Dorothy Harris, Hondo, Tex.
08/29/15	Oklahoma Blues	Willard Robison/Bud Brownie	Bud Brownie	Bud Brownie, Tulsa, Okla.
10/29/15	Oklahoma Blues	Willard Robison	Willard Robison	Willard Robison, Tulsa, Okla.
09/22/15	Jelly Roll Blues (The)		Ferdinand Morton	Will Rossiter, Chicago
10/01/15	Snakey Blues (The)		William Nash	William Nash, Hot Springs, Ark.[20]
10/13/15	Old Kentucky Blues [fr. *George Washington Bullion Abroad*]	J. Homer Tutt / S. Tutt Whitney	James J. Vaughan	Joseph Stern, New York
*10/21/15	Tipperary Blues		Euday L. Bowman	Euday L. Bowman, Fort Worth, Tex.
01/05/16	Tipperary Blues		Euday L. Bowman	Euday L. Bowman, Fort Worth, Tex.

1. © Date	2. Title	3. Words	4. Music	5. Name & Location of © Holder
10/25/15	Weary Blues (The)		Artie Matthews	John Stark, St. Louis
11/06/15	Rice Hotel Blues		Jimmie Marten	Homer D. Matthew, Houston, Tex.
11/18/15	Bunch of Blues (A)		H. Alf Kelley / J. Paul Wyer	Will Rossiter, Chicago
*12/04/15	Coburn Blues		William K. Phillips	William K. Phillips, Jacksonville, Fla.
?—/—/18[21]	Coburn Blues		William K. Phillips	William K. Phillips, Jacksonville, Fla.
12/22/15	Joe Turner Blues	W. C. Handy	W. C. Handy	Pace & Handy, Memphis
—/—/15	Irish Blues— The Meanest Kind, The Greenest Kind	J. Brandon Walsh	Ernie Erdman	Will Rossiter, Chicago

1. Later adapted and published as a solo piano composition under the title "Tar-Heel Blues" (see entry for 05/25/15).
2. See also the entry for "Dallas Blues" (Leighton Brothers 01/02/17 in the full listing at www.longlostblues.com), which is musically related to this number.
3. The copyright entry for the original version gives the composer as anonymous, arranged by Robbins.
4. This version was never registered for copyright. It is musically distinct from the earlier version, with two separate sections rather than a single one.
5. This version was never registered for copyright. It is musically similar to the preceding version, but, unlike both earlier versions, has lyrics.
6. This edition was never registered for copyright. Publication date as given by Handy in *Father of the Blues*, 107.
7. Copyright transferred to Theron Bennett, New York, later in 1912 and published by him.
8. It would seem the first edition was published by White. At an unknown date (probably 1913–1914), the publisher changed to Gerts & Bush, Dallas.
9. This version is an arrangement for band.
10. Published by W. Kirkus Dugdale Co, Washington D.C.
11. Published by W. Kirkus Dugdale Co, Washington D.C.
12. Published by Chicago Music Bureau, Chicago.
13. Published by Pace & Handy, Memphis.
14. This edition was never registered for copyright.
15. Published by Pace & Handy, Memphis.
16. This, the retitled version of the work, was never independently registered for copyright. According to Hurwitt ("W. C. Handy as Music Publisher," 109), the work was referred to as a blues by the press from at least 1916.
17. Published by Pace & Handy, New York.
18. This item was never registered for copyright.
19. This composition is an instrumental adaptation of "The Blues" (1/11/12, q.v.).
20. Published by Pace & Handy, Memphis.
21. Published by W. C. Handy. The published version was not copyrighted, and the date of publication is uncertain: 1918 is suggested by Hurwitt ("W.C. Handy as Music Publisher," 571).

NOTES

A Word About the Music Examples

1. Muir, "Before 'Crazy Blues,'" 167.

Introduction

1. William W. Westcott, "City Vaudeville Classic Blues: Locale and Venue in Early Blues," in *Ethnomusicology in Canada: Proceedings of the First Conference on Ethnomusicology in Canada,* ed. Robert Widmer (Toronto: University of Toronto Press, 1990).

2. See, for instance, Charters, *The Country Blues,* 34–46; and Davis, *The History of the Blues,* 58–60.

3. See especially the work of Lynn Abbott and Doug Seroff, notably "'They Cert'ly Sound Good to Me,'" and *Ragged but Right.*

4. Muir, "Before 'Crazy Blues,'" 21–49.

5. Fred Hoyle, *Of Men and Galaxies* (Amherst, N.Y.: Prometheus Books, 2005), 58.

6. Wald, *Escaping the Delta,* 4.

7. Richard A. Reuss, *American Folk Music and Left-Wing Politics, 1927–1957* (Langham, Md.: Scarecrow Press, 2000), 19. The term *traditional* is often used to describe such music. However, I avoid this, since it suggests that such music is old: in fact, all the evidence suggests that the blues idiom developed quite rapidly around the turn of the century.

8. This definition, one of many used in writings about popular music, is discussed in Richard Middleton, "Popular Music/I. Popular Music in Europe & North America/1. Definitions," in *New Grove Dictionary of Music and Musicians,* 2nd ed.

9. Bradford, *Born with the Blues,* 115. Bradford is often not a particularly reliable witness, and this figure of 75,000 copies sold may well be an exaggeration, perhaps a considerable one; even so, the record must have sold well.

10. Giles Oakley, *The Devil's Music: A History of the Blues* (London: Ariel Books, 1983), 84.

Chapter 1. The Popular Blues Industry, 1912–1920

1. Gardner, *Popular Songs of the Twentieth Century,* 289, estimates the song to be the twenty-first most successful of the year.

2. Howard W. Odum, "Folk-Song and Folk-Poetry," 272.

3. "Too Mean to Cry Blues," Paramount 12496.

4. *Indianapolis Freeman,* April 16, 1910; quoted in Abbott and Seroff, "'They Cert'ly Sound Good to Me,'" 413.

5. Abbott and Seroff, "'They Cert'ly Sound Good to Me,'" 414; and Doug Seroff, interview with the author, July 8, 2005.

6. Lynn Abbott and Doug Seroff, "The Life and Death of Pioneer Bluesman Butler 'String Beans' May: 'Been Here, Made His Quick Duck, And Got Away,'" *Tributaries: Journal of the Alabama Folklife Association* 5 (2002): 15.

7. Ibid., 9. Italics in original.

8. Ibid., 15.

9. Ibid.

10. See longlostblues.com. See also appendix 1 in Muir, "Before 'Crazy Blues,'" 383–502.

11. For a more detailed discussion about the statistical relationship of instrumental to vocal blues, see Muir, "Before 'Crazy Blues,'" 374–75.

12. A discography and a rollography of blues recordings are to be found on this book's website, longlostblues.com. See also Muir, "Before 'Crazy Blues,'" Appendices 2 and 3, respectively.

13. Muir, "Before 'Crazy Blues,'" 548–90.

14. It is impossible to determine at this date piano roll sales with any precision. Probably the best indicator comes from the *U.S. Census of Manufactures* for the years 1914 and 1919, where annual sales of perforated music rolls (which included not just piano rolls, but also rolls for other instruments, such as mechanical organs) were only about 7 percent of cylinder and disc recordings combined. The figures are as follows: for 1914, $11.1 million for records, and $0.8 million for rolls; for 1919, $44.7 million for records, and $3.1 million for roles. *U.S. Bureau of the Census: Census of Manufactures* (Washington, D.C.: Government Printing Office, 1916, 1921).

15. Ibid.

16. See appendix 1 for details.

17. Handy, *Father of the Blues*, 106; see also Jasen and Jones, *Spreadin' Rhythm Around*, 232–35.

18. See Brooks, *Lost Sounds*, 415, for a different perspective than the straightforward tale of exploitation presented by Handy in *Father of the Blues*.

19. Handy, *Father of the Blues*, 109.

20. Brooks, *Lost Sounds*, 414.

21. Gardner, *Popular Songs of the Twentieth Century*, 305.

22. Abbe Niles, "The Story of the Blues," in *Blues: An Anthology*, ed. W. C. Handy, 19 (New York: Albert & Charles Boni, 1926).

23. Listed in Muir, "Before 'Crazy Blues,'" 513–14, 555–56.

24. This trend is shown by the following statistics: in the first four years of popular blues production (1912–15), 64 percent of blues were published in the South, while only 27 percent were published in the North (the remaining 9 percent appeared in the West and the Midwest). But for the second half of the decade, this situation reversed: over the years 1916–20, only 36 percent of blues were published in the South, while 60 percent were published in the North.

25. Of the 1912 batch, three were composed by blacks. Of the other two, White's "Nigger Blues," as its name would suggest, was undoubtedly of black origin, and this is also probably true of Wand's "Dallas Blues."

26. "Origin of 'Blues' Numbers," *Sheet Music News*, October 1923, 41.

27. The advertisement is on the back of "It's Nobody's Business But My Own," by Skidmore and Walker, published by Walker; however, it refers to Joseph Stern, one of the major New York publishers, as the exclusive selling agent. The blues listed are all published by Stern's company, though one of them, "I've Got the Army Blues," is in fact by the white partnership of L. Wolfe Gilbert and Carey Morgan.

28. "The Enigmatic Folksongs of the Southern Underworld," *Current Opinion* 67 (July–December 1919): 165.

29. Victor 18097.

30. I am grateful to Michael Garber for contextualizing the song (personal communication, February 3, 2008).

31. Abbott and Seroff, "'They Cert'ly Sound Good to Me,'" 409–11.

32. See discography on this book's website (longlostblues.com) for details of these recordings, or appendix 2 of Muir, "Before 'Crazy Blues.'" For discussion of Bernard's recording career, see Bernard's entry in Gracyk, ed., *The Encyclopedia of Popular American Recording Pioneers,* 40–42.

33. Abbott and Seroff, *Ragged But Right,* 211–12.

34. *Indianapolis Freeman,* November 9, 1912. Quoted in Abbott and Seroff, *Ragged But Right,* 177.

35. "J. C. Miles' Band And Minstrels," *Indianapolis Freeman,* May 16, 1914. Quoted Abbott and Seroff, *Ragged But Right,* 179.

36. Marshall Wyatt and Bengt Olssen, booklet essays (p. 47) to *Good for What Ails You: Music of the Medicine Shows 1926–1937,* Old Hat CD-1005.

37. Lawrence Gushee, *Pioneers of Jazz: The Story of the Creole Band* (New York: Oxford University Press, 2005), 289.

38. Columbia A2941, A2979, and A2877, respectively.

39. Brooks, *Lost Sounds,* 143. The number of records shipped means the number sent by the record company to retail outlets for sale. Not all of the items sent would necessarily have been sold, though presumably most would have been. Therefore, although the two figures may be similar, the number of records shipped is probably slightly greater than the number sold. No figures of any kind are available for "I'm Sorry I Ain't Got It, You Could Have It If I Had It Blues," though all of Williams's recordings were selling very well at this point in his career.

40. Information taken from Brooks, *Lost Sounds,* 353. Note that I have included Sweatman's "Slide, Kelly, Slide" (Columbia A2775) as a blues disc in this reckoning: the subtitle of this work is "Trombone Blues."

41. They are Artempo 12286; Rhythm E 17933; Universal 2335; Arto 228X; and Singa 5228.

Chapter 2. The Identity and Idiom of Early Popular Blues

1. Rudi Blesh, *Shining Trumpets: A History of Jazz* (New York: Knopf, 1946), 11–12.

2. Hughes Panassié, *The Real Jazz* (New York: Smith & Durrell, 1947), 21.

3. For more on the anticommercialism of blues commentators, see Muir, "Before 'Crazy Blues,'" 21–33.

4. See Oliver, *Songsters & Saints,* chap. 3.

5. See Wald, *Escaping the Delta,* esp. chap. 3.

6. Wald, *Escaping the Delta,* 58 and 292 fn. 27.

7. Ibid., 53–54.

8. See table 1.

9. Abbott and Seroff, "'They Cert'ly Sound Good to Me,'" 410.

10. I am oversimplifying here to make my point. Many folk blues are thematically cohesive, and indeed many folk blues artists recorded both noncohesive and cohesive types. Perhaps the most striking example is Blind Lemon Jefferson, whose recording career moved from the noncohesive to the cohesive type (Evans, *Big City Blues,* 75–81). Nevertheless, folk blues are at their most distinctive when thematically noncohesive. I should add that the term *thematically noncohesive* does not in any way imply a negative criticism; indeed, in writing about folk blues, such blues are usually aesthetically more valued than the cohesive type.

11. Memphis: W. C. Handy, 1914.

12. Chicago: Roger Graham, 1916.

13. Blind Blake, "Early Morning Blues," Paramount 12387, 1926. Transcribed by Titon, *Early Downhome Blues,* 73–74. This blues is in AAB format, so that the first line of each verse is repeated. I have omitted two spoken interjections on the repeat of the first line of the second and third verses.

14. For the circumstances surrounding the composition of the song, see Laurence Bergreen, *As Thousands Cheer: The Life of Irving Berlin* (New York: Viking, 1990), 81–85.

15. New York: Waterson, Berlin & Snyder.

16. Words and music by Lew Berk (Rochester, N.Y.: Lew Berk, 1916).

17. New York: F. B. Haviland.

18. Titon, *Early Downhome Blues,* 179.

19. Spoken during a performance at the 1969 Ann Arbor Blues Festival, Ann Arbor, Mich.; quoted Titon, *Early Downhome Blues,* 179.

20. Muir, "Before 'Crazy Blues,'" 115–16.

21. Words by Charles A. Mason, music by Charles S. Cooke and Richard M. Whiting (New York: Jerome Remick).

22. Note that in "Broadway Blues" (example 4), this process is reversed: in this song it is the place where the singer currently is (Manhattan) that gives the song its title, not the countryside he yearns for.

23. New York: Joseph Stern, 1917. For an excerpt from the song, see example 17.

24. Odum and Johnson, *Negro Workaday Songs,* 30.

25. Words by Arthur Holt, music by William T. Pierson (New York: William T. Pierson).

26. New York: Broadway Music Corp., 1918.

27. The disc, cylinder, and piano roll recordings are listed in Muir, "Before 'Crazy Blues,'" 537–38, 551.

28. See, for example, Oliver, *Blues Fell This Morning,* 153–61; and Titon, *Early Downhome,* 183–85.

29. Music by Mitch Le Blanc, words by Jimmie Marten (Houston: Thomas Goggan and Bro.).

30. General 4001, 1939.

31. Words and music by Eldon B. Spofford (San Francisco & New York: Earl Music Publishing).

32. New York: W. C. Handy, 1918.

33. Words and music by "Kid" Howard Carr, Harry Russell, and Jimmie Havens (New York: Shapiro Bernstein, 1918).

34. Words by Carey Morgan, music by Charles McCarron (New York: Broadway Music Corp., 1918).

35. The major study on the subject is Michael G. Garber, "Reflexive Songs in the American Musical."

36. New York: Theron Bennett, 1913.

37. The convention is examined in some depth in Garber, "Reflexive Songs in the American Musical," 62–96.

38. Words by Albert R. Cunha, music by John A. Noble (Honolulu: A. R. Cunha & J. A. Noble).

39. A clear link between the song version of "Memphis Blues" and "Alexander's Ragtime Band" is their shared tonal structure. One of the most distinctive features of "Alexander's Ragtime Band" is that the verse and chorus are in different keys, the chorus moving to the subdominant (F major). Berlin's song was not the first to use this structure, but it was certainly very unusual at the time. The song version of "Memphis Blues" uses an identical scheme with the verse in F and the chorus in B♭.

40. Discussed in Garber, "Reflexive Songs in the American Musical," 70–71.

41. Words by Jim Burris, music by Chris Smith (New York: Stern).

42. Memphis: W. C. Handy. I assume that the unusual title refers to the distinctive serpentine quintuplets in the first strain at mm. 1 and 4.

43. The use of this term is anomalous, for mood indications in English-based music scores are given either in Italian or English; the Italian equivalent is *luttuoso.*

44. Respectively: Ideal 6000, date unknown; and Columbia A-2421, 1917.

45. Published by Walter Jacobs, Boston. This work appeared in *The Tuneful Yankee,* the monthly house magazine of the publisher, vol. 1, no. 2 (February 1917): 19–21.

46. New York: Metropolis Music.

47. W. C. Handy, "How I Came to Write The 'Memphis Blues,'" *New York Age*, 7 December 1916, 6; quoted in Hurwitt, "W. C. Handy as Music Publisher," 114. As just discussed, "Snakey Blues" is an example of another instrumental blues that uses a blues sequence for two of its strains.

48. For further examples of the interchangeability between blues and ragtime, see Berlin, *Ragtime*, 158. Note also that Antonio Maggio's "I Got the Blues," the 1908 instrumental composition that was the first to associate the concept of having the blues with the twelve-bar sequence, is subtitled "An Up-to-Date Rag."

49. W. C. Handy, *Father of the Blues*, 198–99.

50. Muir, "Before 'Crazy Blues,'" 85.

51. Bryant, "Shaking Big Shoulders," 171. Bryant also mentions the claim of African American pianist-bandleader Hughie Woolford. I assume, however, that Woolford's involvement was at a musical, rather than a choreographic, level, and therefore that his claim is not relevant to the present inquiry.

52. Badger, *A Life in Ragtime*, 281 fn. 12.

53. The most detailed telling and examination of this account is Badger, *A Life in Ragtime*, 115. See also Samuel B. Charters and Leonard Kunstadt, *Jazz: A History of the New York Scene* (Garden City, N.Y.: Doubleday, 1962), 34.

54. Badger, *A Life in Ragtime*, 281 fn. 12.

55. "Castles Dance Foxtrot; Call It Negro Step," *New York Herald*, undated clipping (Fall 1914) in the Castle Scrapbooks, Billy Rose Theater Collection, New York Public Library; quoted in Badger *A Life in Ragtime*, 116.

56. "The Tango is of Negro Origin: All Late Dances Were Used by Colored People Before Whites Took Them Up," *Indianapolis Ledger*, January 30, 1915; quoted in Bryant, "Shaking Big Shoulders," 172.

57. Handy, *Father of the Blues*, 226.

58. Bryant, "Shaking Big Shoulders," 172–73.

59. For my understanding of the nature and evolution of the one-step, I am indebted to Richard Powers of the dance department of Stanford University (personal communication, April 2005).

60. Thornton Hagert, liner notes to the LP *Instrumental Dance Music 1780s–1920s* (New World Records, NW 293), 3.

61. Richard M. Stephenson and Joseph Iaccarino, *The Complete Book of Ballroom Dancing* (Garden City, N.Y.: Doubleday, 1980), 25.

62. Ibid., 27.

63. Another contender was another Latin dance, the maxixe, of Brazilian folk origin, which reached New York around the same time as the tango and remained popular throughout the decade. It was, however, even more specialized than the tango, and hence never gained widespread acceptance. Ibid., 44.

64. Hagert, *Instrumental Dance Music 1780s–1920s*, 3. Although these tempo indications are only approximations, this distinction of tempos was maintained for the fox-trot and one-step for most of the rest of the decade. There are hundreds of examples of dance records from the era where one side is labeled a fox-trot and the other a one-step. In such instances, the one-steps are nearly always performed faster than the fox-trots.

65. "Negro Composer on Race's Music," *New York Tribune*, November 22, 1914; quoted in Badger, *A Life in Ragtime*, 116. See also "Says Colored People First to Do Modern Dances," *Indianapolis Freeman*, March 16, 1915.

66. "Mr. and Mrs. Vernon Castle's New Dances for this Winter; III: The Castle Fox-trot," *Ladies*

Home Journal, December 31, 1914, 24; quoted in Badger *A Life in Ragtime,* 116. The step "Get Over, Sal," also known as "Get Over, Sally," is obscure. Marshall Stearns in *Jazz Dance: The Story of American Vernacular Dance* (1968; reprint New York: Da Capo, 1994), 108, discusses it in the context of the lyrics of Shelton Brooks's "Walkin' the Dog" (Chicago: Will Rossiter, 1916), the chorus to which begins: "Get 'way back and snap your fingers / Get over Sally one and all. / Grab your gal and don't you linger / Do that slow drag round the hall." Stearns defines the step as "a jump to the side, arms down, and fingers pointing to the floor" (108). This can scarcely be the move Castle had in mind, however; and, as Stearns does not cite a source for his definition, it is not possible to comment further, except to say that the proximity of the Get Over Sally to the slow drag in Brooks's lyric does suggest a possible association between the two. The only other references I have been able to find to the step are the following: a 1914 instrumental composition by Wallie Herzer titled "Get Over, Sal" (New York: Wallie Herzer); "Get Over Sally Blues," words and music by Ray Blick and Charley Straight (publication details unknown), where the title is never explained in the lyric; and James S. Sumner's lyric to Euday Bowman's "Twelfth Street Rag" (Kansas City: J. W. Jenkins, 1919), whose chorus starts: "First you slide, / and then you glide, / then shimmie for a while; / To the left, / then to the right, / 'Lame Duck,' 'Get Over Sal.'"

67. Lomax, *Land Where the Blues Began,* 364.

68. Ibid. Alan Lomax himself saw the slow drag danced in a Delta juke joint in the 1940s and vividly recalled its intimacy: "The couples, glued together in a belly-to-belly, loin-to-loin embrace, approximated sexual intercourse as closely as their vertical posture, their clothing, and the crowd around them would allow" (364).

69. New York: Shapiro, Bernstein & Co. Bevo was a popular nonalcoholic malt beverage brewed by Anheuser-Busch. It was first manufactured in 1916 and sales boomed during the Prohibition era until the late 1920s. See http://en.wikipedia.org/wiki/Bevo (accessed April 23, 2007). Therefore, this blues, although it does not have a lyric, is by implication an example of prohibition blues discussed earlier in this chapter.

70. Berlin, *Ragtime,* 147.

71. I am oversimplifying for the sake of clarity. In fact, the precise ratio between the two notes of the pair subtly varies even within the same performance. Studies have shown that the average, however, is very close to two-thirds to a third. See James Lincoln Collier *Jazz: the American Theme Song* (New York: Oxford University Press, 1993), 77–78.

72. By William H. Fry and John W. Yarborough (Brooklyn: Sterling Piano Co., 1915). The passage quoted is from the end of m. 16 through m. 20.

73. You can see a similar moment on m. 15 of example 7.

74. New York: Broadway Music Corporation, 1915.

75. For example, the Corrente of the Bb Partita BWV 825 (regarding this see the *Urtext* edition [Munich: G. Henle, no date], 114 fn. 1).

76. The earliest schottische I have been able to find using such notation is "Fifteen Dollar Schottische" by Harry Kennedy (Boston: Oliver Ditson, 1838). This score is available for inspection at http://levysheetmusic.mse.jhu.edu/otcgi/llscgi60 (accessed March 11, 2007).

77. By Lawrence B. O'Connor (Boston: Walter Jacobs).

78. Forth Worth, Tex.: Euday L. Bowman.

79. Kansas City: J. W. Jenkins' Sons Music Co. The arrangement is by C. E. Wheeler. See Berlin, *Ragtime,* 149–150.

80. I would stress that no two performances exactly correspond with example 14c. Each of these performances, however, is undoubtedly closer to example 14c than to either example 14a or b.

81. Columbia 35663.

82. Brunswick 3316.

83. Columbia A-3972.

84. Okeh 8051.

85. Aoelian Vocalion X-9044.

86. Chicago: Will Rossiter, 1915.

87. Solo recordings: Gennett 5552 (1924); Library of Congress Recordings, Circle 4 (1938); Vocal-style 50505 (1924, piano roll). Band recordings, Jelly Roll Morton's Red Hot Peppers: Victor 20405 (1926); Bluebird B-10255 (1926).

88. According to Morton, the piece was composed in 1905; see James Dapogny, ed., *Ferdinand "Jelly Roll" Morton: The Collected Piano Music* (Washington, D.C.: Smithsonian Institution Press, 1982), 293. If so, it would be fascinating to know if the piece was originally conceived in swing rhythm, or whether it began life with a regular ragtime "even eighths" feel and was later rhythmically transformed when swing rhythm was coming into fashion, perhaps around 1911.

89. Bryant, "Shaking Big Shoulders," 187–88.

90. Oscar Durea, "The Jazzed Fox-trot," *The Two-Step,* October 1917, 23–24; quoted in Bryant, "Shaking Big Shoulders," 187.

91. Chicago *Daily Tribune,* July 11, 1915, E8. I am indebted to Dr. Lawrence Gushee for drawing my attention to this article.

92. Muir, "Before 'Crazy Blues,'" 145.

93. There was a short period after the start-up of popular blues in 1912 when a number of pieces not called blues, but using the twelve-bar sequence, were published. That was because the blues sequence was not yet exclusively linked with the blues title. Such pieces are rightly considered proto-blues and are discussed in chapter 6 of this book. By 1914 it was established that pieces using the blues sequence were titled blues. The only exceptions I have come across between then and the end of 1920 are the first strain of the instrumental "The Kangaroo Hop," by Melville Morris (New York: Remick, 1915); "Morning Noon and Night," words and music by James White (Chicago: Will Rossiter, 1916), which is basically a blues, though not so titled, and uses a twelve-bar sequence in the first half of the verse; and "The Dirty Dozen," words by Jack Frost, music by Clarence M. Jones (Chicago: Frank Root & Co., 1917), also a blues in all but name, being the first manifestation in print of the blues song-type known as "The Dozens" or "Dirty Dozens" (see Peter Muir, "The Dirty Dozens," in *The Encyclopedia of the Blues,* ed. Edward Komara, 270 [New York: Routledge, 2006]).

94. New York: Metropolis Music, 1914.

95. Memphis: Pace & Handy.

96. New York: W. T. Pierson, 1916. In the example, I have omitted the four-bar introduction and two-bar repeated vamp for clarity's sake.

97. Handy, *Father of the Blues,* 143.

98. New York: Joseph Stern, 1917.

99. Lyrics by Al Wilson, music by Irving Bibo (New York: Irving Berlin Inc., 1920).

100. David Evans, "Blues," in *The Garland Encyclopedia of World Music.* Vol. 3, *The United States and Canada,* ed. Ellen Koskoff, (New York: Garland, 2001), 642.

101. Memphis: W. C. Handy, 1914.

102. The E♭ is here spelled as a D♯, as is conventional with blue thirds in published blues.

103. Notice that while the blues third resolves upward (here D♯–E), the blue seventh resolves downward (B♭–A). This is the strong tendency in both folk and popular blues.

104. For more detailed discussion on these issues, see Muir, "Before 'Crazy Blues,'" 159–62.

105. A comparison of popular blues and pop songs suggested that 88 percent of popular blues use blue notes as compared with 56.6 percent of pop songs. See Muir, "Before 'Crazy Blues,'" 159–162.

106. The term is suggested by the association of this device with the barbershop-quartet style; see, for example, Sigmund Spaeth, *Barber Shop Ballads: A Book of Close Harmony* (New York: Simon & Schuster, 1925), 18. I have not explored its roots, however, and would not want to suggest that it necessarily derived from that style. This type of cadence is also associated with African American sanctified music.

107. An earlier survey reported 35 percent as opposed to 16.5 percent. See Muir, "Before 'Crazy Blues,'" 165.

108. See Peter Muir, "Skip James," in *The Encyclopedia of the Blues,* ed. Edward Komara, 504 (New York: Routledge, 2006).

109. My earlier survey suggested the motif was used in 61 percent of popular blues, but only in 25 percent of non-blues. Muir, "Before 'Crazy Blues,'" 163.

110. The motif is also used in the 1913 song version of "The Memphis Blues" at the start of the chorus.

111. Muir, "Before 'Crazy Blues,'" 122.

112. New York: Palmetto Music Publishing, 1921. Although the work was not published until after our cut-off date for this study (December 31, 1920), it was copyrighted in November of the previous year, hence its inclusion here.

113. Words and music by L. Wolfe Gilbert and Carey Morgan (New York: Joseph Stern, 1916).

114. Words by Max C. Freedman, music by Harry D. Squires (New York: Jerome Remick, 1919).

115. Words and music by Charles A. Arthur (Detroit: Charles Arthur, 1920).

116. Words and music by Frank N. Vuille (Murphysboro, Ill.: Central Music Company, 1919).

117. They are: Mississippi John Hurt's "Got the Blues, Can't Be Satisfied" (Okeh 8724, 1928; transcribed in Titon, *Early Downhome Blues,* 76–78); and Blind Willie McTell's "Mama 'T'ain't Long fo' Day" (Victor 21474, 1927; transcribed in Titon, *Early Downhome Blues,* 101–02).

118. Taft, *The Blues Lyric Formula,* 193–94. Extracting from figures provided elsewhere in the same chapter, the travel formulas are found 1,675 times, the relationship formulas 1,050 times, but the "I have the blues" formula only 190 times.

119. I should mention in passing that all five of these devices are examples of what are called *topics* in semiotically oriented music analysis. Topics are defined as "patches of music that trigger clear associations with styles, genres, and expressive meanings" (Robert S. Hatten, *Interpreting Musical Gestures, Topics, and Tropes: Mozart, Beethoven, Schubert* [Bloomington: Indiana University Press, 2004], 2). Topical analysis of Tin Pan Alley–based jazz and blues material has been illuminatingly undertaken, notably by Jeffrey Magee in "'Everybody Step': Irving Berlin, Jazz, and Broadway in the 1920s," *Journal of the American Musicological Society* 59/3 (Fall 2006): 697–732. In this article, devices in Tin Pan Alley songs that are associated with blues, such as blue notes and the twelve-bar sequence, are termed (along with parallel devices that suggest ragtime or jazz) *black topics,* that is, topics with "African American resonance" (700). Note, however, that the four-note chromatic motif is slightly different from the examples Magee discusses, as it does not seem to be derived from African American styles, even though it is used in popular blues to suggest those styles. Furthermore, Magee's use of *topic* is limited to music and, as far as I am aware, would not include textual elements like "I've Got the Blues." I have elsewhere discussed these elements using a different paradigm, that of what the popular music historian Peter Van der Merwe terms *matrices,* with a *matrix* being defined as "one of the basic patterns that give coherence to a piece of music" (Van der Merwe, *The Origins of Popular Style,* 320). See Muir, "Before 'Crazy Blues,'" 173–78. Detailed examination of the five blues elements isolated here in terms of either Van der Merwe's matrices or Magee/Hatten's black topics is too theoretical for the scope of this discussion.

Chapter 3. Curing the Blues with the Blues

1. *The New Grove Dictionary of Music and Musicians,* 2nd ed., s.v. "Blues."

2. Harold Courlander, *Folk Music U.S.A.* (New York: Columbia University Press, 1963), 124.

3. I have abstracted the information in this paragraph from two sources: *New Grove Dictionary of Music and Musicians,* 2nd ed., s.v. "Tarantella" (by Erich Schwandt); and "Tarantism," in *Music as Medicine: The History of Music Therapy Since Antiquity,* ed. Peregrine Holden, 250–312 (Aldershot: Ashgate Publishing, 2000). The latter source is at this writing the fullest and most up-to-date treatment of this subject.

4. In fact, this is only a loose parallel—not an exact one. Whereas blues music is named for the condition of "having the blues," the tarantella was not named for tarantism; rather, both words are named for Taranto, a town in southern Italy. The etymological relationship between tarantella and tarantism is hence an indirect one.

5. Abstracted from the *Oxford English Dictionary,* 2nd ed.: "blue" (adj.), definitions 1a. and 2a.; also "blae" and "blo."

6. Theodore Thass-Thiemann, *The Interpretation of Language:* Volume 1: *Understanding the Symbolic Meaning of Language* (New York: Jason Aronson Inc., 1973), 306.

7. Ibid., 306–07. Thass-Thiemann also argues that there is an etymological connection between the two words. This argument, however, is controversial and is discredited by the *Oxford English Dictionary* ("blue" [adj.], etymology).

8. *Oxford English Dictionary,* 2nd ed.: "blue" (adj.), 3a.

9. Quoted in the *Oxford English Dictionary,* 2nd ed.: "blue devil," 2a.

10. Quoted in the *Oxford English Dictionary,* 2nd ed.: "blue" (noun), 12.

11. New York: E. B. Treat and Co.

12. New York: Putnam's Sons.

13. A. D. Rockwell, "Some Causes and Characteristics of Neurasthenia," *New York Medical Journal* 58 (1893), 590.

14. Francis G. Gosling, *Before Freud: Neurasthenia and the American Medical Community 1870–1910* (Urbana: University of Illinois Press, 1987), 10.

15. "The Problem of Finding a Cure for Our National Malady," *New York Times,* September 1, 1907; quoted in Gayle Sherwood, "Charles Ives and 'Our National Malady,'" *Journal of the American Musicological Society* 54, no. 3 (Fall 2001): 558.

16. Sherwood, "Charles Ives and 'Our National Malady,'" 560.

17. New York: E. B. Treat and Co., 1904.

18. Tom Lutz, "Curing the Blues: W. E. B. Du Bois, Fashionable Diseases and Degraded Music," *Black Music Research Journal* 11, no. 2 (Fall 1991): 141.

19. Quoted in Warren D. Anderson, *Ethos and Education in Greek Music: The Evidence of Poetry and Philosophy* (Cambridge, Mass.: Harvard University Press, 1966), 237 fn. 4.

20. Peter Holman, *Dowland: Lachrimae* (1604) (Cambridge: Cambridge University Press, 1999), 50.

21. Ibid., 51.

22. Richard Burton, *The Anatomy of Melancholy,* vol. 2 (London: Dent, 1932), 115.

23. Boston: W. F. Wellman.

24. For the Lyceum Theatre, Toledo, Ohio, October 1, 1904. I am grateful to Michael Montgomery for drawing my attention to this item.

25. Garber, "Reflexive Songs in the American Musical," 154–55. There are two qualifiers to Garber's discussion of the music-cures-blues motif in musicals. The first is that Garber is not just talking about music, but about music and dance that together form what he terms the music matrix,

the point being that the two modalities are so closely intertwined in the American musical that the presence of one nearly always implies the other (71). Thus songs that concentrate on the effects of dancing on alleviating the blues, of which there are many, are by implication simultaneously also discussing the effects of the music. For instance, in the 1914 song "Dancing the Blues Away" (words and music by Joe McCarthy, Howard Johnson, and Fred Fisher [New York: Leo Feist]), the title phrase refers not just to the curative effects of dancing but also by implication to the music that generated the dancing. The second qualifier to Garber's discussion of the music-cures-blues motif is that the unpleasant feelings that the music matrix dispels are not always referred to in the songs he examines as "the blues," although this is the most frequent term, but also by synonyms such as "troubles," "worries," "the Devil," "the jinx," and "the hoodoo" (175).

26. One of the most remarkable aspects of Garber's findings is just how common the music-cures-blues motif was to become in show songs. Although Garber does not give precise statistics regarding this topic, he does give figures for what he terms the "Come on and" song. This is a class of song whose lyrics invite the audience to become involved in the dramatic action, usually either by singing and dancing, or at least by observing the music and dancing on the stage. The invitation is typically presented in the trope "Come on and . . . ." Perhaps the most famous example is Irving Berlin's "Alexander's Ragtime Band" (1911), whose chorus begins "Come on and hear, / Come on and hear / Alexander's Ragtime Band." Most of the "Come on and" songs make use of the music-cures-blues idea, either explicitly or otherwise, as the reason for the audience's participation is usually to lose the blues (146–47). Therefore, the frequency of such songs is also a clear indicator of the prevalence of the music-cures-blues motif. Garber found that a remarkable 81 percent of the musicals in his survey use "Come on and" songs. This suggests that the music-cures-blues convention was extremely widespread in the American musical.

27. Gordon Seagrove, "Blues is Jazz and Jazz is Blues," *Chicago Daily Tribune,* July 11, 1915, E8. This is the remarkable article quoted in the previous chapter that contains the earliest known use of the word jazz in a musical context.

28. Words by George H. Bowles, music by Euday L. Bowman (Kansas City, Mo.: J. W. Jenkins).

29. Words by Isadore Murphy, music by Paul Biese and F. Henri Klickmann (Chicago: Frank K. Root).

30. This accounts for the finding reported in Garber's dissertation that, from the time of the jazz craze, there was a sharp rise in the number of show tunes whose lyrics use the music-cures-blues motif.

31. Words by Roger Lewis, music by Harry Olsen (New York: Witmark and Sons).

32. Paramount 12493, 1927.

33. Vocalion 03563, 1936.

34. *The American Heritage Dictionary of the English Language,* 4th ed., s.v. "Allopathy."

35. Laws, 790 e8–791 b1.

36. Politics, 1342a.

37. Ibid., translated by Benjamin Jowett. http://classics.mit.edu/Aristotle/politics.8.eight.html, accessed March 12, 2008.

38. *New Grove Encyclopedia of Music and Musicians,* 2nd ed., s.v. "John Dowland" (by Peter Holman, with Paul O'Dette).

39. Quoted by Holman, *Dowland Lachrimae* (1604), 52.

40. Ibid.

41. The lyrics to Dowland's songs are mostly anonymous. Although some may have been composed by him, most were probably not. He was, however, careful and very personal in the selection of his lyrics, so we can assume that his choices reflect his creative and expressive concerns as though

he had composed them himself. "He had a keen and sensitive ear for poetry," writes his biographer, "and a quick appreciation of such verses as were suitable for his purpose." Diana Poulton, *John Dowland* (Berkeley: University of California Press, 1972), 211.

42. Linda Phyllis Austern, "'No Pill's Gonna Cure My Ill': Gender, Erotic Melancholy and Traditions of Musical Healing in the Modern West," in *Musical Healing in Cultural Contexts*, ed. Penelope Gouk, 118 (Aldershot, Hants: Ashgate, 2000).

43. Modern edition in David Nadal (transcriber), *John Dowland's Lute Songs: Third and Fourth Books* (Mineola, N.Y.: Dover Editions, 2002), 130–34.

44. Aeolian Vocalion 12112, 1919.

45. W. C. Handy, "How I Came to Write the 'Memphis Blues,'" *New York Age,* December 7, 1916, 6; quoted in Hurwitt, "W. C. Handy as Music Publisher," 114. For further discussion of this quotation, see Muir, "Before 'Crazy Blues,'" 64.

46. Handy, *Father of the Blues,* 200.

47. Little Wonder 501. The work was recorded twice more before 1921, both times by Hawaiian groups (Pathé 20101, issued ca. March 1917, performed by Louise and Ferara Hawaiian Troupe; and Lyratone 4165, issued ca. September 1919, performed by the Kalawao Hawaiian Orchestra). However, I have not been able to audition these recordings to see whether they are also homeopathic. I also have found two recordings of the work made a few years later, again by Hawaiian guitar duos. These are Brunswick 2926, played by Palakiko and Paaluhi; and Edison 51616, played by Ferara and Paaluhi. Both these recordings are similar in mood to the Little Wonder record. The flipside of the Edison record, incidentally, is Handy's "St. Louis Blues."

48. Words by Jack Mahoney, music by Harold Bloom (New York: Harry von Tilzer).

49. "The Real American Folk Song (Is a Rag)," words by Ira Gershwin, music by George Gershwin. This song was from a Broadway show called *Ladies First,* but it was not published until 1959.

50. Taken from Garber, "Reflexive Songs in the American Musical," 178–79.

51. Words by Frank H. Warren, music by S. R. Henry (New York: Joseph Stern). Emphasis added.

52. Martin Petrey, "Music as a Medicine in the Home," *Ladies' Home Journal* 20 (1903): 49.

53. Mary Angela Dickens, "Margery," *All the Year Round,* third series, vol. 2, issue 33 (August 17 1889): 166. This extract is exceptional in that it explicitly valorizes the homeopathic approach over the allopathic.

54. Gene Lees, "How to Write Lyrics," in *Singers & the Song* (Oxford: Oxford University Press, 1987), 17–23.

55. See this book's online discography (at longlostblues.com) or Muir, "Before 'Crazy Blues,'" 530–31 for details.

56. New York: F. B. Haviland.

57. Paris Green is a common name for copper acetoarsonate, a deadly poisonous substance that has had a wide variety of uses, including as a rodenticide (at one time it was widely used to kill rats in Parisian sewers, hence its popular name). For further information, see http://en.wikipedia.org/wiki/Paris_green (accessed March 18, 2008).

58. Words by Al Bernard, music by H. Qualli Clark (New York: Pace & Handy, 1919).

59. Words and music by Johnny Cooper (Los Angeles: W. A. Quincke & Co.).

60. Words by J. Brandon Walsh, music by Ernie Erdman (Chicago: Will Rossiter, 1915).

61. Victor 18255, 1917.

62. Victor 18483, 1918.

63. Victor 18513, 1918.

64. Victor 18369, 1917.

65. Columbia A-2768, 1919.

66. Frederick Douglass, *My Bondage and My Freedom* (New York: Miller, Orton & Mulligan, 1855); quoted in Eileen Southern, ed., *Readings in Black American Music,* 2nd ed. (New York: Norton & Co, 1983), 84. Emphasis in original.

67. Ibid.

68. Michael T. Coolen, "Senegambian Influences on Afro-American Musical Culture," *Black Music Research Journal* 11, no. 1 (Spring 1991): 8.

69. Ibid., 6, 7.

70. Joseph J. Shipley, *The Origins of English Words: A Discursive Dictionary of Indo-European Roots* (Baltimore: John Hopkins University Press, 1984), 33; American Heritage Dictionary, 4th ed., 2022.

Chapter 4. The Blues of W. C. Handy

1. The place to start with Handy studies is his autobiography *Father of the Blues.* The most important commentary on Handy includes the following: Hurwitt, "W. C. Handy as Music Publisher: Career and Reputation," an admirably thorough and well-researched account of his business affairs but with limited discussion of his music; Hurwitt's "William Christopher Handy," in *International Dictionary of Black Composers,* which offers an excellent summary of Handy's life and career, a complete list of his works, and some detailed discussion of several of his blues; Brooks, *Lost Sounds: Blacks and the Birth of the Recording Industry, 1890–1919,* which includes an excellent chapter on Handy's early recordings; and Jasen and Jones, *Spreadin' Rhythm Around: Black Popular Songwriters, 1880–1930,* which includes a fairly detailed examination of Handy's career focusing on his songs. It is surprising that there has so far been no book-length study of Handy, given his profound importance in American culture. I suspect that in part this is due to the controversial nature of his posthumous reputation, a point discussed at the end of this chapter. The only two books exclusively devoted to him, Richard Cooper's *W. C. Handy: Doctor of the Blues* (Raleigh, N.C.: Creative Productions, 1987) and Elizabeth Rider Montgomery's *William C. Handy: Father of the Blues* (Champaign, Ill.: Garrard, 1973), are both potted biographies for children.

2. This approach was found in another early southern blues, Will Nash's "Snakey Blues," published by Handy in 1915 (see example 5; this work has four strains so that its form is ABCD).

3. The only exception that I am aware is the piano rag version of Chris Smith's "Monkey Rag" from 1911, which, like "The Memphis Blues," uses a twelve-bar sequence for two of its three strains. However, the second of those strains uses a chord sequence that is far removed from regular blues. See Muir "Before 'Crazy Blues,'" 346–51.

4. Niles, "Introduction," 8.

5. See Berlin, *Ragtime: A Musical and Cultural History,* 130–34.

6. The melody of the B strain, mm. 9–12, is also based on secondary ragtime rhythms.

7. Handy, *Father of the Blues,* 93.

8. "Mr. Crump Don't Like It" (Paramount 12552, 1927). One other recording is known, a field recording made for the Library of Congress in 1940 by an old-timer called Noah Moore ("Mr. Crump Don't 'Low It Here").

9. Meade, *Country Music Sources,* 552. Meade lists eight hillbilly recordings. Probably the most important black versions are by Papa Charlie Jackson ("Mama Don't Allow It," Paramount 12296, 1925) and Cow Cow Davenport ("Mama Don't Allow No Easy Riders Here," Vocalion 1434, 1929).

10. The main difference between the second and third versions is harmonic. The third version uses essentially the same sixteen-measure chord sequence as Handy's. The chord sequence of the

second version is also sixteen measures long and consists of the last eight measures of Handy's third version played twice. The first version, incidentally, uses an entirely unrelated chord sequence.

11. Handy, *Blues: An Anthology*, 207.

12. For example "When Sousa Comes to Coon-Town," words by Alex Rogers, music by James Vaughn and Tom Lemonier (New York: Shapiro Bernstein, 1902) and "Sousa's Band is On Parade Today," words by "Add-Vance," music by Charles Kohlman (New York: Paul Dresser, 1905).

13. Handy, *Father of the Blues*, 117.

14. Performed by Prince's Band (Columbia A-2327, 1917).

15. Niles, "Introduction," 31.

16. Ibid., 31–32. Notice that the cell (example 37) uses the same pitches as the three-note motif underlying the breaks in the C strain of "The Memphis Blues" (examples 32 and 33): blues third, regular third, and root. The difference is that the "Jogo Blues" cell *falls* to the root, whereas the "The Memphis Blues" motif *rises* to it. What they also have in common is that they constantly reiterate the motif to build tension (it is used five times in a row for both of the "The Memphis Blues" breaks and five times for the first line [four measures] of the "Jogo Blues" A strain).

17. Handy, *Father of the Blues*, 117–18.

18. Handy composed a parlor song around the same time as "Jogo Blues" called "The Girl You Never Have Met," with words by his business partner Harry Pace (Memphis: Pace & Handy, 1913). Since it was copyrighted at exactly the same time as "Jogo Blues," it is impossible to ascertain the order in which they were composed. The two songs represent opposite poles of Handy's creativity: "The Girl You Never Have Met" is as musically unadventurous as "Jogo Blues" is experimental.

19. Alec Wilder, *American Popular Song: The Great Innovators, 1900–1950* (New York: Oxford University Press, 1990), 20.

20. Jasen and Jones, *Spreadin' Rhythm Around*, 235.

21. Handy, *Father of the Blues*, 118–21.

22. Hurwitt, "William Christopher Handy," 555.

23. Handy, *Father of the Blues*, 123.

24. *Ibid.*, 119.

25. Maggio made this claim in a 1955 article in *Overture*, the magazine of the Los Angeles Musicians' Union (Local 47). The article is quoted and discussed in Hurwitt, "W. C. Handy as Music Publisher," 479–81.

26. Quoted in Hurwitt, "W. C. Handy as Music Publisher," 481.

27. Abbott and Seroff, "'They Cert'ly Sound Good to Me,'" 406.

28. Handy, *Father of the Blues*, 51–53.

29. *Ibid.*, 97–98.

30. Handy mentions the disguised use of the Latin feel in "The Memphis Blues" in *Father of the Blues*, 120. He seems to be referring to the passage quoted in example 44, where the left hand implies a *habanera* figure of two dotted eighth notes followed by an eighth note.

31. Other blues by Handy using Latin rhythms are "Loveless Love" (1921), "Harlem Blues" (1923), "Sundown Blues" (1923), "Friendless Blues" (1926), and "Blue Gummed Blues" (1926).

32. Morton made this statement in 1938 in an extended interview with ethnomusicologist Alan Lomax for the Library of Congress. The interviews were first issued commercially on the Circle label in the 1940s, and the remark quoted is to be found on Circle 28 (matrix 1682).

33. The issue is examined in some detail in John Szwed, *Doctor Jazz*, the accompanying booklet to *Jelly Roll Morton: The Complete Library of Congress Recordings by Alan Lomax* (Rounder, 2005), 33–36.

34. Handy, *Father of the Blues*, 119.

35. *Ibid.,* 74.

36. It was also featured in the very first popular blues, Smith and Brymn's "The Blues" from 1912.

37. "Easy Rider," in *Random House Dictionary of American Slang* (New York: Random House, 1994).

38. I should add, however, that the term "jockey" is a slang word for penis (see the first entry for "Jockey" in *Random House Dictionary of American Slang*). Thus, the song's reference to Susan Johnson's lover as her "jockey Lee," while at one level defusing the sexual implications of the song's title, at another level reinforces it.

39. In fact, I suspect that Norton's use of the device (and therefore Handy's indirectly) derives form an earlier commercial source, Hart A. Wand's "Dallas Blues" (1912); the relevant passage is quoted in example 23.

40. Handy, *Father of the Blues*, 198–199.

41. The recording is by comedian Morton Harvey, with piano accompaniment (Emerson 729, 1915). It was Harvey who had made the first vocal recording of "The Memphis Blues" the previous year for Victor.

42. Handy, *Father of the Blues*, 144–45.

43. Transcription in Taft, *Talkin' to Myself*, 270.

44. "The Hesitation Blues," on *Leadbelly's Last Sessions, Part 3* (Folkways FA 2942). The song is first appears in early 1913, when black vaudevillians George and Nana Coleman were performing it at the Dreamland Theater in Waco, Texas, under the title "How Long Must I Wait?" (Abbott and Seroff, "'They Cert'ly Sound Good to Me,'" 442; it is assumed by the title, though it is not known for certain, that this is the same song that Handy's version was based on).

45. Abbe Niles, "The Story of Blues," in Handy, *Blues: An Anthology,* 34.

46. Published by the composers.

47. White, *American Negro Folk-Songs*, 325–26, 339, and 398. For discussion of these, see Evans, *Big Road Blues,* 61.

48. Published by the composer in Philadelphia.

49. William Broonzy and Yannick Bruynoghe, *Big Bill Blues: William Broonzy's Story* (1964; reprint, New York: Da Capo, 1992), 56.

50. Abbe Niles, "Introduction," 36.

51. Handy, *Father of the Blues*, 145–46.

52. Odum, "Folk-Song and Folk-Poetry as Found in the Secular Songs of the Southern Negroes," 255–94, 351–96, 351.

53. Handy, *Father of the Blues,*146.

54. Broonzy and Bruynoghe, *Big Bill Blues,* 56–59.

55. Words and music by Rowland Howard (St. Louis: Balmer and Weber, 1872). Some measure of the song's success can be gauged from the fact that three pirated versions are known, all from 1874: two from New York, and one from the West Coast. These can be viewed along with the original at the following web site http://memory.loc.gov/ammem/mussmhtml/mussmhome.html.

56. Of the ten recordings of the work made before 1921, eight called the work "Beale Street Blues"; only two used the original title (see Muir, "Before 'Crazy Blues,'" 509–10, for details).

57. In June 1916, six months before "Beale Street Blues," Handy copyrighted a three-strain piano rag called "Ole Miss." This work is sometimes confused with a blues, and indeed it was included in the second edition of *Blues: An Anthology*. However, unlike "Yellow Dog Blues," which is a blues by most definitions of the word, "Ole Miss" really is a rag and not a blues. Certainly it lacks what for Handy was the defining quality of his instrumental blues: having at least one strain that uses the

twelve-bar format. For this reason it is not included in the discussion here. Note also that the piece was only termed a blues in the vocal edition of the work that appeared ca. 1920. The confusion may in part stem from the indication "A la Blues," which heads the second strain in the original edition. This indication apparently refers to the fact that the strain makes prominent use of blue notes in the melody for six of its sixteen bars.

58. Words and music by Charles B. Lawlor and James W. Blake (New York: Howley, Haviland & Co., 1894). For a discussion about the phenomenon of songs celebrating the city, see Garber, "Reflexive Songs in the American Musical, 1898–1947," 179–90.

59. Handy must have been inspired in this by George Norton's lyric to "The Memphis Blues": the first verse begins with a brief celebration of Memphis ("that's where the people smile on you / smile on you all the while"). Despite its name, however, "The Memphis Blues" is far more a celebration of Handy's band and the blues than it is of Memphis: the notion of having Memphis as the prime focus of a song seems to have been Handy's own.

60. To give one measure of the relative popularity of the two works: Tom Lord's *Jazz Discography*, the most chronologically and stylistically comprehensive of the various jazz discographies, lists nearly 1500 recordings of "St. Louis Blues" (www.lordisco.com/tunes/S38.html) as compared with ca. 340 for "Beale Street" (www.lordisco.com/tunes/B8.html; both web pages accessed May 15, 2008)

61. Handy, *Father of the Blues,* 169.

62. Ibid., 178–85.

63. In 1917 Handy published an instrumental work by black clarinetist Douglass Williams titled "The Hooking Cow Blues." Handy is listed as co-composer in some sources. However, according to Abbe Niles ("Introduction," 35), Handy's role was merely as arranger, although he added an eight-bar section tagged to the end of the chorus depicting the bellows of the steer (farmyard calls were all the rage following the success of the Original Dixieland Jazz Band's recording of "Livery Stable Blues" for Victor earlier in the year). Overall, the work is Williams's, not Handy's, and hence it is not included in the discussion here.

64. Handy, *Father of the Blues,* 149.

65. Niles, "Introduction," 34

66. Scarborough, *On the Trail of Negro Folk-Songs,* 271–72.

67. Hurwitt, "William Christopher Handy," 554.

68. Handy, *Father of the Blues,* 133.

69. According to Tim Brooks, by the end of 1920, 51 different recordings of Handy songs had been made (*Lost Sounds,* 423).

70. The early reception of Handy's blues is discussed in Hurwitt, "W. C. Handy as Music Publisher," 99–128.

71. For a discussion of the publicity campaign for the recordings and their sales, see Brooks, *Lost Sounds,* 418–21.

72. Scarborough, *On the Trail of Negro Folksongs,* 264–73.

73. The affair is discussed in Hurwitt, "W.C. Handy as Music Publisher," 419–27.

74. Szwed, *Doctor Jazz,* 13.

Chapter 5. The Creativity of Early Southern Published Blues

1. The main exceptions are major Tin Pan Alley composers trying their hands at the new idiom. Perhaps the outstanding example within the period is Jerome Kern's "Left All Alone Again Blues," one of the most successful pop songs of 1920, which was discussed in chapter 1 (example 3). At their best, such songs are, in their own way, as creative as the southern type of blues.

2. "Baby Seals Blues" was registered for copyright on August 3, "Dallas Blues" on August 6. Note,

however, that the order of copyright does not necessarily reflect the order in which they were published, and so it is possible that "Dallas Blues" appeared for sale before "Baby Seals Blues." Indeed, according to the composer, who was interviewed in the 1950s by the historian Samuel Charters, "Dallas Blues" was published as early as March 1912 (*The Country Blues,* 34). That would make it the first blues to be published after Smith and Brymn's "The Blues" in January of that same year. However, Wand's assertion is problematic. The main evidence given is that the copy of the work registered for copyright in the Library of Congress has printed at the bottom of the first page of music that it is the "third edition." The argument then is that the work was copyrighted only after the first two editions had sold out. In fact, I have compared several of these different "editions," which are all identical. Thus "edition" here, if it means anything at all, can only refer to the print run. In Charters's interview with Wand, the latter claimed the first two print runs sold out very quickly, the first in less than a week, the second almost as fast. If the work was really published in March and the first two printings sold out in less than three weeks, why had the third printing not sold out by August? The greatest likelihood is that Wand is not a reliable source, a suspicion reinforced by his dubious claims to the work's authorship, discussed below.

3. Abbott and Seroff, "'They Cert'ly Sound Good to Me,'" 418.

4. As a rule, the only popular songs from the era routinely published as vocal duets were those taken from musicals or revues.

5. Paramount 12354 (1926), take 2, verse 4. The lyric is transcribed in Titon, *Early Downhome Blues,* 113.

6. Abbott and Seroff, "'They Cert'ly Sound Good to Me,'" 419–22.

7. K. C. E., "New Crown Garden," *Freeman,* October 5, 1912, 5; quoted in Abbott and Seroff, "'They Cert'ly Sound Good to Me,'" 418.

8. "Sing 'Em Blues," Okeh 8124, 1923.

9. Abbott and Seroff, "'They Cert'ly Sound Good to Me,'" 421.

10. See www.lordisco.com/tunes/D1.html (accessed May 15, 2008).

11. 88–Note 65950, unknown date.

12. This new melody is in fact related to the original, with mm. 7–11 of each being essentially the same (compare mm. 7–11 of examples 55 and 57). The second edition of "Dallas Blues," incidentally, is rather mysterious: the sheet music is extremely rare—more so than the other versions—and it is not clear for what purpose it was produced or exactly when. The only recording is by Wilbur Sweatman (Columbia A-2663, 1918).

13. Charters, *The Country Blues,* 35.

14. These versions are discussed in Abbott and Seroff, "'They Cert'ly Sound Good to Me,'" 408–09, 411–12.

15. Dugdale was also the publisher of Baxter's "I've Got the Blues." For details of the company, see www.songpoemmusic.com/dugdale.html (accessed February 13, 2007).

16. Library of Congress registration number Cl E 305797.

17. Valentine was the arranger for the 1916 copyright deposit of Charles Hillman's "Preparedness Blues," which was published by Handy the following year. This fact does not imply any direct relationship between Handy and Valentine—just between Hillman and Valentine.

18. Handy, *Father of the Blues,* 100.

19. Brief biography in *The ASCAP Biographical Dictionary of Composers, Authors, and Publishers,* 2nd ed. (New York, Thomas Y. Crowell, 1952).

20. Bruce Vermazen, *That Moaning Saxophone: The Six Brown Brothers and the Dawning of a Musical Craze* (Oxford: Oxford University Press, 2004), 69.

21. This background comes from Abbott and Seroff, "'They Cert'ly Sounds Good to Me,'" 443–44.

22. Muir, "Before 'Crazy Blues,'" 297–304.

23. Library of Congress registration number Cl E 347980.

24. "Porter's Rag," incidentally, bears more than a little resemblance to Euday L. Bowman's "Twelfth Street Rag," published earlier in the year in nearby Fort Worth.

25. There is a question with Bowman's works as to whether their dates of copyright registration (the dates quoted here) reflect the dates of their creation. It is conceivable that a number of them predate their registration by some time, perhaps years. In this line of argument, Bowman simply copyrighted the works for publication and, being of limited means and publishing the works himself, did so piecemeal in order to stagger the costs of printing and distribution. It is more likely, however, that he copyrighted each work shortly after its completion, in which case the copyright dates would reflect the dates of composition fairly accurately. The only work possible to date with reasonable certainty is "Kansas City Blues," copyrighted August 1915, which, since it quotes Handy's "Yellow Dog Blues," must have been written after the publication of the latter at the end of 1914. Even then, however, one cannot be sure about this: it is possible—though unlikely—that there is no direct relationship between the works, but rather that they simply borrow from the same folk material. If so, "Kansas City Blues" could theoretically predate "Yellow Dog Blues."

26. In Richard Zimmerman, *Gems of Texas Ragtime* (Grass Valley, Calif: American Ragtime Company, 1996). This anthology contains all of Bowman's known ragtime and blues compositions from the 1910s.

27. According to Tim Brooks, a remarkable 180,000 copies of this recording were shipped (*Lost Sounds*, 348).

28. The only obvious blues reference in Bowman's rags is the use of the theme "Make me a Pallet on the Floor" in his unpublished "Tenth Street Rag" (1914). However, despite the fact that this theme was later published under the title "Atlanta Blues" by W. C. Handy, it is strictly speaking a proto-blues, not a blues, and uses a sixteen-bar rather than a twelve-bar structure. Interestingly, the distinctive chord sequence of this theme was also used by Bowman in the introductions to "Eleventh Street Rag" (1918) and "Twelfth Street Rag" (1914), although in both of these instances the melodies employed are different from the familiar version of the theme. For further details, see Peter C. Muir, "Make Me a Pallet on the Floor," in *Encyclopedia of the Blues,* ed. Edward Komara (New York: Routledge, 2006).

29. See Muir, "Before 'Crazy Blues,'" 363–64.

30. For discussion on this point, see Peter C. Muir, "Blind Lemon Jefferson," in *Encyclopedia of the Blues.*

31. There are two other blues by Thomas known from this period: "Cuban Blues" (ca. 1917), mentioned on the 1917 published edition of "New Orleans Hop Scop Blues," and "I've Got the Aggravating Blues" (ca. 1919), known only from a coin-operated piano roll. Neither song was copyrighted, and no copy of "Cuban Blues" has ever been found. The only known copy of the piano roll with "I've Got the Aggravating Blues" was not available for inspection.

32. I am grateful to John Penney of Detroit for providing me with accurate biographical information about Thomas, drawn from his and Ron Harwood's forthcoming book about the Thomas family.

33. Michael Montgomery, "The Several Editions of 'New Orleans Hop Scop Blues,'" unpublished article.

34. The editions of 1919 and 1923 also include a conventional vamp between the introduction and verse.

35. Peter Silvester, *A Left Hand Like God: The Story of Boogie-Woogie* (London: Quartet Books, 1988), 47. The extract from House and Patterson's "Blues" quoted in example 66 uses an equally

idiomatic boogie bass-line and was copyrighted two years before "New Orleans Hop Scop Blues." It was, however, never published.

36. *Boogie Woogie Blues* (New York: Clarence Williams, 1940).

37. See discussion in Silvester, *A Left Hand Like God,* 47–52.

38. All recordings of the work, including Waller's, used the song version as their basis: the original version for piano, being unpublished, was, as far as I know, never recorded.

39. There are only two major sources for biographical and musical commentary for Bradford. The first is his autobiography, *Born With the Blues,* a colorful, if rather rambling and embittered, memoir. The other is the section devoted to him in Jasen and Jones, *Spreadin' Rhythm Around* (255–78). This is a much more balanced account of Bradford's career, with some serious discussion of his music.

40. The account of the "Crazy Blues" recording session by the session's pianist, Willie "the Lion" Smith, downplays Bradford's role. However, Jasen and Jones have persuasively argued that Smith's account is inaccurate in this regard (*Spreadin' Rhythm Around,* 263–64).

41. This work bears no relationship to Bradford's 1921 published composition of the same title.

42. Bradford, *Born with the Blues,* 96, 99.

43. In doing so, of course, Bradford fundamentally departs from the *musical* approach of traditional blues, which typically uses the same music for every stanza, providing a fundamental coherence to the song no matter how wayward the lyrics.

44. It is inaccurate to suggest, as Bradford does in his autobiography, that "Crazy Blues" is essentially "Harlem Blues" with the title changed (*Born with the Blues,* 124–25).

45. This is suggested by the fact that considerably more cover versions were recorded of "Crazy Blues." As late as 1938, for instance, the vocalist Georgia White recorded a version of "Crazy Blues" (Decca 7807) closely modeled on Smith's recording.

46. Jasen and Jones, *Spreadin' Rhythm Around,* 278.

47. His authorship of this song is disputed. See Jasen and Jones, *Spreadin' Rhythm Around,* 169–70.

48. The melodic use of riffs had previously only been used very rarely in ragtime compositions like Euday Bowman's "Twelfth Street Rag" (1915).

Chapter 6. Published Proto-Blues and the Evolution of the Twelve-Bar Sequence

1. See Muir, "Before 'Crazy Blues,'" 189–91, for a discussion of this evidence.

2. Troy, N.Y.: Firth, Pond & Co.

3. Brooklyn: J. W. Smith, Jr.

4. Quoted in Dale Cockrell, *Demons of Disorder: Early Blackface Minstrels and Their World* (Cambridge: Cambridge University Press, 1997), 201. The article later appeared in the *Boston Post* on January 1, 1840.

5. Published by Tell Taylor, Chicago. Another example from the 1910s is a line from the chorus of John E. McKinnon's "I Got the Blues" (St. Louis: Syndicate Music, 1914): "I'm blue, blue as indigo blues." A more famous, though later, example of this image is Duke Ellington's "Mood Indigo" (1930). Note also the following line in the first verse of Chapman's "Oh, Ain't I Got the Blues!": "The sky is 'blue' as indigo; The ground is black as ink."

6. Cockrell, *Demons of Disorder,* 201.

7. New York: Lyceum Publishing.

8. Detroit: Grinnell. This song is discussed in Muir, "Before 'Crazy Blues,'" 217–18.

9. Papa Charlie Jackson, "I'm Alabama Bound" (Paramount, 1925); Jelly Roll Morton "Don't You Leave Me Here" (General, 1939); Blind Lemon Jefferson, "Elder Green's in Town" (Okeh, 1927); Charlie Patton, "Elder Green Blues" (Paramount, 1929). The song was widely known throughout the

South before World War I. See Oliver, *Songsters and Saints,* 296, fn. 10, and 115–17 for fuller discussions. The song has, incidentally, no connection with the 1924 song-hit "Alabamy Bound" by the Tin Pan Alley team of DeSylva, Brown, and Henderson.

10. For further discussion on the history of the song, see Muir "Before 'Crazy Blues,'" 220.

11. For details of Cannon's published proto-blues, see Muir "Before 'Crazy Blues,'" 223.

12. "Song Writer Cannon Was Devoted Son," *Daily Courier* (Connelsville, Penn.), November 11, 1971.

13. Ed. F. Smith, "Well, Anyhow," *Jackson Citizen Patriot,* April 23, 1944.

14. Gardner, *Popular Songs of the Twentieth Century,* 252.

15. Aside from the sources already named, biographical information about Cannon is taken from a series of articles by Don Durst that appeared in the *Jackson Citizen Patriot,* January 29–February 8, 1966. Other sources on Cannon include: Untitled and unattributed article, *The Referee* (San Francisco), January 29, 1910; "Stencils and Booze His Undoing," *The Presto,* February 10, 1910; "Yes, Bill Bailey Has Gone Home," *Toledo Blade,* June 18, 1912; George Swetnam, "How 'Bill Bailey' Came Home," *Pittsburgh Press,* July 25, 1965; Alice Jarrett, "Young Musician Delves Into History of Noted Song Writer Hughie Cannon," *Daily Courier* (Connelsville, Penn.), November 10–12, 1971. There is also one scholarly study of Cannon's work, a privately distributed newsletter of the Vernacular Music Research Center, Arlington, Virginia, dated March 24, 1971; it was written by Thornton Hagert and contains a serious discussion of Cannon's contribution to the twelve-bar sequence, along with a list of his published compositions.

16. The songs are listed in Muir, "Before 'Crazy Blues,'" 223. The exception is "Alic Busby, Don't Go Away" (1904), which uses an expanded form of the twelve-bar sequence for its chorus (247).

17. This system of structural analysis of blues and blues-related music is taken from Titon, *Early Downhome Blues,* 141–42.

18. For a review of the research supporting this theory, see Muir, "Before 'Crazy Blues,'" 242 fn. 65.

19. Laws, *Native American Balladry,* 240.

20. See Cecil Brown, *Stagolee Shot Billy* (Cambridge, Mass.: Harvard University Press, 2003), and George M. Eberhart, "Stack Lee: The Man, the Music, and the Myth," *Popular Music and Society* 20, no. 1 (Spring 1996): 1–70. The song occurs in several different forms. However, the main version is closely related to "Frankie and Johnnie," even at times using the same melody (Eberhart, 37).

21. John Garst, "The Ballad of Delia Green and Moses 'Cooney' Houston," http://hem.passagen .se/obrecht/backpages/chords/36_wgw/ballad_of_delia_green.htm (accessed September 15, 2007).

22. Oliver, *Songsters and Saints,* 250. The boll weevil is here seen as a metaphorical outlaw because of its ruinous behavior. Oliver suggests that the popularity of the song among blacks stemmed from its symbolism: "[the boll weevil's] indestructibility, its covert behavior, attacking the white crop from within had its symbolic appeal" (250).

23. In addition to these five songs, there is also "I Wonder Why Bill Bailey Don't Come Home" (1902) by Frank Fogerty, Matt C. Woodward, and William Jerome. As its title suggests, it fits into the narrative between "Bill Bailey, Won't You Please Come Home" and "Since Bill Bailey Came Home." However, neither music nor text is related to proto-blues.

24. Muir, "Before 'Crazy Blues,'" 287–88.

25. "Ain't Dat a Shame" was apparently the thirteenth most popular song of 1901, and "Bill Bailey" the sixth most popular of 1902. See Gardner, *Popular Songs of the Twentieth Century,* 254 and 258.

26. Pages 89–90. The informant for this song, a Mrs. Tom Bartlett of Marlin, Texas, notes that "a hop-joint is the vernacular for a drug-shop, and all that implies, and 'drug' to a Negro means cocaine, 'coke,' 'dope,' etc., being synonymous with 'hops'" (89).

27. Counterarguments are considered in Muir, "Before 'Crazy Blues,'" 289–94.

28. Bob Emmet, "Minstrelsy," *Billboard,* September 3, 1932.

29. Edward Le Roy Rice, *Monarchs of Minstrelsy: From "Daddy" Rice to Date* (New York: Kenny Publishing Co., 1911), 358.

30. Ibid.

31. The two other songs are "Don't You Never Take No Ten Cent Drink on Me" (New York: Howley, Haviland & Dresser, 1901); and "I Hates to Get Up Early in the Morn" (New York: Howley, Haviland & Dresser, 1901).

32. Thornton Hagert, privately circulated newsletter of Vernacular Music Research, March 27, 1971, 5.

33. Biographical information on Queen comes from his obituary in the *New York Dramatic Mirror,* March 1, 1902, 16.

34. New York: Feist & Frankenhaler.

35. Frank and Bert Leighton, "Origin of 'Blues' (or Jazz)," *Variety,* January 6, 1922; reprinted in *Jazz in Print (1856–1929): An Anthology of Selected Early Readings in Jazz History,* ed. Karl Koenig. 164–66 (Hillsdale, N.Y.: Pendragon, 2002).

36. Information derived from posting in the relevant issues of *Variety.*

37. The entire song is quoted in Muir, "Before 'Crazy Blues,'" 249–52.

38. Columbia A-2968. The work was also recorded at around the same time by Al Bernard (Bell P-120), who, like Cannon, was a minstrel and a pioneer white promoter of the blues. His recording is far lass bluesy than Harris's, however.

39. *Big Road Blues,* 44.

40. D. K. Wilgus and Eleanor R. Long, "The Blues Ballad and the Genesis of Style in the Traditional Narrative Song," in *Narrative Folksong: New Directions: Essays in Appreciation of W. Edson Richmond,* ed. Carol L. Edwards and Kathleen E. B. Manley, 455 (Boulder, Col.: Westview Press, 1985).

41. Oliver, *The Story of the Blues,* 22–25; Evans, *Big Road Blues,* 44.

42. *Father of the Blues,* 143 (emphasis in original).

43. I do not mean to suggest that blues ballads were never *performed* after 1920, but rather that almost no songs were *created* in the genre after that date, at least in black culture.

44. These songs are quoted and discussed in Muir, "Before 'Crazy Blues,'" 290–98; 311–19.

45. St. Louis: Joseph Lacht.

46. For further discussion, see Muir, "Before 'Crazy Blues,'" 343–44.

47. I have argued elsewhere against the theory put forward by Joyner that such sixteen-bar expansions of the twelve-bar blues theme as found in "Texas Blues" were inspired by commercial pressures. See Muir, "Before 'Crazy Blues,'" 363.

48. These songs are quoted and discussed in Muir, "Before 'Crazy Blues,'" 343–51. Regarding the composer of "Monkey Rag," this is the same Chris Smith who was co-composer of both "The Blues," copyrighted a few months after "Monkey Rag," and "I've Got de Blues," the pioneering proto-blues song from 1901. Smith's contribution to early popular blues was therefore unique: it began just after the turn of the century, and he was still actively composing blues in the mid-1920s (Jasen and Jones, *Spreadin' Rhythm Around,* 144). "Monkey Rag," incidentally, is exceptional in that it uses twelve-bar structures for both its verse and chorus, making it the only proto-blues song to do so aside from Cannon's "You Needn't Come Home" from 1901. However, the sequence used by Smith in the chorus departs a long way from a regular blues sequence (see Muir, "Before 'Crazy Blues,'" 348–50). "Monkey Rag" was also issued as a piano rag with three strains, the first two corresponding to the verse and chorus of the song and the third using a conventional sixteen-bar structure with no blues relationship. This is the first published instrumental rag to use a twelve-bar structure for two

strains, thereby anticipating the publication of Handy's "The Memphis Blues" by approximately a year (though "The Memphis Blues" was composed in 1909, almost certainly before "Monkey Blues"; furthermore both its twelve-bar strains use a straight blues sequence).

49. Quoted and discussed in Muir, "Before 'Crazy Blues,'" 311–12.

50. Gardner, *Popular Songs of the Twentieth Century*, 294, 295, 297, and 299.

51. Barry Kernfield, "Call and Response," in the *New Grove Dictionary of Music and Musicians*, 2nd ed.

52. For background, see Abbott and Seroff, *Out of Sight*, 454–55.

53. Titon, *Early Downhome Blues*, 162.

54. David Evans, *Big Road Blues*, 45; Muir, "Before 'Crazy Blues,'" 376–77.

55. The reference is to "Kansas City girls [who] can't play anything on pianos except 'rags' and the worst 'rags' at that. 'The Bully' and 'Forty Drops' are their favorites" (*Leavenworth Herald*, December 8, 1894, quoted in Abbott and Seroff, *Out of Sight*, 448). This quotation is also notable in that it contains "the earliest-known printed reference to the word 'rags' to indicate a particular kind of music." "Forty Drops" was an early ragtime instrumental composition.

56. *Father of the Blues*, 27–28, 119–20.

57. See Norm Cohen, album notes to *Minstrels and Tunesmiths*, JEMF LP 109.

58. Listed in Muir, "Before 'Crazy Blues,'" 255.

59. Trevathan's version was in fact titled "May Irwin's Bully Song" to distinguish it from the pack (New York: White-South Music Publishing, 1896). For further discussion, see Muir, "Before 'Crazy Blues,'" 254–55.

60. James L. Ford, *Forty-Odd Years in the Literary Shop (New York: Dutton, 1921)*, 275–76; James J. Geller, *Famous Songs and Their Stories* (New York: Macaulay, 1931), 97–98.

61. The very first published version of the song, "Looking for a Bully" by Joseph E. Howard (New York: Joseph Stern, 1895), uses the twelve-bar theme in its chorus rather than the verse. See Muir, "Before 'Crazy Blues,'" 261.

62. Ibid.

63. For instance, Laws, *Native American Balladry*, 239–40. However, it is different from externalized blues ballads like "Frankie" and "Stagolee" in that the song is sung in the first person—and to very gripping effect.

64. Aside from the rhythmic shift, the only divergence from the original in this example is the raising of the second note of m. 8 by a step in order to accommodate the altered relationship between the melody and the harmony (the original melody note, D, sounds odd over the E minor chord).

65. Van der Merwe, *The Origins of Popular Style*, 185–86.

66. The full version of the song is given in L. W. Payne, Jr., "Some Texas Versions of 'The Frog's Courting': The Way of the Folk with a Song," in *Rainbow in the Morning*, ed. J. Frank Dobie (repr., Denton, Tex.: University of North Texas Press, 2000), 14–15

67. Ibid., 5–6.

68. Payne quotes numerous African American examples ("Some Texas Versions of 'The Frog's Courting'").

69. See Muir, "Before 'Crazy Blues,'" 322–31.

70. Ibid.

71. The reference is an announcement in a black Kansas City newspaper, the *Leavenworth Herald*, August 21, 1897, of a forthcoming performance at the Kansas City Negro Press Association by a "piano thumper" called Charlie Lee performing "Stack-a-Lee" "in variations." The announcement

was unearthed by ragtime historian Edward A. Berlin and can be found on his website at www
.edwardaberlin.com/disc.htm#stag (accessed June 13, 2008). One wonders if the variations were
pre-composed or improvised. Either way, the event is the earliest to be documented that might be
claimed as a blues performance.

72. Quoted at www.pbs.org/theblues/ (accessed May 17, 2008).

73. Susan McClary, *Conventional Wisdom: The Content of Musical Form* (Berkeley and Los Angeles: University of California Press, 2000), 32.

MAJOR WORKS CONSULTED

Note: This listing contains only works cited frequently in this book. Works that are cited less often are given full bibliographic reference the first time they are cited within the relevant note.

Abbott, Lynn, and Doug Seroff. *Out of Sight: The Rise of African American Popular Music, 1889–1895.* Jackson: University Press of Mississippi, 2002.

———. *Ragged but Right: Traveling Shows, "Coon Songs," and the Dark Pathway to Blues and Jazz.* Jackson: University Press of Mississippi, 2007.

———. "'They Cert'ly Sound Good to Me': Sheet Music, Southern Vaudeville, and the Commercial Ascendancy of the Blues." In *Ramblin' on My Mind: New Perspectives on the Blues,* edited by David Evans, 49–104. Urbana: University of Illinois Press, 2008.

ASCAP Biographical Dictionary of Composers, Authors, and Publishers. 2nd ed. New York: Thomas Y. Crowell, 1952.

Badger, Reid. *A Life in Ragtime: A Biography of James Reese Europe.* New York: Oxford University Press, 1995.

Berlin, Edward A. *Ragtime: A Musical and Cultural History.* Berkeley: University of California Press, 1980.

Bradford, Perry. *Born with the Blues.* New York: Oak Publications, 1965.

Brooks, Tim. *Lost Sounds: Black and the Birth of the Recording Industry, 1890–1919.* Urbana: University of Illinois Press, 2004.

Bryant, Rebecca A. "Shaking Big Shoulders: Music and Dance Culture in Chicago, 1910–1925." PhD diss., University of Illinois, 2003.

Charters, Samuel. *The Country Blues.* 1959. Reprint, New York: Da Capo, 1975.

———. *The Bluesmen: The Story and the Music of the Men Who Made the Blues.* New York: Oak Publications, 1966–67.

Davis, Francis. *The History of the Blues.* New York: Hyperion, 1995.

Dixon, Robert M. W., John Godrich, and Howard W. Rye. *Blues and Gospel Records, 1890–1943.* 4th edition. Oxford: Oxford University Press, 1997.

Evans, David. *Big Road Blues: Tradition and Creativity in the Folk Blues.* Berkeley: University of California Press, 1982.

Ford, Robert. *A Blues Bibliography: The International Literature of an Afro-American Genre.* Bromley, Kent: Paul Pelletier, 1999.

Garber, Michael G. "Reflexive Songs in the American Musical, 1898 to 1947." PhD diss., The City University of New York, 2006.

Gardner, Edward Foote. *Popular Songs of the Twentieth Century: Volume 1—Chart Detail & Encyclopedia, 1900–1949.* St. Paul, Minn.: Paragon House, 2000.

Gracyk, Tim, ed. *The Encyclopedia of Popular American Recording Pioneers.* Granite Bay, Calif.: Victrola and 78 Journal Press, 1999.

Handy, William Christopher. *Father of the Blues: An Autobiography.* 1941. Reprint, New York: Da Capo, 1991.

———, ed. *Blues: An Anthology.* New York: A. & C. Boni, 1926.

Hurwitt, Elliott S. "William Christopher Handy." In *International Dictionary of Black Composers,* edited by Samuel Floyd Jr., 549–58. New York: Routledge, 1999.

———. "W. C. Handy as Music Publisher: Career and Reputation." PhD diss., City University of New York, 2000.

Jasen, David, and Gene Jones. *Spreading Rhythm Around: Black Popular Songwriters, 1880–1930.* New York: Schirmer, 1998.

Laws, G. Malcolm, Jr. *Native American Balladry.* Rev. ed. Philadelphia: American Folklore Society, 1964.

Lomax, Alan. *The Land Where the Blues Began.* New York: Pantheon Books, 1993.

Meade, Guthrie T., Jr., with Richard Spottswood and Douglas S. Meade. *Country Music Sources: A Biblio-Discography of Commercially Recorded Traditional Music.* Chapel Hill: University of North Carolina Press, 2002.

Muir, Peter C. "Before 'Crazy Blues': Commercial Blues in America, 1850–1920." PhD diss., City University of New York, 2004.

Niles, Abbe. "Introduction." In *Blues: An Anthology,* edited by W. C. Handy, 1–24.

Odum, Howard W. "Folk-Song and Folk-Poetry as Found in the Secular Songs of the Southern Negroes." *Journal of American Folklore* 24 (1911): 255–94, 351–96.

Odum, Howard W., and Guy B. Johnson. *Negro Workaday Songs.* Chapel Hill: University of North Carolina Press, 1926.

Oliver, Paul. *Songsters and Saints: Vocal Traditions on Race Records.* Cambridge: Cambridge University Press, 1984.

———. *Blues Fell this Morning: the Meaning of the Blues.* Cambridge: Cambridge University Press, 1960.

———. *The Story of the Blues.* London: Design Yearbook, 1969.

Scarborough, Dorothy. *On the Trail of Negro Folk-Songs.* 1925. Reprint, Cambridge, Mass.: Harvard University Press, 1963.

Taft, Michael. *The Blues Lyric Formula.* New York: Routledge, 2006.

———. *Talkin' to Myself: Blues Lyrics, 1921–1942.* New York: Routledge, 2005.

Titon, Jeff Todd. *Early Downhome Blues: a Musical and Cultural Analysis.* 2nd ed. Chapel Hill: University of North Carolina Press, 1994.

Van der Merwe, Peter. *The Origins of Popular Style.* Oxford: Oxford University Press, 1989.

Wald, Elijah. *Escaping the Delta: Robert Johnson and the Invention of the Blues.* New York: Harper Collins, 2004.

White, Newman I. *American Negro Folk-Songs.* Cambridge, Mass.: Harvard University Press, 1928.

GENERAL INDEX

Abbott, Lynn, 10, 146
Abernathy, Seymour, 128, 200
Abraham, Maurice, 203
Abrams, Albert, 82
Aeolian Vocalion (record company), 26
African music, 101
allopathic blues, 89–103, 198
All Star Trio, 96
Anderson, Charles, 146
Anderson, Pink, 25
animal dances, 58
Armstrong, Howard "Louie Bluie," 29–30
Armstrong, Louis, 64, 154, 205–6
Arto (record company), 26
Autry, Gene, 29
Ayer, Nat D., 200, 203

Badger, Reid, 57
Bailey, Willard, 195
barbershop ending, 75, 169, 198–99, 228n106
Barlow's Minstrels, 196, 198
barrelhouse, 102, 155
Barron, Ted S., 55–56, 152
Bauer, June, 176
Baxter, Philip, 148
Bayes, Nora, 20
Beard, George M., 82
Bennett, Theron C., 17–18, 106, 111
Berk, Lew, 41
Berlin, Edward, 61
Berlin, Irving, 40, 43, 47–48
Bernard, Al, 22, 96, 100, 240n38
Bevo, 226n69
Birch, Billy, 83
Bird, Billy, 43
black vaudeville. *See under* vaudeville
Blake, Blind, 40, 42
Blake, Eubie, 26, 95, 200
Bland, James, 43
Blesh, Rudi, 29
Blessner, Gustave, 182

blue devils, 81, 97, 98
blue notes, 7–8, 38; in allopathic blues, 93; in
   the blues of W. C. Handy, 108–9, 113, 117,
   233n16, 235n57; definition of, 71, 73–74; in early
   Southern published blues, 142, 149, 178; and
   false relations, 92, 93; in homeopathic blues,
   93; in popular blues idiom, 49, 55–56, 74–75,
   100, 227n105; in popular non-blues, 227n105; in
   proto-blues, 198
Blues: An Anthology (Handy), 137–38, 139, 151, 157
blues, allopathic, , 198
blues, definitions of, 2. *See also* blues, titular
blues, folk, 1, 2; African origins of, 103; in the
   blues of W. C. Handy, 113, 117, 123, 125, 127–28,
   134, 129–30, 132, 136; defined, 3, 28, 221n7; drink
   as theme in, 45; emerges from blues ballad,
   203–7; homeopathic nature of, 88–89, 99–100,
   103; influence on early Southern published
   blues, 143, 146, 147, 152, 156, 173, 174, 176–78;
   influence on popular blues, 7–8, 38, 40, 42–43,
   48–49; influence on published proto-blues,
   186–87; personal nature of, 39; relationship with
   popular music, 29–30; titles of, using place-
   names, 43–44. *See also* blue notes; blues ballads;
   blues lyrics; call and response; "Frankie and
   Johnny" song family; twelve-bar blues sequence
blues, hokum, 102
blues, homeopathic, 88–103, 169, 178, 198, 231n47;
   anticipated in proto-blues culture, 206–7, 210
blues, instrumental, 26; and dance, 49; defined,
   11; and the fox-trot, 56–62; and ragtime, 55–56,
   225n48; structure of, 55; survey of, 48–66
blues, popular: defined, 1, 2; emerges from folk
   blues, 7–8; historiography of, 1–2, 29–30; idiom
   of, 66–79; influence of popular music on, 1, 19,
   28–30, 38–39; performance of, 20–26; personal
   vs. impersonal quality of, 39; relationship to
   jazz, 62–66, 87–88; white vs. black blues, 19–20.
   See also barbershop ending; blue notes; blues,
   instrumental; blues, titular; blues, vocal; call
   and response; four-note chromatic motif; "I've

SONG INDEX

This is an index of titles of all songs and instrumental works referred to in the text. Author attributions are given in parenthesis in instances where two different numbers share the same or similar titles. This index is for individual numbers only: for collections, such as *W. C. Handy's Collection of Negro Spirituals,* and musicals, such as *The Night Boat,* see the general index.

Aframerican Hymn, 135
Ain't Dat a Shame?, 195, 196, 215
Alabama Blues (Bird), 43
Alabama Blues (Hoffman). *See* I'm Alabama Bound
Alcoholic Blues, 44–45
Alexander's Ragtime Band, 47–48, 224n39, 230n26
Alic Busby, Don't Go Away, 239n16
All Alone, 197–98
All Night Long, 200, 203
Atlanta Blues, 136, 137
Aunt Hagar's Blues, 118, 134–35, 137
Aunt Hagar's Children. *See* Aunt Hagar's Blues

Baby Seals Blues, 9, 25, 142–46, 173–74, 235–36n2
Back Home Again in Indiana, 43
Bad-Rag, 203
Ballad of the Boll Weevil, The, 192–93, 194, 195, 199, 212; popularity of, 239n22
Ballin' the Jack, 48
Baltimore Blues, 200
Basement Blues, 135, 136
Basin Street Blues, 130, 176
Beale Street. *See* Beale Street Blues
Beale Street Blues, 22, 101, 112, 121, 130–33, 138; influence of "The Memphis Blues" on, 131, 235n59; theme of prohibition in, 44
Bevo Blues, 59–61, 60, 93, 95
Big Chief Blues, 22, 101, 139
Bill, You Done Me Wrong (Leighton Brothers), 195, 200

Bill Bailey, Won't You Please Come Home?, 189, 192–93, 215
Billy's Request, 83–85, 97
Black and White Rag, 109
Blowin' the Blues Away, 98
Blues (Burrows/Stanley), 148
Blues (House/Patterson), 154–56, 157, 237–38n35
Blues, The (Smith/Brymn), 7–9, 11, 17, 25, 26; use of four-note chromatic motif, 76, 234n36; use of "I've got the blues" phrase, 77
Blues in the Night, 29
Bluin' the Blues, 101
Boll Weevil. *See* Ballad of the Boll Weevil, The
Bone Dry Blues, The, 176–177
Bone-Head Blues, 49, 53–55, 59, 61; as example of allopathic blues, 93, 95
Broadway Blues (Swanstrom/Carey), 30, 43, 49, 77, 78–79; analysis of, 31–34, 37–39; as example of allopathic blues, 95
Broadway Blues (Walsh/Sherman), 20, 21
Broken Hearted Blues, 168, 174
Bucket's Got a Hole in It, 154
Bull Frog Blues, 21
Bully Song, The (folk song), 210–13, 215. *See also* Looking for a Bully; May Irwin's Bully Song
Burst Forth, My Tears, 91

Careless Love, 135
Carolina Blues, 44
Carry Me Back to My Old Virginny, 43
Chasin' the Blues, 97
Chattanooga Choo-Choo, 29
Chinese Blues, 18–19, 101
Colorado Blues, 156, 157, 159
Come After Breakfast, 7
Crazy Blues, 3–4, 26, 102, 167–69, 221n9; analysis of, 174; musical sources of, 238n44; popularity of, 174, 238n45
Creole Love Call, 200
Cuban Blues, 237n31

An internationally recognized pianist, composer, scholar, and conductor, **PETER MUIR** is the cofounder and codirector of the Institute for Music and Health in Verbank, New York.

MUSIC IN AMERICAN LIFE

Lonesome Cowgirls and Honky-Tonk Angels: The Women of Barn Dance Radio
    Kristine M. McCusker
California Polyphony: Ethnic Voices, Musical Crossroads   *Mina Yang*
The Never-Ending Revival: Rounder Records and the Folk Alliance   *Michael F. Scully*
Sing It Pretty: A Memoir   *Bess Lomax Hawes*
Working Girl Blues: The Life and Music of Hazel Dickens   *Hazel Dickens and Bill C. Malone*
Charles Ives Reconsidered   *Gayle Sherwood Magee*
The Hayloft Gang: The Story of the National Barn Dance   *Edited by Chad Berry*
Country Music Humorists and Comedians   *Loyal Jones*
Record Makers and Breakers: Voices of the Independent Rock 'n' Roll Pioneers   *John Broven*
Music of the First Nations: Tradition and Innovation in Native North America
    Edited by Tara Browner
Cafe Society: The wrong place for the Right people   *Barney Josephson,*
    with Terry Trilling-Josephson
George Gershwin: An Intimate Portrait   *Walter Rimler*
Life Flows On in Endless Song: Folk Songs and American History   *Robert V. Wells*
I Feel a Song Coming On: The Life of Jimmy McHugh   *Alyn Shipton*
King of the Queen City: The Story of King Records   *Jon Hartley Fox*
Long Lost Blues: Popular Blues in America, 1850–1920   *Peter C. Muir*

The University of Illinois Press
is a founding member of the
Association of American University Presses.

———————————————————————

Composed in 10.25/14.5 Adobe Minion Pro
with Univers display
by Jim Proefrock
at the University of Illinois Press
Designed by Kelly Gray
Manufactured by Cushing-Malloy, Inc.

University of Illinois Press
1325 South Oak Street
Champaign, IL 61820-6903
www.press.uillinois.edu